# Do-it-yourself Yearbook

# Popular Science

## Do-it-yourself Yearbook

# 1990

Popular Science Books
SEDGEWOOD® PRESS, New York

Cover photo by Mike Mitchell Photography, courtesy of *Popular Science* magazine.

Copyright © 1989 by Meredith Corporation, Des Moines, Iowa.

Published by
  Popular Science Books
  Sedgewood® Press
  750 Third Avenue
  New York, New York 10017

Distributed by Meredith Corporation, Des Moines, Iowa.

ISBN: 0-696-11020-2

Manufactured in the United States of America

10  9  8  7  6  5  4  3  2

# introduction

In the eight years this Yearbook has been compiled, I can't recall a more exciting collection of material mainly from the pages of *Popular Science* magazine. When I was asked to write the Introduction once again, I reminded the editors of this volume that I've just taken early retirement from *Popular Science* and, after 25 years, am no longer in charge of all do-it-yourself material there. The Yearbook editors responded that most articles selected for this year had been written or edited by me in my final year at *Popular Science;* and they felt I'd bring a fresh eye to the material reprinted here from other magazines—*Homeowner* and *Home Mechanix*.

## Why other sources?

*Popular Science,* long shackled to its cover label, "The What's New Magazine," is limited in what it can include in its editorial mix. In the home improvement area, I had to tie projects to new materials, for example, and there was never any possibility for us to treat basic construction or repairs. To broaden such coverage in a book like this, then, it's necessary to tap outside sources—magazines of comparable quality with less restrictive editorial policies. The criterion for selection of Yearbook articles remains the same for these articles as for those from *Popular Science:* They must offer ideas and provide instruction that will prove of value to any owner of a home or workshop who wishes to enrich his or her lifestyle.

Most of the articles in this volume bear authors' names you'll recognize from the pages of *Popular Science*. At least three of these authors have served as president of the National Association of Home and Workshop Writers (NAHWW), whose membership includes nearly every major do-it-yourself writer in America. This association continues to be sparkplugged by popular how-to writer Richard Day from his California outpost atop Palomar Mountain.

Rich recently returned my visit to *his* mountain by driving down from Montreal (where he's a regular consultant on a series of how-to books) to check out *my* mountain in Pennsylvania's Poconos. There I've built the Lockbox leisure home. Right up until I retired, I employed the Lockbox as a showcase house for new home improvement products; you'll find one of the last of these articles in this book, under the headline "Float a Fancy Floor."

Rich Day and I put our feet up before my fireplace and spent several hours bewailing the decline of the market for quality do-it-yourself writing. The chief editors of two large-circulation technology-and-home-improvement magazines have admitted to a lessening commitment to how-to projects, leaving publications such as *Homeowner* and *Home Mechanix* to take up the slack. We speculated on why this was so, especially since sales in home-improvement tools and products continue to break records each year, and since home centers are booming. Housing costs have spiraled out of the reach of trade-up buyers, who must settle for improving the modest home they own or investing sweat equity in a handyman's special.

A major reason for the shift in magazine policy, we decided, is that the type of material you'll find in this book is among the hardest for any magazine to generate.

Finally Rich rose: "Enough talk! Let's memorialize my visit with a project." I gave him a choice of installing a replacement for a rotting wood window (for which the manufacturer's instructions were dauntingly inadequate) or assembling a firewood rack from pressure-treated 2 x 4s. As we completed the firewood rack, we agreed that any American home without an improvement or a repair crying for attention was an anomaly. And virtually any homeowner can tackle such jobs with proper inspiration and instruction. Rich and I—along with fellow professionals like R. J. DeCristoforo, who has two great workshop jigs in the Indoor Projects section of this book—have made careers on just such a conviction. And we remain delighted that the best of our work is acknowledged and preserved in books such as this one.

## The struggle for quality

As I've said, such articles don't come easily. Every project in this book has its own story of struggle and triumph. Each had to be creatively proposed, fought for and nurtured through months of research and development. Take the three articles that make up Part I, for example. The striking collection of house designs grew from my long-standing Leisure Home of the Month series, which *Popular Science* has since discontinued. I chose to rally the contributing architects I'd assembled over the years for one final blast and am happy to report that detailed plans for all six houses are available to readers of this Yearbook. To balance this emphasis on house *plans,* I decided *Popular Science* should report on reader experience with house *kits*. My search for a company that could cooperate in a field experiment took me several years and trips to the Midwest. Once we had commitments from our two pairs of novice homebuilders, I asked fellow staffer Elaine Gilmore to monitor one of the construction sites while I kept tabs on the "control" site. The story took months to assemble, but the unique results made it worth our effort. Finally, my report on the joys (and woes) of enlarging a period house developed from my long association with Bob Vila's *This Old House* on public television. When the Boston PBS station that produces that show described an upcoming project to me, I flew to the West Coast to sit in on the taping of early episodes to be certain the project was right for *Popular Science* readers.

As I've said in my introductions to previous *Do-It-Yourself Yearbooks,* the magazine staffs and their regular freelancers expend so much energy on getting these articles exactly right, we're all pleased to see our best efforts rescued from the ephemeral magazine world of instant disposability for hardcover permanence. Where my own work is concerned, I find this especially true this year, since these covers preserve much of my last (and, perhaps, best) work for *Popular Science*. And you benefit from this material's having been pre-tested in the marketplace: Since a million readers have already "approved" these projects, you can be doubly assured of the accuracy and completeness of this material.

Oh, and Rich Day (if you're reading this): I've noodled out the window-maker's installation muddle, so any time you're back this way . . .

Alfred Lees
Home and Shop Editor (retired)
POPULAR SCIENCE

# contents

# 6 summer houses for year-round living

Bill Phillips

Menike Phillips

## atrium house

**The latest design** from Alfredo De Vido combines the appeal of sunny semi-outdoor spaces with energy-efficient features. The heart of this house and its conservation system is a sun-oriented patio that draws solar heat through its glass roof and holds it in the masonry mass of its paved floor. Energy-saving aspects include a compact shape with a minimum of exterior surfaces; air-lock vestibules at front and back; and insulating shutters. Window walls close off the house when the atrium is cool. This same glazed core helps cool the house in summer by letting warm air escape through a top vent.

**FIRST FLOOR**

ENTRY HALL — FAMILY ROOM
DINING ROOM — ATRIUM/SUNSPACE
KITCHEN — LIVING ROOM

**SECOND FLOOR**

BALCONY — OPEN TO BELOW — OPEN TO BELOW
BEDROOM — OPEN TO BELOW
BEDROOM — BATH — BATH — BEDROOM

2 5 10

When I contacted the five architects whose house plans had been reader favorites in previous Yearbooks, I asked each to design a home that comfortably embraces today's technologies and bolder sense of design without sacrificing traditional comforts.

One architect found the challenge so stimulating that he submitted two houses; the others presented flexible designs that will adapt to a variety of sites—*by Al Lees.*

(For data on ordering plans, see page 8.)

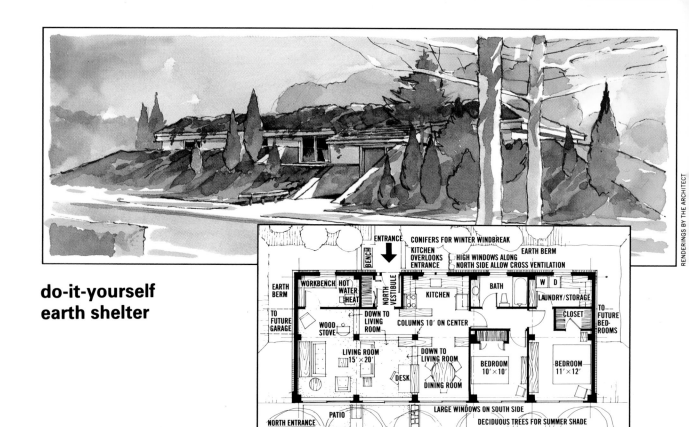

# do-it-yourself earth shelter

ENTRANCE  CONIFERS FOR WINTER WINDBREAK

BENCH

KITCHEN OVERLOOKS ENTRANCE

EARTH BERM

HIGH WINDOWS ALONG NORTH SIDE ALLOW CROSS VENTILATION

EARTH BERM

WORKBENCH  HOT WATER HEAT

KITCHEN

BATH

W  D

TO FUTURE GARAGE

NORTH VESTIBULE

DOWN TO LIVING ROOM

LAUNDRY/STORAGE

CLOSET

TO FUTURE BEDROOMS

WOOD STOVE

COLUMNS 10' ON CENTER

LIVING ROOM 15' × 20'

DOWN TO LIVING ROOM

BEDROOM 10' × 10'

BEDROOM 11' × 12'

DESK

DINING ROOM

NORTH ENTRANCE  PATIO

LARGE WINDOWS ON SOUTH SIDE

DECIDUOUS TREES FOR SUMMER SHADE

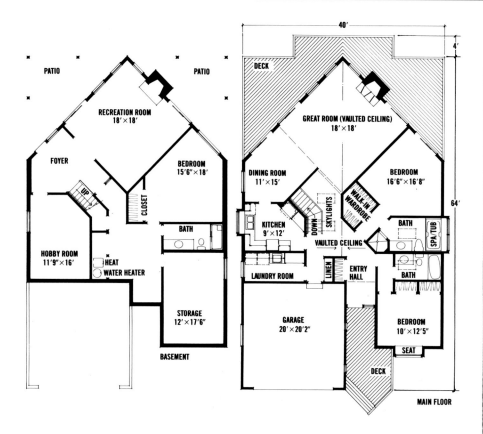

PATIO  PATIO

DECK

40'

4'

RECREATION ROOM 18' × 18'

GREAT ROOM (VAULTED CEILING) 18' × 18'

FOYER

BEDROOM 15'6" × 18'

DINING ROOM 11' × 15'

BEDROOM 16'6" × 16'8"

UP

CLOSET

SKYLIGHTS

WALK-IN WARDROBE

64'

BATH

KITCHEN 9' × 12'

DOWN

BATH

SPA/TUB

HOBBY ROOM 11'9" × 16'

HEAT

WATER HEATER

VAULTED CEILING

LINEN

ENTRY HALL

BATH

STORAGE 12' × 17'6"

LAUNDRY ROOM

BEDROOM 10' × 12'5"

BASEMENT

GARAGE 20' × 20'2"

SEAT

DECK

MAIN FLOOR

# two-story prow

**Designed for fullest use** of a narrow lot with the major view at the back (the case with most waterside or canyon sites), this house offers a sweeping vista through a two-story window wall that wraps around the great-room fireplace. The stone chimney, shake roof, and vertical cedar siding tie the house to any natural setting, also make a design statement on a city lot. An angled deck invites visitors into a snug entry.

**Flat land,** hilly land, north slope, south slope—you name it, this 1,000 square-foot two-bedroom house by Cape Cod-based architect Malcolm Wells offers two floor plans to fit almost any snowbelt site. Farther south, where air conditioning is the main concern, a south-to-north reversal solves the orientation problem. Columns support a timber-and-joist deck that carries a rooftop wildflower garden. A simple duct system pulls solar-heated air down into the floor mass.

Floor plan labels:

CONIFERS FOR WINTER WINDBREAK
EARTH BERM
HIGH WINDOWS ALONG NORTH SIDE ALLOW CROSS VENTILATION
EARTH BERM
WORKBENCH  W  D  HEAT
HOT WATER  UTILITY ROOM
WOOD STOVE
TO FUTURE GARAGE
SUMMER DOOR
BUILT-IN SEAT  BATH  STORAGE 5'×11'
DINING AREA
COLUMNS 10' ON CENTER
DOWN TO LIVING ROOM
LOW WALL
BREAKFAST AREA
KITCHEN
CLOSET
TO FUTURE BEDROOMS
LIVING ROOM 12'6"×15'6"
SOUTH VESTIBULE
BEDROOM 10'×10'
BEDROOM 11'×12'
PATIO
SOUTH ENTRANCE
ENTRANCE
LARGE WINDOWS ON SOUTH SIDE
DECIDUOUS TREES FOR SUMMER SHADE

# radiant house

**Designed by** Charles G. Woods (who lives in one of his underground houses), the Radiant is a 3,500-square-foot house with protective earth berms on all but its south-facing chord. Construction plans include a section for building a single-story version on a flat lot, with an optional 1,750-square-foot basement. The wedge-shaped rooms radiate from a central skylighted atrium, and several of them open onto a wraparound deck, with steps down to a patio.

RENDERING BY JAY AND TRACY BOYLE

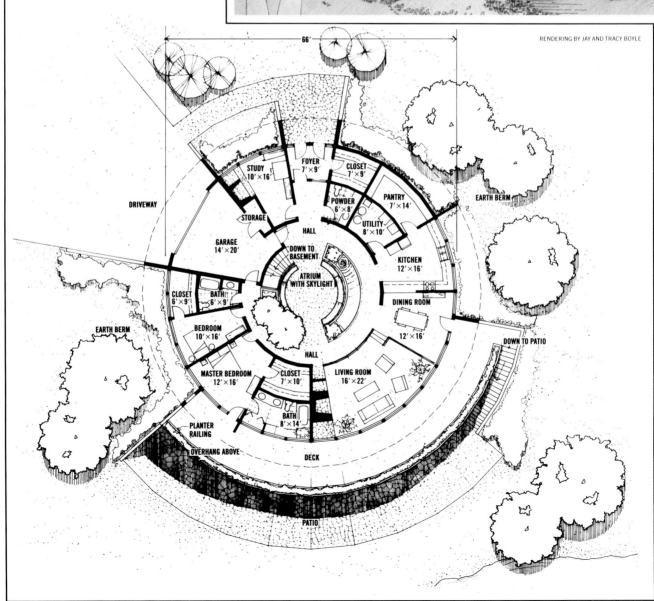

66'

DRIVEWAY

STUDY
10' × 16'

FOYER
7' × 9'

CLOSET
7' × 9'

EARTH BERM

STORAGE

POWDER
6' × 8'

PANTRY
7' × 14'

GARAGE
14' × 20'

HALL

UTILITY
8' × 10'

DOWN TO
BASEMENT

KITCHEN
12' × 16'

ATRIUM
WITH SKYLIGHT

CLOSET
6' × 9'

BATH
6' × 9'

DINING ROOM
12' × 16'

DOWN TO PATIO

EARTH BERM

BEDROOM
10' × 16'

HALL

MASTER BEDROOM
12' × 16'

CLOSET
7' × 10'

LIVING ROOM
16' × 22'

BATH
8' × 14'

PLANTER
RAILING

OVERHANG ABOVE

DECK

PATIO

# omega house

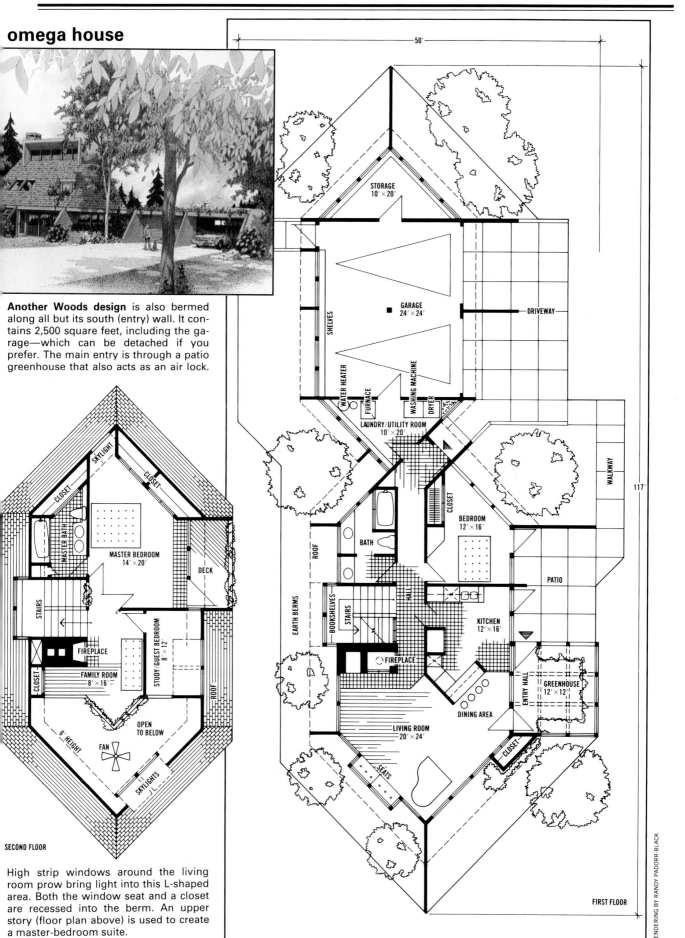

**Another Woods design** is also bermed along all but its south (entry) wall. It contains 2,500 square feet, including the garage—which can be detached if you prefer. The main entry is through a patio greenhouse that also acts as an air lock.

High strip windows around the living room prow bring light into this L-shaped area. Both the window seat and a closet are recessed into the berm. An upper story (floor plan above) is used to create a master-bedroom suite.

SECOND FLOOR

**SECOND FLOOR labels:**
SKYLIGHT
CLOSET
CLOSET
MASTER BATH
MASTER BEDROOM 14' × 20'
DECK
STAIRS
CLOSET
FIREPLACE
FAMILY ROOM 8' × 16'
STUDY/GUEST BEDROOM 8' × 12'
ROOF
OPEN TO BELOW
6' HEIGHT
FAN
SKYLIGHTS

**FIRST FLOOR labels:**
50'
117'
STORAGE 10' × 20'
GARAGE 24' × 24'
DRIVEWAY
SHELVES
WATER HEATER
FURNACE
WASHING MACHINE
DRYER
LAUNDRY/UTILITY ROOM 10' × 20'
WALKWAY
CLOSET
BEDROOM 12' × 16'
BATH
ROOF
PATIO
EARTH BERMS
BOOKSHELVES
STAIRS
HALL
KITCHEN 12' × 16'
FIREPLACE
DINING AREA
ENTRY HALL
GREENHOUSE 12' × 12'
CLOSET
LIVING ROOM 20' × 24'
SEATS
FIRST FLOOR

RENDERING BY RANDY PADORR-BLACK

RENDERING BY EDWARD J. KELBISH

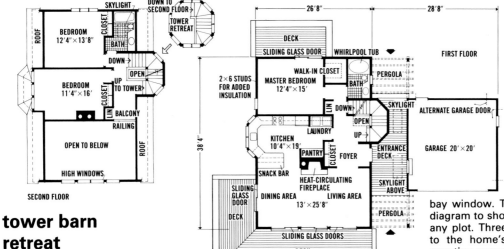

## tower barn retreat

Though influenced by old barns, this house uses its gambrel roof to tuck in a partial second story with extra bedrooms and a bath—plus a balcony that shares the spectacular view that the two-story living/dining room has through the glazed end wall. Turn from the balcony and climb another story up the octagonal tower to a unique retreat. Downstairs a large country kitchen extends into a bay window. The plans include a siting diagram to show the best positioning for any plot. Three decks add activity areas to the home's 1,677 square feet (not counting garage—or the tower retreat).

## HOW TO ORDER HOUSE PLANS

● Atrium house plans are $125 per set, $175 for four sets, from Alfredo De Vido Assoc. (699 Madison Ave., New York, NY 10021).

● Detailed construction plans for the Radiant and Omega can be ordered from Charles G. Woods (Natural Architecture, RD 3, Box 538, Honesdale, PA 18431), for $150 per set. A set for both houses: $275. Additional sets of the same plan are $25 each. Phone (717) 253-5452 for Visa or MasterCard orders.

● A set of four Two-Story Prow plans is $225 (with daylight basement) or $200 (without). Mirror reverse plans are available, as is a materials list ($30 extra). Write Kenneth Gephart AIBD CSI, 9630 S. W. Eagle La., Beav-erton, OR 97005. Phone (503) 641-7584 for Visa or MasterCard orders.

● The adaptable earth shelter house is available as one set of plans for $100, showing both north- and south-entry versions. Send payment to Malcolm Wells, Box 1149, Brewster, MA 02631.

● Tower Barn plans are $150 per set; five sets $195. Mirror reverse plan is $15 extra; materials list: $30. Homes for Living, 363 Seventh Ave., New York, NY 10001.

Please add $10 handling and shipping to all orders sent to U.S. addresses. Canadian and overseas orders are subject to added costs.

# kit houses
# new tech vs. old

## 600 hours
## —new tech

**Chris and David Ademmer's** house in Minnesota is shingled, sided, and trimmed, with windows and doors installed, after 600 hours (and 15 minutes) work. David and his father were the prime movers, with Chris's father not far behind. David's uncle helped, as did friends. Chris handled the painting, decorating —and moral support.

**For comparison story on building an old tech house, see page 12.**

Last June, when David Ademmer carried his bride, Chris Hadac Ademmer, across the threshold, they entered their own sparkling new house. No starter home this: It's a 2,392-square-foot split entry with four bedrooms, two baths, and a 528-square-foot garage.

As the dream of homeownership eludes ever more Americans, how did this young couple (he's 26, she's 21) manage to bring it off?

With a great deal of labor—their own and that of a few relatives and friends. They built the house themselves, starting with a panelized kit from a Miles Homes catalog.

Shortly before the Ademmers decided to build, *Popular Science* and Miles agreed to an owner-builder field test (see companion story for details). That required two couples with similar skills building identical houses. The Ademmers became our component builders when they chose a Miles design called the Foxwood. Their building site was near the southern Minnesota town of New Prague. Population: 2,952.

Outside of town, gently rolling pastures alternate with plowed fields. Fences separate one from another like stitches edging the patches of an oversize quilt. Asphalt roads, usually as straight and purposeful as the people, for no apparent reason will occasionally curve or twist.

David Ademmer is a strapping young man with a bit of little boy still in his face and a mop of curly blond

**An accessible home site** in Minnesota allowed Miles to drive its flatbed delivery truck right to foundation. After David Ademmer (center) and helpers unloaded small bundles, the special truck bed's powered rollers eased the bundled components off the truck and onto ground. Items needed first were on top.

**Floor trusses** span 27-foot width of the Ademmers' house. Not normal kit components, they were supplied by Miles to test pros and cons. The pros: They saved time and left the lower level unobstructed by support posts. Some cons: They arrived off-square and had to be shimmed. And Miles questions cost effectiveness.

hair topping off his mid-height frame. He works as a welder at Minnesota Valley Engineering, seven miles away. David is a man of few words, at least with strangers. And neither he nor Chris, who works in the sales department of the same company, has been bitten by wanderlust. They intend to spend their lives in New Prague.

One good reason to start with a house of their own. "At first we figured we'd rent for a year, but we heard about Miles and the build-it-yourself homes, so we went there one Saturday to a seminar," Chris says in her shy but matter-of-fact way. "My uncle built a Miles kit twenty years ago," David volunteers. "He had good luck with it." Miles soon had a deal.

That was August 1987. Chris and David had already set June 11, 1988, as their wedding date. To start married life in the new house, they'd have to build through a Minnesota winter. David's father, Jerry Ademmer (a foundation contractor), volunteered to help. Chris's father, George Hadac (a retired butcher), also signed on. Neither they nor David had had much carpentry experience, but all were knowledgeable about tools.

A Miles house can be customized to a considerable extent. The Ademmers added an exterior door, a deck to the kitchen, and another door on the back of the lower level. Miles does the customizing on CAD terminals in its Minneapolis headquarters, and computer-generated cutting diagrams go off to one of its three plants.

The Ademmers' house was cut and the components assembled at a Miles plant in nearby Owatonna. On my visit I didn't find an automated factory. Components are cut on radial-arm saws. Framing panels are assembled by hand on big tables with metal edges for squaring and red-painted stripes indicating stud placement. Workers use pneumatic nailers to put the pieces together.

All pieces and assemblies are numbered or lettered to match identical codes on the blueprints. "And they're in sequence," manager Vince Bakken points out, "so that as the builders put the house together they don't end up with a twelve-foot wall section that they can't get into the house."

The Ademmers broke ground in late August, and Jerry and David Ademmer laid the block foundation. "It was letter perfect," says Scott Gerber of Miles. The kit arrived on November 12th, a Thursday. David took the day off work. (In all, he took only five days' vacation to work on the house. But it pretty much ate up his free time when weather permitted working, he confirms.)

On delivery day the sky was clear, the ground was dry, and the temperature reached a balmy 60 degrees F. The preassembled framing panels went up fast.

On the second day, with the two dads working, they hit a snag. "One framing panel wasn't square and it threw off a corner," David says.

The only real framing problem they had—indeed the biggest problem of all (aside from the weather)—was the angled stairway (see plan). Miles did not panelize the framing around the stair. "Too many site variables," Gerber explains. So like the Rafters, our stick-building couple in Pennsylvania, the Ademmers had to cut 2 x 4s to size and deal with odd angles in the installation. That was the hard part. "Blueprints didn't explain it well," David wrote in the log they kept daily. "I don't think the Miles people knew exactly how to do that stairway," he confided to me later. "It was our first," Gerber admits.

On November 18th the Ademmer team discovered another problem: The floor trusses weren't square. Not a standard component for a Miles kit, the company bought them from a local fabricator. "It wasn't a serious problem," says Gerber, "but the Ademmers didn't know what to do." David called Miles and was instructed how to shim to square the ends.

By November 23rd the second-story wall framing was up. "It's finally starting to look like something, and I want to work on the house even more," David wrote in the log. With the Thanksgiving weekend coming, he knew he'd get in four good days.

The weather had other ideas.

On November 28th, the Saturday after Thanksgiving, freezing rain was falling. "We chipped ice off the studs for two hours, worked an hour, then gave up," David laments softly.

The next day they put a propane heater in the lower level and cranked on the heat to melt the ice, then worked 12 hours under numbing conditions.

But by this time Chris was beginning to see her dream house materialize. "It was so neat to walk around in the upstairs and tell where the rooms are and how big they're going to be," she wrote on November 29th.

December 5th: Another problem. It was time to put up the roof trusses, which were numbered, but inexplicably their blueprints didn't have the number codes on them. The builders guessed which went where, called it wrong, and had to add some bracing to a truss as a result.

"Taking time off work tomorrow so that I can close off the roof because of coming rain and snow," David noted in the log on December 6th. He called on two additional helpers to get the job done fast. And they did. "As I put up the last sheet of roof sheathing it started raining," David recalls.

Soon after Christmas winter arrived with a vengeance. "Some days it was twenty below with strong winds," David tells me. They logged only 9½ hours in January. February saw some improvement. By mid-month they were working about half the days, albeit with gloves and layers of clothes.

In March the weather improved, and the Ademmer team began the final phase of exterior work: the siding and trim. Siding came primed, and Chris added another coat of gray primer.

On Sunday, March 13th, David worked for seven hours finishing the trim and siding and installing the garage doors. By the end of the day he'd completed the exterior to the point

**Factory-assembled** wall-framing panels used in Minnesota house were light enough for two-person handling—the longest was 12 feet. "We just lifted them up, tacked them down, then leveled and squared everything," says Ademmer. "It went fast—faster than I thought it would."

**David Ademmer** and helpers put up roof trusses in 61 hours, though location codes were not on the blueprints at the site. (That caused some mislocation that necessitated fixes.) Compare that time with the 199 hours that the Rafters spent cutting and installing rafters.

*Popular Science* and Miles had determined would end our "contest." Gerber added up the hours logged: 600 hours, 15 minutes.

## Sweat equity

"If you were to start now, what would you do differently?" I ask David. "I'd start in the spring," he replies. But he admits to no real regrets.

And no wonder. He and Chris have a lovely new home for which they paid about half the market value. Base price for the kit is $45,000. They bought kitchen cabinets, carpeting, paint, and plumbing fixtures locally, so they actually paid Miles a little less, even with the interest on the construction loan. Based on what other houses in the area are selling for, David thinks the house could sell today for about $90,000 (including a small portion of land).

Not that he'd consider that. But he is toying with the idea of building another house to sell, preferably with a partner. Now that he's got an education, would he go to the lumberyard and buy the raw materials?

"Too much work," he replies, with just the hint of a grin. "I'd get another Miles kit—with panelization" —*V. Elaine Gilmore. Photos by Billy Robin McFarlin.*

# 594 hours —old tech

**Dorothy and Marty Rafter** stand before their Pennsylvania home after they invested 594 hours in its construction. There's a roof over their head (albeit unshingled), but no windows or doors are installed and no siding or trim has been applied. It was to take them an additional 340 hours to get their home to the state of completion seen on page 9.

**Floor plan** was identical for both homes, but the Rafters opted to flop it, putting the garage on the left. Angled entry stairs of the split-level house lead up to the main level (shown) and down to semi-excavated living level below. Both owner-builders found framing around stairs tricky and slow. Walls are 2 × 4 studs with fiberglass insulation. Foam sheathing on the outside boosts the insulation value to R-20. Ceiling has two layers of fiberglass batts for an R-40 rating.

My first visit to the Pennsylvania site was on a raw November day just after Marty Rafter had bulldozed a driveway up his hill to plunk a mobile home on a ledge for his family to live in during construction of its new home. The family—wife, Dorothy, and three small children—seemed surprisingly chipper at the prospect of roughing it through a mountain winter while their house was built farther up the wooded hill.

The Rafters had put their house in suburban Philadelphia on the market and would invest the profit realized from its sale in a Miles Homes kit; base price: under $45,000 (including plumbing, heating, and bathroom fixtures). Dorothy and Marty had worked several years on renovations at their old home, so they weren't intimidated that they'd never built a house from scratch.

Dorothy had begun investigating

kit packagers when she spotted a newspaper ad for a local Miles Homes seminar. She and Marty attended and liked what they heard about how the company operated. But it was their choice of the Miles' Foxwood model that brought them to the attention of *Popular Science.*

Several months earlier I had visited Miles headquarters outside Minneapolis to discuss a major article based on field research Miles hoped to do. My discussions with Miles executives solidified our plans. We needed two couples who had comparable skills, both tackling their first home-building project, and both choosing the same model. But we needed one couple to opt for all the preassembly Miles could offer, while the other must be willing to invest more "sweat equity" by taking a discounted package with *nothing* precut—even though it wasn't a standard Miles package.

Fortunately, the Miles operation is efficiently computerized so that the company was able to canvass its national sales to match up two couples for this "contest." *Popular Science* had selected the Foxwood as an attractive, challenging project for publication. By choosing to buy this model in a nothing-precut kit, Dorothy and Marty Rafter had qualified for the "Great House Race."

What Miles hoped to learn was which "new tech" assemblies—some common to most Miles kits, some under consideration—benefitted the novice builder most. *Popular Science* wanted to know just how much time factory assembly of some components could save.

Actually nobody told the couples they were in a contest. We didn't want to skew the results by instilling a determination to surpass the other couple. In our frequent monitoring of both projects, Miles and *Popular Science* revealed only that we had parallel projects afoot in an effort to compare construction experiences. Both couples were provided with identical daily log sheets in which they agreed to enter, after each work day, the number of hours all adults had spent working on the house. Both couples were asked to follow the same logical work sequence, through the 15 construction phases that would bring their houses to a weathertight state, with exteriors completed. (We asked for no record keeping on the subsequent interior work because such jobs as insulating would be identical for both projects, and decisions about finishing and trimming interior surfaces

**Delivery of kit** isn't made until the foundation is in. Mountainous Pennsylvania site kept truck at some distance. Organized stacking is vital and helps simplify checking against load list to make sure that no pieces are missing or damaged.

**Because all joists** had to be hand cut on old-tech home, framing around the skewed entry stair only added tricky angles to the chore. But in absence of long-span trusses, a central support beam was needed for second-story joists.

**Once floor deck** was added, every sill and stud had to be cut by hand. Here, Marty is framed by the stairwell. Only after all walls were sheathed could the crew begin the roof framing.

**Owner-builder Marty Rafter** is seen here in a forest of hand-cut rafter assemblies. By far the most time-consuming part of his construction, rafters have no place in Rafter's future now.

## BOX SCORE

Miles and Popular Science broke the construction into 15 phases. Here's what the two kits contained for each phase—and how many hours each step took the owner-builders.

| | Rafters (hrs.) | Ademmers (hrs.) |
|---|---|---|
| 1 LOWER WALL FRAMING—The Rafters got uncut 2 × 4s; the Ademmers got assembled framing panels. | 42½ | 23½ |
| 2 LOWER BEARING STRUCTURE—The Rafters' house (with floor joists, see below) required a beam and supporting posts in the center of the lower level. The Ademmers' house (using floor trusses) did not require a center support. Both owner-builders had to erect identical bearing-wall framing around the angled stairway. | 49 | 22 |
| 3 FLOOR SUPPORTS—The Rafters were supplied with joists, which they cut and installed 16 in. on center. The Ademmers got factory-assembled floor joists to install 24 in. on center. | 61 | 20½ |
| 4 FLOOR SHEATHING—The Rafter kit contained standard ply subflooring, which would be topped with ⅝-in. underlayment. The Ademmer kit contained ¾-in., single-layer, tongue-and-groove flooring, designed to be used with trusses. It is glued as well as nailed. | 39* | 31 |
| 5 UPPER WALL FRAMING—The Rafters got uncut 2 × 4s; the Ademmers got preassembled framing panels. | 63 | 42 |
| 6 WALL SHEATHING—An "apples to apples" comparison that proved to be anything but equal in the doing (see Scoring the Builders, below). | 14 | 56 |
| 7 GARAGE WALL FRAMING—Uncut 2 × 4s to the Rafters; assembled framing panels to the Ademmers. | 32½ | 24½ |
| 8 ROOF FRAMING—The Rafters used rafters; the Ademmers used roof trusses. | 199 | 61 |
| 9 GABLE-END OVERHANGS—The Ademmers received preassembled overhangs with the soffit boards already applied. The Rafters received material only. | 39 | 12½ |
| 10 ROOF SHEATHING | 23½* | 68¾ |
| 11 OVERHANG CONSTRUCTION | 32½* | 58 |
| 12 ROOFING (metal edging, felt, roof vents, shingles) | — | 68 |
| 13 WINDOWS AND EXTERIOR DOOR | — | 13½ |
| 14 GARAGE DOORS | — | 10 |
| 15 TRIM AND SIDING | — | 88 |
| TOTAL | 594 | 600¼ |

*Incomplete at "contest" end. Rafters spent 17 more hrs. on roof sheathing—which put them 28 hrs. faster than Ademmers on this identical task. The prime reason: Ademmers tackled the job in the midst of a Minnesota winter. Rafters also spent 32 more hrs. on overhang construction. And as we go to press Marty Rafter has not laid the underlayment over the subfloor.

**Box score** tabulates hours of construction for old and new tech houses.

would introduce incomparable variables.)

By chance, the building sites couldn't have been more different: One was in the middle of 40 acres of flat Minnesota cornfield; the one I monitored was on a rocky knoll in a Pennsylvania forest. Further, the Rafters, after receiving their blueprint, decided that flopping the floor plan to put the garage on the left made more sense for their site.

("Made all the difference," Dorothy tells me. "The garage now hides a neighbor's barn from our living room. And that's one of the great things about a sophisticated company like Miles: It's flexible about changes—the computer made the switch with all dimensions and labels reversed.")

By my November visit to the Rafters, Marty had already staked out the position of the house on the hip of a hill that falls away sharply in two

directions. He'd made a first lame attempt at excavating for the lower floor, and was hoping to get his foundation in before the freeze set in (his property isn't far from Valley Forge, where George Washington and his troops spent a memorable winter).

Because of last-minute snarls in the sale of their old home, the Rafters couldn't schedule delivery before February 6th. (Miles won't deliver until the purchaser documents—with a snapshot—that his foundation is in. In all sales, Miles handles the construction financing, so the company is highly motivated toward getting each house built. It doesn't want to inherit an abandoned project.)

## A memorable start

When I visit again in mid-May, I find that the Rafters remember that February day all too well. Marty tells me he "called in all his debts," and was surprised at the number of friends who showed up to help unload. But he wasn't able to keep the day organized, and later regretted he had involved so many inexperienced hands.

"It was a bitterly cold day," Marty recalls, "and care wasn't taken to stack parts in the order they'd be needed later. Not all our counts against the load list were accurate, either."

"Did that mean you had to buy additional materials?" I ask.

"No. When I notified Miles what was short and that a piece or two had come damaged, they delivered replacement material right away. And they supplied *everything*—down to the nails and bolts. I don't think I spent one hundred dollars at the local home center during construction."

Were the blueprints clear and accurate? "A few details were omitted, or confused me," Marty admits. "But Miles supplies phone numbers for its specialists in construction, financing,

heating, electricity. There's always help available."

How about on-site help? "It was mainly us," Marty says, tossing an arm around Dorothy. "My dad and uncle helped out when they had weekends free. But I was surprised how scarce my friends became once construction started. This has been strictly a weekend project. Dot and I developed a game plan, spending Monday through Friday getting prepared; then we'd charge out into the snow on Saturday and sometimes mess things up, spending the afternoon redoing things we'd done wrong in the morning.

"Sundays were always the best days. Somehow we didn't feel the Saturday pressure of 'so much to do this weekend.' But by Sunday night the site looked like a battlefield, and it was important to save some time before dark to clean up and reorganize for the next work session."

Other tips from the front:
● "If you're going to alter or add to the floor plan, do it before you start building. The nice thing about working with an outfit as well-organized as Miles is that its computer system can bang out a revised set of working drawings in no time. But it messes up all calculations if you change your mind *after* you're very far along."
● "One great boon with a kit is that it eliminates shopping, saving you hours at the lumberyard and

hardware store. And because kit packagers buy in quantity, they can get the best quality in lumber and plywood. There's no comparison between what they can supply and the stuff you find in local lumberyards."
● "Find a company that's not pushy about accepting complete packages. For instance, I canceled the Miles electrical package, figuring I'd buy that locally, and we upgraded our bathroom fixtures, getting credit for the basic units that come with the Foxwood kit."

What's been the *worst* part of the experience? "The rafters!" Marty and Dorothy shout in unison. "Add up the hours we spent just building the roof," Marty continues: "Two hundred ninety-three! That's nearly half of the time we've spent on the whole house —and we haven't even applied the flashing, felt, and shingles! All those angle cuts for each rafter brace . . . !"

The most telling question you can put to anyone at the end of an owner-builder project is: "Would you do it again?" Marty thinks this over, then flashes an appreciative grin at Dorothy: "With a wife as supportive and helpful as mine, a guy can tackle anything. We've learned enough so that the next one would go quicker." Dorothy picks up his thought: "One thing we've learned is to start building in the spring," she says. "And we'd buy a kit with trusses," he adds. For a catalog of plans, write Miles Homes, Box 9495, Minneapolis, MN 55400—*by Al Lees. Photos by Greg Sharko.*

---

## Scoring the builders

Miles marketing manager and corporate architect Scott Gerber monitored both sites and analyzed the daily logs of the participants to determine whether our two families were, indeed, equal in skill and efficiency (one of the reasons to include identical steps in our test).

His conclusion: "The Ademmers and Rafters were equal in skill, but they were not necessarily equal in efficiency." He gives the nod to the Rafters. They lost the race only because of the stacked deck.

"Marty Rafter would read the instructions very carefully, get them in his mind, then go ahead," said Gerber. Rafter's superior efficiency showed up most on the wall sheathing. "He rented scaffolding," Gerber explained. "He spent a couple of hours erecting it to form a continuous bridge around the house. Then he put on the sheathing in twelve hours. The Ademmers walked the sheathing up a ladder a piece at a time. It took them fifty-six hours."

But when it came to roofing (step 12) the Ademmer crew proved more efficient: They did the job in 69 hours; the Rafters took 95½. The reason: "Ademmer called in some friends that day who really knew what they were doing," says Gerber.

Efficiency might have been improved with more sophisticated tools. Both groups used only the basics—circular saw, table saw, reciprocating saw, drills, and hand tools. "But the Rafters went for professional tools —twenty-four-ounce framing hammer, worm-drive circular saw," Gerber reported. "The Ademmers tended to use handyman-grade tools." No doubt they would have reduced the man-hours significantly if they had rented (or bought) power nailers and staplers. "But," Gerber cautions, "those can be dangerous, especially the pneumatic nailers capable of driving framing nails. You've got to know what you're doing."

Gerber's advice: Take a systems approach to each task; try to organize it like a production line. And always work with two or three people."—*V. E. G.*

# decked dormer

When Santa Barbara homeowner David Dickinson told me he'd paid $150,000 for the modest bungalow I was visiting, I had to suppress a gasp. Sure, this was an attractive example of the Craftsman style that spawned many such homes across the country from 1905 through the early 1920s, distinguished by deep roof overhangs, exposed rafter ends, full-width porches with fat tapered piers, and clipped gables. But the Dickinson home was only a single-story bungalow with six cramped rooms. The roof dormer was a nice architectural detail, but it brought light only into an attic storage area, access to which was by means of a pull-down ladder stair in the tight hallway.

I knew that Santa Barbara was one of those elegant and coveted Southern California addresses where new housing was scarce and wildly expensive, but I wasn't prepared when Dickinson went on to say: "We bought it four years ago. The house as is would now bring $250,000."

At the time of my visit, the Dickinsons were at the low point of a building adventure that was to add at least another $150,000 to the value of their home. David's wife, Susan, sensing that new son, Sam, would soon outgrow his small nursery and need *their* bedroom, had spotted an announcement in the local paper that one of public television's most popular series, "This Old House," was looking for a Craftsman-style bungalow to remodel over the

**Not much difference?** That's the point. The house near downtown Santa Barbara was a pure example of the Craftsman style: Its street face had to be preserved. Yet this single-story home crowded its growing family, and the only way to go was up. The original dormer (which brought light to cramped attic storage area) was retained while a giant dormer was added to the rear of house, offset from each side so its bulk is hidden from the street. A handsome pergola (soon to sport wisteria vines) and matching balcony deck—both of redwood—were bonuses.

PHOTOS BY FRED LICHT, AL LEES

final six weekly episodes this past spring. From over 100 responses, hers was chosen, and thus host Bob Vila and carpenter Norm Abram entered their lives. Boston's Public Broadcasting Service outlet, WGBH, which produces the show, had invited me to document the project in print.

The Dickinsons knew how "This Old House" works: The selected homeowners must cover the costs of all professional labor (which they're encouraged to keep down by doing most of the unskilled work themselves). The show generates publicity donations of building products and appliances (in this case over $80,500 worth). It's a good deal, and the homeowner is assured that the project will move fast because of the inexorable demands of a weekly TV show. "This Old House" works so close to its PBS deadlines, it gives goose bumps to a print journalist like me.

### An architect for integrity

On the advice of Bob Vila, the Dickinsons worked with local architect Brian Cearnal, who built them an expert scale model to show how the decked dormer would look. Cearnal was determined not to fudge the original architecture, so he simply extended the existing roof pitch up to a new ridge (see drawing), set the dormer several feet in at each side wall to minimize its bulk when viewed from the street, and (best touch of all) matched the clipped gables of the original roof.

Once the demolition was launched, Vila and Abram took a trip south to Pasadena to visit the Gamble House, perhaps the most striking example of the Craftsman style created by brother architects Charles and Henry Greene. From this truly handcrafted mansion Abram brought back inspirations that he incorporated into the Santa Bar-

bara project—notably in the handsome redwood pergola he spliced onto the driveway side of the house, which replaced an unattractive aluminum canopy over the kitchen entry.

At the time of my visit, there were still two episodes to shoot, and the project swarmed with workmen. Homeowners David and Susan were a bit glassy-eyed as they worked alongside the pros—David hanging a fiberglass mesh (using heavy-duty wallpaper paste) over all the cracked plaster downstairs, while Susan laid a ceramic-tile floor in the new upstairs bathroom.

With any old-house remodeling, unexpected extras will be encountered, raising cost estimates; but the Dickinsons got more than their share. The first and most critical jolt was an inadequate foundation. When the house was built (in 1923 for $3,500), it was local practice to use sand from the nearby ocean beach in concrete mixes. Over the decades, the salt in the sand dissolved, leaving crumbly concrete. Abram's early inspection of the Dickinson foundation confirmed that it would not support the additional weight of an upper story with a new bathroom. The entire house had to be jacked up so the existing foundation could be removed, excavation for a new one dug, and new concrete poured.

Of course, this meant the homeowners had to pack up and move out, because all utilities would have to be disconnected. Once the concrete had set, the jacks were lowered so the house could settle gently onto its new foundation. But the workmen hadn't thought to remove an unused central chimney; the house hung up on it and cracks shot across the plaster walls like lightning strikes, and several interior doors no longer closed. It was to repair those plaster cracks that the contractor came up with that fiberglass mesh (called FibreWall) David was hanging. It's made by Regal of Scandinavia (433 S. Spring St., Los Angeles, CA 90013), and once it was painted over, it created a textured wall surface that hid all the cracks.

Meanwhile, it had been discovered that all original roof framing (including attic floor joists) were 2x4s. There's no snow-load problem in Santa Barbara, but this structure was wholly inadequate for the added weight and had to be strengthened. Then a large section of the rear roof was stripped away, and though a weather tarp was stretched across at the end of the day, it was blown back by that night's storm (unluckily the worst of the season). Water poured into the two back rooms below wrecking both ceilings.

When it came time for wiring and plumbing extensions, the pros found existing runs inadequate, so rewiring was done and new piping had to be installed all the way out to the city main. True, the Dickinsons would have eventually had to deal with both these problems, but coming all at once, the solutions soon ate up David's $50,000 home-improvement loan, and, despite all their sweat equity, the couple was scrambling for additional cash.

What the Dickinsons got for their investment is a spacious master bedroom suite with a bathroom featuring two vanities and a separate tub and shower, plus a walk-

PHOTO CREDITS: MIKE ELIASON, AL LEES, FRED LICHT

**Key to the project** was the addition of a Craftsman-style stair for access to the new bedroom suite (top left). Premortised posts were notched for bolting to stairwell walls; top and bottom rails were pre-grooved to take square balusters with spacer blocks. True Craftsman touch: The window through living room partition (in which homeowner perches son Sam). At lower left, erection of the back wall frame, after a giant hole had been chopped in the roof. Note cantilevered extensions nailed to existing joists for upper deck. Cramped side stoop would be replaced by a pergola-covered side porch that connects with the spacious pressure-treated rear deck.

in closet large enough for a built-in counter of cabinets to serve as Susan's craft bench. Specific Craftsman-style features include the Greene-inspired pergola handcrafted by Abram and a shallow deck-balcony cantilevered across the back dormer with access (through low-emissivity glass sliders) from both the bedroom and Susan's workroom. Access to this new suite is by means of a handsome Craftsman-style stair, space for which was borrowed, downstairs, from Susan and David's former bedroom. Sam's crib is now tucked under the boxed-in risers in that room.

In the final moments of the show's sixth episode—after taking the camera on a tour of a far-from-finished project,

71 days from the initial demolition—host Bob Vila confronted the Dickinsons with cost totals. By then they had poured $57,000 into the project. Vila asked the inevitable question: "Would you do it again?" "Absolutely," replied David.

In actuality, David soon after published a report with a national news service on the "nightmare" experience and the fact that after the TV crew had departed, much work remained. A few weeks later, the show's executive producer Russell Morash was in Los Angeles to accept a fifth Emmy award for the series. As "This Old House" continues on PBS, he's still seeking homes to remodel. Any volunteers?—*by Al Lees. Photos by Mike Eliason.*

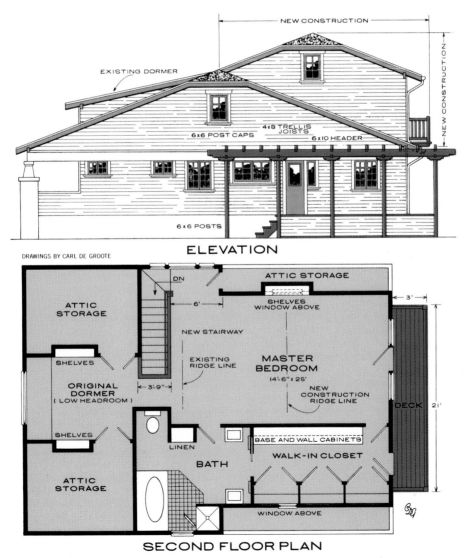

**Elevation drawing** shows relationship of new construction to existing dormer.

# ways to expand your home

**well-rounded room addition**

**The owners** of this ranch-style house in Guilford, Connecticut, found their living space too cramped and humdrum. They set several criteria for the room addition they planned to improve it: There had to be space to store their extensive book collection, the atmosphere had to be pleasant for reading and relaxing, and they wanted a lot of natural light and a dramatic design.

Noyes, Vogt Architects, also of Guilford, provided two distinct spaces. A sun-room (far right), connected to the original house, is topped with eight skylights. This room also serves as a transition between the house and the new library and provides access to the front and side yard gardens.

The "round room" (center) is really a square. Columns support a dome within it. Floor-to-ceiling book shelves are built into the corners, and there are window seats along the walls.

*Reprinted by permission of Homeowner magazine.*

It happens to many homeowners. The house that seemed entirely adequate when they made the decision to buy seems to shrink over the years, whether by dint of additions to the family, changes in lifestyle or merely an expanded vision of the comforts of home. But most homes can grow with their owner's needs and horizons—you can add a room, build on a second story, convert an unused attic or transform the garage into living space.

By adding on rather than moving out, you get to keep the house, neighborhood and schools you're comfortable with, while increasing your living space. You also increase your property's value. You may be able to recoup a good portion, if not all, of your investment when you do finally sell your house. For example, a *HomeOwner* survey of real estate appraisers, projected a cost recovery of 105 to 116 percent for a room addition if you do all the work yourself. If the job is done by a professional, the cost recovery would be 50 to 75 percent.

## Planning what's right for you

To plan your new space, consider your needs, where the space should be located and how it will affect the rest of your home. Start by drawing a floor plan of your house the way it is right now. Then draw in the space you want to add, including the location and relative size of doors, windows, stairs, electrical and plumbing connections, closets and any built-in features. Next, step outside and determine how the new space will change the appearance of your home's exterior. It's a good idea to keep the new space in scale with the rest of the house. Remember that *scale* is not exactly the same as *size*. Scale also relates to proportion. The proportions of the new structure and all its elements should respect and relate to those of the existing house.

You'll also need to familiarize yourself with the local building code. It sets standards for the types, sizes and performance of structural materials; electrical wiring, plumbing, heating, cooling, ventilation, interior ceiling heights and minimum provisions for light and fresh air (see "Minimum Space Requirements" on page 23 for requirements listed in a national building code).

Before you begin construction, you'll have to submit your plans to the local code official. If your plans are in accord with the local code, he'll issue a building permit. Once the work is complete, the official will inspect your work and if it's up to snuff, issue final approval.

If this sounds a bit complicated, seek the help of an architect or remodeling contractor. Even if you plan on doing all or part of the work yourself, a pro can provide valuable advice during the planning and start-up stages.

An architect or contractor can also help you come up with a cost estimate for your project. The amount you'll need to spend will depend on your plans, labor costs in your area, the price and quality of materials you select and how much of the work you do yourself. In areas with high labor costs, expect to pay about $85 per square foot for extensive remodeling work. In some areas, the cost will be much lower, and if you put your own sweat into the project, the price will drop further. If your plans are growing beyond your budget, revise them before cutting corners on materials, or try phasing in your plans over time.

## Building a room addition

The way your house is situated on its lot will help you determine where to build a room addition. Generally speaking, room additions are best placed in the side or backyard where they will have the least impact when your house is viewed from the street. Many local codes set minimums on the distance from the house to the property line, usually 20 feet for side and backyards, and 40 feet for front yards.

Of course, you must balance your original floor plan with the uses of the added space. Keep in mind that a new family room or bedroom placed toward the backyard will probably be more private and better insulated from street noise. You'll save on plumbing and electrical costs by placing a kitchen addition near your existing kitchen.

When it comes to building the addition, you can forego the expense of building a basement, even if the original house has one. Make sure the foundation on which it's built matches the height of the existing foundation. And check the location of existing sewer and water lines before starting to excavate.

The simplest kind of room addition is one that's tied into the existing house frame. You'll have to remove some of the house's siding and sheathing to determine sill and floor heights and to locate existing studs. From there, you can usually use standard wall-framing techniques to enclose the new space. Follow local requirements for floor- and roof-fram-

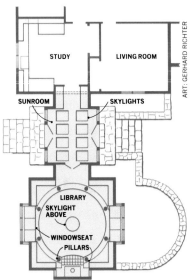

PHOTOS BY ROBERT PERRON-BLACK

STUDY    LIVING ROOM

SUNROOM    SKYLIGHTS

LIBRARY
SKYLIGHT
ABOVE

WINDOWSEAT
PILLARS

ART: GERHARD RICHTER

ing systems and insulation levels.

In addition to cutting a doorway through the wall from your house to the new space, you may have to remove what used to be the exterior finish of your house. You can put up drywall and paint or paper as you wish, or you can incorporate the exterior finish, such as stone or wood siding, into the design of the new room. Outside, match the siding and roofing to those on the existing house. For a look at a two-story addition that's attached to a sidewall of the original house see "Double-Decker Addition," on page 23. For a look at a room addition attached to the house by a breezeway see "Well-Rounded Room Addition," on page 20.

Room additions require heat and power. Many existing oil and gas heating systems can handle up to 50 percent additional load. New ducts or radiators may be all you'll need. If you heat with electricity, you'll have to install baseboard heaters. Check with a contractor for specifics.

Your current electrical service should provide enough power for a simple room addition. Create a new circuit at the service panel to feed power into the room. If you're adding a bath or kitchen, you'll need to tie into the existing water and drain systems. It's a good idea to get the advice of a plumber even if you plan on making the connections yourself.

## Building up

Building up or adding an extra story to your house is a good way to gain living space when there's not enough room on your property for an addition to a sidewall of your home. However, keep in mind that a new story will have a major impact on the exterior of your home, so its design requires careful consideration. See how a second story build-up actually improved the design of a home on page 23.

If you can avoid covering the entire first floor with a new second floor, do so because such an addition can overwhelm a small one-story house and destroy its scale. For example, a second-story addition will have less of an impact on a split-level than on a tiny Cape Cod.

Second-story additions seem to work best when confined to a wing or portion of your house (the shorter leg of an L-shaped plan, for example, or

## double-decker addition

**After 14 years,** this North Shore, Long Island, New York, house was too dear to its owners to give up. They created additional space by attaching a two-story addition to their original house (highlighted area in floor plan).

Contractor Nick Vissicelli of Marnick Construction Corp., Searington, New York, created a large first-floor living room/sunroom (center) and a large master suite on the second floor (far right). The contractor blended the new exterior with the original but enhanced the design by setting the first floor back slightly and using the second floor to cover a narrow deck (above).

The owners did most of the finish work themselves. The cost for the entire project, which included constructing a full basement underneath the addition and installing a completely new heating system for the entire house, was about $90,000.

PHOTOS BY STEVEN FAY

over a one-story garage attached to a two-story house). Locate a large build-up project in the rear of the house, where it will have the least impact on your home's most visible side.

Before starting work, be sure to check two things: Code restrictions that might limit building heights in your area, and the structural integrity of your house. Unlike building a room addition on to a sidewall, a sec-

ond-story build-up must be supported by your house's existing structure and foundation. The existing ceiling joists will be the floor joists for the new space, and they must be able to support the new load. An architect or contractor can help you determine if the structure can support a new floor. But if your ceiling joists are smaller than 2 x 8 or spaced farther than 16 inches on center, you'll have to beef up the floor framing.

Adding a new floor could lead to some rearranging of first-floor spaces because you'll need a stairway leading to the new rooms. If, however, you're building over a wing or garage, or expanding a small attic, you may be able to keep disruptions to a minimum. Try to place the new stair adjacent to a hallway or a foyer, areas that get a lot of traffic. Professionals try to build new stairs directly above existing ones. Chances are there's a

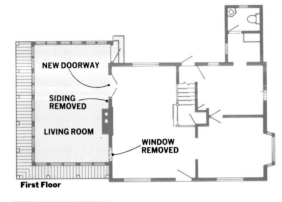

**First Floor**

NEW DOORWAY

SIDING REMOVED

LIVING ROOM

WINDOW REMOVED

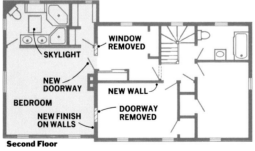

**Second Floor**

SKYLIGHT

WINDOW REMOVED

NEW DOORWAY

NEW WALL

BEDROOM

DOORWAY REMOVED

NEW FINISH ON WALLS

## minimum space requirements

When you add living space, local codes will have something to say about the way you do it. Here are minimums from the "One- and Two-Family Dwelling Code," a national building code. Your code will meet or exceed these standards.

● Kitchens must have at least 50 square feet of space.

● All other rooms, except bathrooms, must have at least 70 square feet of space.

● Hallways and stairways must be at least 3 feet wide.

● Ceilings must be at least 7 feet, 6 inches high for half the room area and no lower than 5 feet for other areas.

● Glazing in each room, except bathrooms, must equal or exceed 8 percent of the floor area, and half the window area must be operable.

● Baths require at least 3 square feet of glazing, unless mechanically ventilated.

closet in this space in an existing house.

One great disadvantage to building up is that you have to remove the roof to frame the new space. It's a fairly simple matter to strip the shingles and sheathing and dismantle the framing structure, but since a roof helps to hold a house together, you should get advice on bracing requirements before removing it. And taking the old roof off exposes your work area to the weather until the new walls and roof are constructed. Be sure to cover the exposed areas with tarps at the end of every workday to protect against overnight cloud bursts.

Aesthetically, the new roof should match the old, or complement the adjoining roof. Most of the materials removed from an old roof can be reused on the one.

Supplying utilities to a new second

**raise high
the roof beams**

**A few years ago,** the house pictured at left was a one-story Cape in dire need of paint. But rather than settle for a facelift, the owners improved the quality of their home by enlarging the attic and building up the rear section. Except for cosmetic changes, the front of the house (not shown) looks as it always did.

The New York City architectural firm of Buck, Cane added only 60 square feet to the existing attic space, but in doing so, they were able to design a master suite (far right) and study.

The architects changed what was a dining room into a living room/dining area. By doing this, they were able to create a new study on the first floor and by removing two closets, design a hallway that leads from the front door straight back to the kitchen, stairs and rear of the house. The cost: $80,000.

story is simply a matter of extending your home's present mechanical systems. Unless your second-floor addition includes a bathroom, plumbing work will be limited to diverting and extending vent pipes.

Second-story build-ups generally yield a large amount of added space. You'll probably need one or more new electrical circuits, especially if your addition includes a kitchen or if you plan to use electric baseboard heat. As in the case of a room addition, check the excess capacity of your present oil or gas heating system; you may be able to simply add on to it.

### Attic conversions

An attic is a perfect out-of-the-way spot for a guest bedroom, quiet study, art studio or kids' playroom. With its dramatically sloped ceilings and windows that probably provide the best views in the house, your attic may hold your best solution to the problem of needing more space.

A quick inspection will tell you how much work is necessary before the attic can be considered suitable for living space. Since the space is already framed and roofed, all you may have to do is add a few windows or skylights, provide for heat and electricity and finish the walls and floors.

Unfortunately, only older homes come equipped with a full-height attic. Most newer houses tend to lack sufficient headroom. For a living space, the roof peak should be at least 8 feet above the attic floor. You can gain added headroom and more wall space for windows by building shed or gable dormers. Dormers are best placed to the rear of the house, where they offer more privacy. A shed dormer should have no less than a 3-in-12 pitch, where the roof rises 3 inches for every foot of horizontal run. Gable dormers should have about a 12-in-12 pitch, which will look good with just about any existing roof pitch.

As in the case of a second-story build-up, make sure the attic floor joists will support the additional load you'll be placing on it. And remember to remove any insulation from between the joists. You can always put insulation between the roof rafters.

You'll need a conventional stairway to get to the new living space—a ladder or pull-down stair probably violates the building code for living space. If you have a conventional

PHOTOS: TOM YEE

**First Floor**

LIVING/ DINING

BED-ROOM

STUDY

BEDROOM

**Second Floor**

DECK

OPEN TO BELOW

MASTER BEDROOM

ATTIC

CLOSET

STUDY

OPEN TO BELOW

ATTIC

ATTIC

stair that's unfinished, you'll need to install a handrail or bannister and finish the treads and risers with hardwood or carpeting. At the top of the stairs, enclose the opening with a railing, or build a full- or half-wall as a safety measure.

If your present ladder or pull-down stair is located in a convenient space, try to build the new stair there. If, however, it's located in the ceiling of a hallway or other inconvenient area, you'll have to find a new location. Again, try to build a new stair over an existing one. Straight-run stairs are most efficient, while U-return stairs, L-stairs, winder stairs or cir-

cular stairs may better serve the configuration of your attic space.

Build the stairs last, but cut a hole for them in the attic floor at the start of construction. This will allow you to move construction materials up to the space with ease.

Converting your attic to living space could deprive you of a good chunk of storage area. You can regain some of it by using the low areas around the perimeter of the attic for storage. As a rule of thumb, build knee walls to enclose the space under rafters that is less than 4 feet high. But rather than nailing up drywall, consider installing built-in shelves or

bookcases. The space behind the knee walls provides handy chaseways for utilities.

Depending on how you plan to use the space, you can leave it as one large space or partition it off into separate rooms. A middle ground is to separate areas with movable storage units or bookcases. This allows you to make quick, inexpensive layout changes.

If you're planning on adding a bath, place it directly above one on the floor below to simplify plumbing connections. Follow the same procedures for heating and electricity as described for the second-story build-up. And in

## child's play

**The vaulted ceiling** in this Wilsonville, Oregon, house, provided the look the owners wanted when they bought it, but as their family grew and space shrank, the 16-foot-high ceilings came to be viewed as wasted space. So, the owners turned their do-it-yourself skills to transforming the space into a loft play area for their kids.

In the space behind the wall in the top photo, there's a stairway leading to the second floor. Originally, an opening looked out over the dining room from the upstairs. The owners removed the rail and some of the drywall to find the existing floor frame. They also exposed the top plate and joist header.

They began construction by attaching 2 x 10 ledgers on both sides of the dining room and installing 2 x 10 joists to create the loft floor frame (see drawing). The 3-foot-high rail (top photo) was anchored to the wall studs at both ends of the loft. They tapped into an existing circuit to bring electricity to the loft.

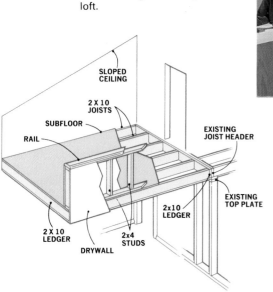

SLOPED CEILING

2 X 10 JOISTS

SUBFLOOR

RAIL

EXISTING JOIST HEADER

EXISTING TOP PLATE

2x10 LEDGER

2 X 10 LEDGER

2x4 STUDS

DRYWALL

Local contractors installed the skylight (bottom photo) and the drywall. The owners did the rest themselves. The total cost for the materials and the labor came to about $1,200.

**The tinted area** of the floor plan (far right) was all the first-floor living space this Orange, Connecticut, house offered. While the attached garage was a logical choice for expansion, the owners didn't want to give up the parking and storage space.

Since the location of the existing garage was perfect, the architectural firm of Maier & Giannelli, New Haven, Connecticut, decided to convert the existing garage to a living room and build a new garage for parking.

The architects got the most out of the space by keeping the original soaring ceiling of the room and designing a variety of built-ins, including a work area (far right) and shelves and cabinets (center). The cabinets are made of birch plywood and particleboard and finished with natural oak half-round edge moldings. New windows along the open walls provide natural light. The conversion allowed the owners to change their old living room into a new master bedroom.

The project came to about $60,000, including the conversion shown here, remodeling of a breezeway, construction of the porch behind the breezeway and the new garage.

both cases, remember that hot air rises; a few floor registers to channel heat from the downstairs up to the attic may be all you need.

### Transforming a garage

When it comes to transforming a garage into living space, the bigger it is and the closer it is to the house, the more sense such a project makes. In converting a garage, your renovation work will be limited to finishing the interior, adding a few windows, dealing with the garage door opening and,

perhaps, softening the view with landscaping. Actually, the presence of a garage door gives you a couple of options: You can remove it and build a standard wall, you can glaze the opening, or you can even find a way to leave the door in place and open it on warm days to extend the interior onto a patio.

The exposed roof structure in many garages gives you a chance to create the feeling of expansive space by simply insulating and cladding the rafters with drywall. Or, if the roof is

PHOTOS: ROBERT PERRON

DEN    PORCH

SHELVES ABOVE

FIREPLACE

RENOVATED
GARAGE

GARAGE
(NEW CONSTRUCTION)

BUILT-IN
CABINETS

pitched high enough, you can create a finished loft space.

Add insulating blankets between the wall studs and finish the interior with drywall. You'll get the best use out of a tight space by installing built-in shelving, bookcases, cabinets and entertainment centers. See the garage conversion above for an example of how built-ins can help to make a conversion work.

Finishing the concrete floor may be your biggest renovation challenge. In most cases, it's best to lay a plastic vapor barrier over the entire floor, build a floor frame with 2 x 4s filling the spaces between the joists with batt insulation, and nail down sheet underlayment, topping it off with finish flooring or carpeting.

Most garages are already wired for electricity, although you'll probably need to add a few more receptacles. And again, look into extending your present heating system. Or, depending on your plans, a cozy wood-burning stove may be the only heat you'll need—by Michael J. Crosbie.

# double your pleasure

**Bottom photo** is an exterior view of three-bay sunspace. The unit is built into the house addition—an option made possible because the unit's manufacturer customizes each order. The upper skylights were added by the owner—lower three came with kit. **Before** photo, above, shows the original projection from the back wall of this two-story tract house—a cramped breakfast nook with two bow windows that received little direct sun. As shown in floor plan (facing page) and **After** photo (right), the owner expanded the projection from the existing ridge line and incorporated a sunspace at eaves.

When a homeowner in Brewster, New York, decided to expand a little breakfast-nook projection from his south-facing rear wall, he knew he wanted to incorporate a kit sunspace into a side wall. But he couldn't decide which side, so he ended up ordering a kit for both. Because these units had to be custom-made to fit the framing of the new wing, he contacted Solar Additions, a sunspace company that's well-known for working with homeowners. (See source list at end of article.)

Solar Additions had just introduced a new "window room" it calls Nature's Window. Basically, it's a four-foot-deep, nine-foot-high extension with 46-by-76-inch window bays (three, four, five, or more) set vertically between laminated arches of either yellow pine or redwood.

Exterior shots of both the three- and four-bay units added to the Brewster wing are on these pages.

To order a kit tailored to your needs you send a photo or sketch of your home's south-facing wall to Solar Additions. Its designers respond with design sketches and estimates. When you buy the custom-made unit it arrives in pieces with instructions for assembly. (Or the company will help you find a qualified local contractor.)

Often you'll have to cut out a section of the wall where Nature's Window will be spliced on; but in the case of the Brewster house, the kit frames were simply tied into the wall and roof framing for the new wing. The new roofing was extended down over the insulated roof deck of the sunspaces at both eaves. (Solar Additions recommends a venting skylight for each bay, but this feature is optional.) Once the new siding was applied, the kits all but disappeared when viewed from the exterior. They were absorbed into the general structure of the extension.

But that aspect of this project is atypical. It's more common for kits of this type to be spliced onto a southfacing wall of a living room, bedroom, or kitchen. The erection procedure is basically the same—and basically as simple. I watched the complete four-bay unit in Brewster go up in one day with a crew of three.

The unit must sit on its own foundation, poured or concrete block. The floor can be an insulated slab or subflooring over wood joists. Either way, you'll probably want to face it with ceramic tile to provide a heat-absorbing masonry mass.

No flooring material comes with the kit, which does include the laminated arches, the ledger and floor plates the arches span, glass, the roofing system, all required fasteners, hardware, and redwood trim. Options include the operable skylights and sun screens.

As the assembly photos indicate, erection isn't especially tricky because, as with most other factory-made kits, parts are designed to fit together. The critical starting point is checking that the redwood floor plate and wall plate are precisely parallel, because each comes with brackets already mounted at the proper spacing to take the laminated arches that bridge these brackets to support the glazing. If the plates diverge from parallel, some arches will be too long or too short.

You run two continuous parallel beads of silicone sealant along the full width of the subfloor before setting the floor plate in place. The wall plate may have to be notched into the siding or shimmed out. Do a neat job because it remains visible after assembly.

Next, insert the preassembled knee-wall panels, sealing all joints and anchoring the frames to the arches. At our site the bottom frames of these panels hadn't been factory-notched to clear the bolt heads securing the arch brackets, so a router came in handy. Insert header strips between the hips of the arches, then add the end walls. You can opt for these solid panels to be factory-as-sembled. We put ours together on site.

Now nail the tongue-and-groove 2 x 6s across the arches to form a roof deck. And if you've chosen the skylight option, cut a rough opening centered on each bay for which a skylight has been supplied. Staple four-mil polyethylene (a vapor barrier) over the roof deck, then cut out the holes for the skylights and install the preassembled H frames, centering them around the skylight holes. Cover the whole deck with rigid insulation, notching it to fit snugly around the projections from the H frames. After dropping in the skylights, apply head and bottom flashing.

In our project the tongue-and-groove roof deck butted against the ends of the 2 x 6 rafters of the main structure. When we nailed on the half-inch plywood sheathing (as a base for shingling) it came flush with the sheathing on the main roof. We drove five-inch ring nails down through the rigid insulation and into the 2 x 6 decking.

To install the glass, run an unbroken bead of the silicone caulk around the redwood casing and set in the double-glazed panel. Hold it temporarily in place with the blocking provided. Fill all voids between the panel edges and casing with silicone. Next day, install the redwood trim supplied.

The order in which you tackle these

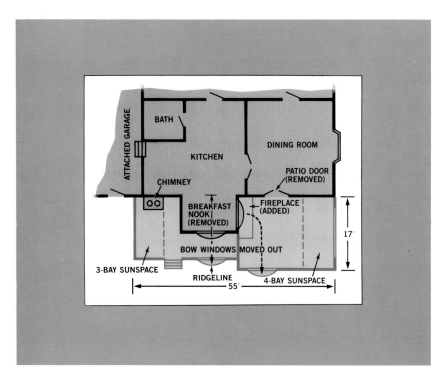

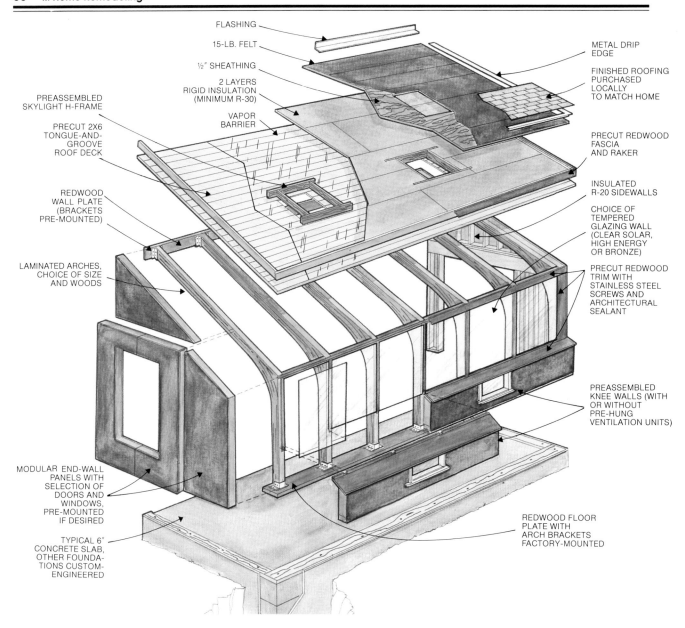

FLASHING

15-LB. FELT

½" SHEATHING

2 LAYERS RIGID INSULATION (MINIMUM R-30)

VAPOR BARRIER

PREASSEMBLED SKYLIGHT H-FRAME

PRECUT 2X6 TONGUE-AND-GROOVE ROOF DECK

REDWOOD WALL PLATE (BRACKETS PRE-MOUNTED)

LAMINATED ARCHES, CHOICE OF SIZE AND WOODS

MODULAR END-WALL PANELS WITH SELECTION OF DOORS AND WINDOWS, PRE-MOUNTED IF DESIRED

TYPICAL 6" CONCRETE SLAB, OTHER FOUNDATIONS CUSTOM-ENGINEERED

METAL DRIP EDGE

FINISHED ROOFING PURCHASED LOCALLY TO MATCH HOME

PRECUT REDWOOD FASCIA AND RAKER

INSULATED R-20 SIDEWALLS

CHOICE OF TEMPERED GLAZING WALL (CLEAR SOLAR, HIGH ENERGY OR BRONZE)

PRECUT REDWOOD TRIM WITH STAINLESS STEEL SCREWS AND ARCHITECTURAL SEALANT

PREASSEMBLED KNEE WALLS (WITH OR WITHOUT PRE-HUNG VENTILATION UNITS)

REDWOOD FLOOR PLATE WITH ARCH BRACKETS FACTORY-MOUNTED

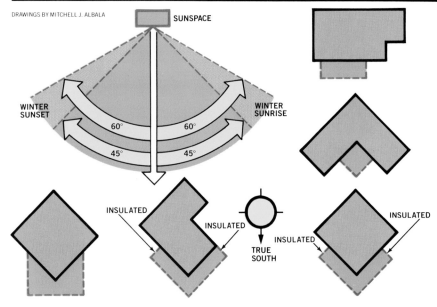

DRAWINGS BY MITCHELL J. ALBALA

SUNSPACE

WINTER SUNSET

WINTER SUNRISE

60°   60°

45°   45°

INSULATED

INSULATED

INSULATED

TRUE SOUTH

INSULATED

INSULATED

## How to site a sunspace

The survey map of your lot will show true north and south, but might not show how your house is oriented. If you site with a compass, you may have to apply a correction of as much as 23 degrees. (Compass and true south agree only on a line through Michigan and Florida.) Once you've found true south you can determine the area that should be free of obstructions. Use compass or protractor to locate 60 degrees east and west of true south as seen from your intended site. These are the points where the sun rises and sets in midwinter. Most solar heat is gained between the time from about 45 degrees east of south (9 a.m. solar time) to 45 degrees west (3 p.m.), so obstructions outside this zone are no problem. Floor-plan sketches show best ways to position a sunspace.—*John H. Mauldin*

*Mauldin is a designer-builder of solar structures and the author of* Sunspaces—Home Additions for Year-Round Natural Living *($14.60 paperback; Tab Books, Blue Ridge Summit, Pa. 17294-0859), from which sketches at right have been adapted.*

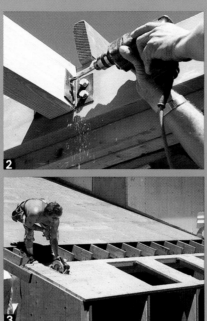

**After floor plate** with pre-mounted brackets is anchored to foundation's sill plate, laminated arches are tipped in place [1] and drilled through bracket holes at top [2] and bottom; then they're bolted in place. Holes for skylights (one per bay) are cut through tongue-and-groove roof deck [3]. Note that deck is recessed below sheathing of adjacent structure to accommodate rigid insulation. Final sheathing on unit—for nailing on shingles—will set flush with the adjacent roof. The vertical glass is carefully tipped into rabbets as seen in frame [4]. Note the sealed edge of the double glazing.

steps may vary. You'll note in the photos that we installed the vertical glazing before dropping in the skylights. This gave us more flexibility in handling the big, heavy panels of glass (a three-person job) because we could pop up—or down—through the open roof holes. Roofing the entire structure with fiberglass shingles over 15-pound roofing felt was the final job.

What's the difference between these add-on sunspaces and the old shed greenhouse? "Energy management," says Lee Stanley, pioneer sunspace designer and director of Solar Additions. "These units—installed for less than a new car would cost—are designed to tap solar energy for human comfort. And though you can certainly grow flowers and food in them all winter, they're meant as added living space. So they must be engineered for efficiencies well beyond those required by a greenhouse. Our models feature double glazing plus insulated roof and side walls to allow storage of solar heat in winter.

They're ventilated to prevent overheating in summer. It's this kind of comfort that explains why over 150,000 sunspaces have been added to United States homes in the past decade, and why this is one of the best ways to upgrade a house for resale."

You can't just tack a sunspace onto any wall, however. These units should be oriented within 30 degrees of true south (see sidebar). So how does this project manage a sunspace on both ends of the south-facing extension? By compromising proper siting.

A sunspace that doesn't face south can be a net loss as far as heat is concerned. If it's not in direct winter sun, not only will it fail to contribute any solar gain, it can be a big heat loser—unless you equip it with elaborate insulating drapes or shutters (see "Outfit Your Sunspace"). And that could cancel out the main reason for installing a sunspace: To open up your home to outdoor views.

I asked John Mauldin (author of the sidebar) which compromise was best when a *corner* of a house points true south, and it's impractical to wrap a sunspace around it. Do you add the unit to the wall angled east or west?

Mauldin told me his advice would depend on local weather patterns and family lifestyle. "Are winter mornings overcast or foggy while afternoons tend to be clear?" he asked. "Then your orientation should favor the west. Do you like an early-morning warmup and perhaps a cozy breakfast in the sunspace? Or will you use it for unwinding?"

The Brewster homeowner has a choice. The "morning" sunspace gets direct sun earlier and longer, so its position off the kitchen makes it a good breakfast nook. The "evening" sunspace gets less sun, later, so it sports only three bays and is comfortable for cocktails.

But if you must settle for only one, you'll be happiest with a sunspace you've tailored to your site, life-style, and local weather—*by Al Lees. Photos by Geoffrey Gross.*

# sun-sational sun rooms

Today's sunspaces come in almost any size—from a window bump-out to a two-story unit that spans the side of a house. They include greenhouses used to grow plants that can't survive outdoors, as well as sun rooms used for living space and solar heat collection.

If you have the time and talent, you can add a sunspace to your home with one of a new generation of kits that include all the materials you'll need. Here's what you should consider if you're thinking about purchasing a sunspace kit.

First, do you have the skills you'll

need? You can hire others to pour the foundation and do the electrical wiring, but you'll still need some carpentry experience. Most experts don't recommend erecting a sunspace without the help of a local dealer.

"Back in the old days, when sunspaces were strictly greenhouses, leaks weren't critical," says Dr. Harold Gray, executive director of the National Greenhouse Manufacturers Association. But modern sun rooms may contain fine furniture. "It takes a little expertise to make the sunspace leak-proof," Gray says.

Also, the old greenhouses used single glazing, says Gray. "The standard lights [panes] of glass were much easier to handle." Today the sunspace may be glazed with slabs of double glass (see "Get Smart About Glazing"). Even the smallest panels, 10 feet square, weigh about 50 pounds.

Do you have time to build a sunspace? Professionals can build one in a few days, but it often takes them much longer. "Allow a sufficient amount of time and expense to get the project completed," says Larry Chavez, president of Sunlite Industries, a sun-space-kit maker. And don't forget that the foundation, wiring, accessories, and finishing are "extras" that may cost as much as the kit itself.

If you've decided to build your own sunspace, how do you choose from the many kits available? The two most important considerations are the engineering and the ease of assembly.

"Before you buy any system, be sure the manufacturer is willing and able to provide stamped engineering calculations [prepared by a registered professional engineer] verifying the integrity of the unit you propose to buy," advises William B. Gilmer, president of Regal Manufacturing, a maker of skylights and sun rooms. "The company may charge an extra $150 to $250 for the service, but it's cheap insurance," he says.

It's also essential to look carefully at the instructions beforehand. Manufacturers like The Sun Co. make your job easier by numbering parts to match step-by-step directions. But some companies sell kits that are extremely difficult for a do-it-yourselfer to assemble, warns Ed Overberger, vice president of Creative Structures, a sunspace manufacturer. "I would look for a professionally produced installation video, one that shows you details," he recommends. He estimates that phone calls from confused buyers have dropped by three-quarters since his company introduced a

An insulated wood roof (facing page) keeps out heat in summer, while angled glass lets in the low winter sun. Habitat's Solar Room has one-piece laminated cedar rafters, so there's no need to measure the angle. Pre-glazed aluminum frames fit neatly between rafters. The kit sells for $11,544: A finished room costs about twice that amount. The aluminum-framed Sunspot (above) comes with an installation video. Two people can assemble the basic 8-by-11-ft. room in about 12 hrs., claims the manufacturer, ODL Inc. This model, which can be ordered by your local home center or lumberyard, has a straight eave. Aluminum frames are more common than wood ones.

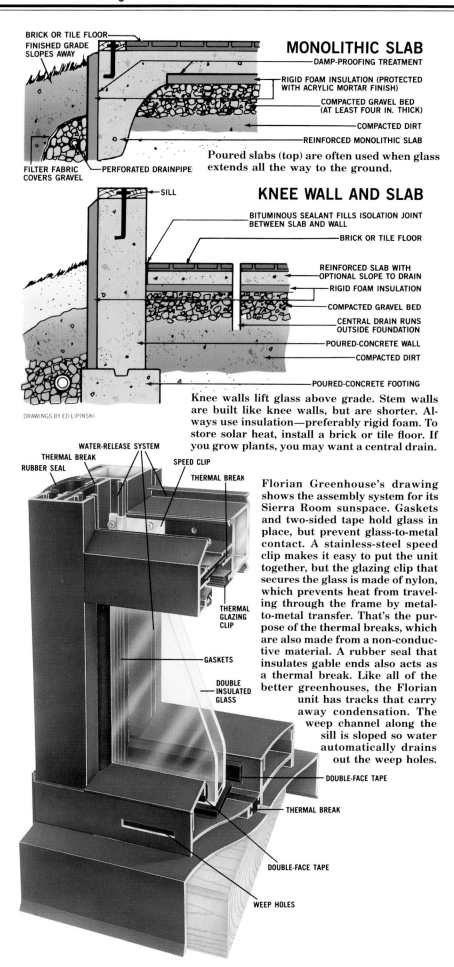

## MONOLITHIC SLAB

BRICK OR TILE FLOOR
FINISHED GRADE
SLOPES AWAY

DAMP-PROOFING TREATMENT

RIGID FOAM INSULATION (PROTECTED WITH ACRYLIC MORTAR FINISH)

COMPACTED GRAVEL BED (AT LEAST FOUR IN. THICK)

COMPACTED DIRT

REINFORCED MONOLITHIC SLAB

FILTER FABRIC COVERS GRAVEL    PERFORATED DRAINPIPE

**Poured slabs (top) are often used when glass extends all the way to the ground.**

## KNEE WALL AND SLAB

SILL

BITUMINOUS SEALANT FILLS ISOLATION JOINT BETWEEN SLAB AND WALL

BRICK OR TILE FLOOR

REINFORCED SLAB WITH OPTIONAL SLOPE TO DRAIN

RIGID FOAM INSULATION

COMPACTED GRAVEL BED

CENTRAL DRAIN RUNS OUTSIDE FOUNDATION

POURED-CONCRETE WALL

COMPACTED DIRT

POURED-CONCRETE FOOTING

DRAWINGS BY ED LIPINSKI

**Knee walls lift glass above grade. Stem walls are built like knee walls, but are shorter. Always use insulation—preferably rigid foam. To store solar heat, install a brick or tile floor. If you grow plants, you may want a central drain.**

WATER-RELEASE SYSTEM
THERMAL BREAK
RUBBER SEAL
SPEED CLIP
THERMAL BREAK
THERMAL GLAZING CLIP
GASKETS
DOUBLE INSULATED GLASS
DOUBLE-FACE TAPE
THERMAL BREAK
DOUBLE-FACE TAPE
WEEP HOLES

Florian Greenhouse's drawing shows the assembly system for its Sierra Room sunspace. Gaskets and two-sided tape hold glass in place, but prevent glass-to-metal contact. A stainless-steel speed clip makes it easy to put the unit together, but the glazing clip that secures the glass is made of nylon, which prevents heat from traveling through the frame by metal-to-metal transfer. That's the purpose of the thermal breaks, which are also made from a non-conductive material. A rubber seal that insulates gable ends also acts as a thermal break. Like all of the better greenhouses, the Florian unit has tracks that carry away condensation. The weep channel along the sill is sloped so water automatically drains out the weep holes.

video a year ago. Ask to borrow or rent the video and manual, and make sure you feel confident about putting the sunspace together before you buy it.

For an extra fee some companies will send a carpenter to your home to check the alignment of the sunspace's sills before you begin erecting the framing. Ask the dealer if such a service is available.

One way to assess the difficulty of building a sunspace is to check references. "Get a list of satisfied customers and inspect a finished sunspace," says Overberger. "I would be skeptical of a dealer who can't give you the name of another do-it-yourselfer who has built a sunspace."

Once you've found a sunspace that's properly engineered, and you're certain you can build it with the instructions provided, you need to make some other decisions:

● Purpose and size. A room used to grow plants has different glazing and ventilation requirements than a living area. If you don't need a fancy room, you might want to look at sun porches like those made by Vegetable Factory and Solar Resources. "Not everybody can afford twelve or twenty thousand dollars for a glass structure," says Stephen R. Kenin, president of Solar Resources. His company's Solar Rooms, which sell for under $2,000, switch from solar collectors in winter to screened porches in summer.

● Foundation. Will you build it on a slab or construct a stem wall or knee wall? It's important to properly prepare the site in advance (see drawings and "Pro's Tips").

● Framing. Aluminum framing is almost always cheaper than wood. It usually comes in bronze, white, and mill-finished aluminum—but at least one homeowner has turned his greenhouse into a *pinkhouse*. Whatever the color, the metal should be anodized to prevent corrosion. Some aluminum structures have a baked-on enamel coating instead. If you choose one of these, make sure the coating is even, or the surface may crack and peel.

Wood systems may be more attractive than aluminum, but they are usually more difficult to install and maintain. Laminated beams, for example, may need occasional varnishing.

Both aluminum- and wood-framed sunspaces can be made watertight. The sunspace should not only keep out rain and melting snow, but should also eliminate condensation that may accumulate on inside sur-

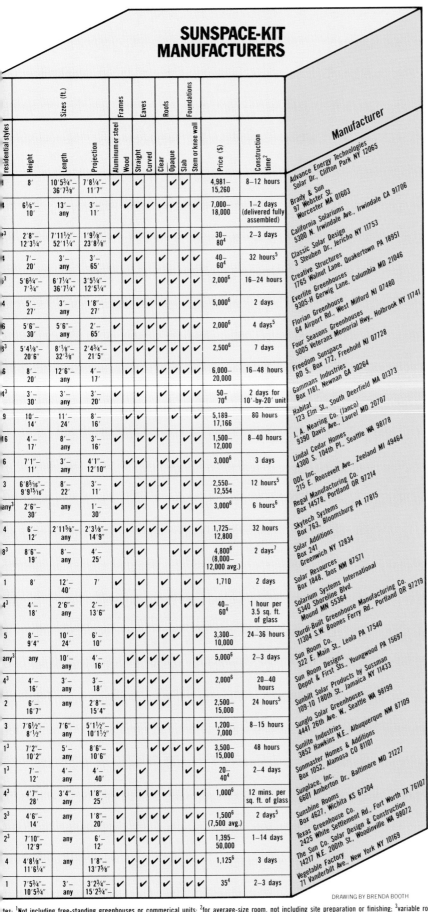

## SUNSPACE-KIT MANUFACTURERS

| Residential styles | Sizes (ft.) | | | Frames | | Eaves | | Roofs | | Foundations | | | | |
|---|---|---|---|---|---|---|---|---|---|---|---|---|---|---|
| | Height | Length | Projection | Aluminum or steel | Wood | Straight | Curved | Clear | Opaque | Slab | Stem or knee wall | Price ($) | Construction time[2] | Manufacturer |
| 1 | 8′ | 10′5¾″–36′7⅜″ | 7′8¼″–11′7″ | ✔ | | ✔ | | | ✔ | ✔ | | 4,981–15,260 | 8–12 hours | Advance Energy Technologies Solar Dr., Clifton Park NY 12065 |
| 4 | 6⅙″–10′ | 13′–any | 3′–11′ | | ✔ | ✔ | ✔ | ✔ | ✔ | ✔ | ✔ | 7,000–18,000 | 1–2 days (delivered fully assembled) | Brady & Sun 97 Webster St. Worcester MA 01603 |
| [3] | 2′8″–12′3¼″ | 7′11½″–52′1¼″ | 1′9⅞″–23′8⅞″ | ✔ | | ✔ | ✔ | ✔ | ✔ | ✔ | ✔ | 30–80[4] | 2–3 days | California Solariums 5300 N. Irwindale Ave., Irwindale CA 91706 |
| 4 | 7′–20′ | 3′–any | 3′–65′ | | ✔ | ✔ | | ✔ | | ✔ | ✔ | 40–60[4] | 32 hours[5] | Classic Solar Design 3 Steuben Dr., Jericho NY 11753 |
| [3] | 5′6¾″–7′¾″ | 6′7¼″–36′7¼″ | 3′5¼″–12′5¼″ | | ✔ | ✔ | | ✔ | ✔ | ✔ | ✔ | 2,000[6] | 16–24 hours | Creative Structures 1765 Walnut Lane, Quakertown PA 18951 |
| 4 | 5′–27′ | 3′–any | 1′8″–27′ | ✔ | ✔ | ✔ | ✔ | ✔ | | ✔ | ✔ | 5,000[6] | 2 days | Everlite Greenhouses 9305-H Gerwig Lane, Columbia MD 21046 |
| 6 | 5′6″–30′ | 5′6″–any | 2′–65′ | ✔ | | ✔ | ✔ | ✔ | | ✔ | ✔ | 2,000[6] | 4 days[5] | Florian Greenhouse 64 Airport Rd., West Milford NJ 07480 |
| 3[3] | 5′4⅛″–20′6″ | 8′⅛″–32′⅜″ | 2′4¾″–21′5″ | ✔ | ✔ | ✔ | ✔ | ✔ | ✔ | ✔ | ✔ | 2,500[6] | 7 days | Four Seasons Greenhouses 5005 Veterans Memorial Hwy., Holbrook NY 11741 |
| 6 | 8′–20′ | 12′6″–any | 4′–17′ | | ✔ | ✔ | | ✔ | ✔ | ✔ | ✔ | 6,000–20,000 | 16–48 hours | Freedom Sunspace RD 5, Box 172, Freehold NJ 07728 |
| 4[3] | 3′–30′ | 3′–any | 3′–20′ | ✔ | | ✔ | | ✔ | | ✔ | ✔ | 50–70[4] | 2 days for 10′-by-20′ unit | Gammans Industries Box 1181, Newnan GA 30264 |
| 9 | 10′–14′ | 11′–24′ | 8′–16′ | | ✔ | ✔ | | | ✔ | | ✔ | 5,189–17,166 | 80 hours | Habitat 123 Elm St., South Deerfield MA 01373 |
| 16 | 4′–17′ | 8′–any | 3′–16′ | ✔ | | ✔ | ✔ | ✔ | | ✔ | ✔ | 1,500–12,000 | 8–40 hours | J. A. Nearing Co. (Janco) 9390 Davis Ave., Laurel MD 20707 |
| 6 | 7′1″–11′ | 3′–any | 4′1″–12′10″ | | ✔ | ✔ | | ✔ | ✔ | ✔ | ✔ | 3,000[6] | 3 days | Lindal Cedar Homes 4300 S. 104th Pl., Seattle WA 98178 |
| 3 | 6′8⁵⁄₁₆″–9′9¹⁵⁄₁₆″ | 8′–22′ | 3′–11′ | ✔ | | ✔ | ✔ | ✔ | | ✔ | ✔ | 2,550–12,554 | 12 hours[5] | ODL Inc. 215 E. Roosevelt Ave., Zeeland MI 49464 |
| any[3] | 2′6″–30′ | any | 1′–30′ | ✔ | | ✔ | | ✔ | ✔ | ✔ | ✔ | 3,000[6] | 6 hours[6] | Regal Manufacturing Co. Box 14578, Portland OR 97214 |
| 4 | 6′–12′ | 2′11⅝″–any | 2′3⅛″–14′9″ | ✔ | ✔ | ✔ | ✔ | ✔ | | ✔ | ✔ | 1,725–12,800 | 32 hours | Skytech Systems Box 763, Bloomsburg PA 17815 |
| 8[3] | 8′6″–19′ | 8′–any | 4′–25′ | | ✔ | ✔ | | | ✔ | ✔ | ✔ | 4,800[6] (8,000–12,000 avg.) | 2 days[7] | Solar Additions Box 241 Greenwich NY 12834 |
| 1 | 8′ | 12′–40′ | 7′ | ✔ | | ✔ | | ✔ | | ✔ | ✔ | 1,710 | 2 days | Solar Resources Box 1848, Taos NM 87571 |
| 4[3] | 4′–18′ | 2′6″–any | 2′–13′6″ | ✔ | | ✔ | ✔ | ✔ | | ✔ | ✔ | 40–60[4] | 1 hour per 3.5 sq. ft. of glass | Solarium Systems International 5340 Shoreline Blvd. Mound MN 55364 |
| 5 | 8′–9′4″ | 10′–24′ | 6′–10′ | | ✔ | ✔ | | ✔ | ✔ | | ✔ | 3,300–10,000 | 24–36 hours | Sturdi-Built Greenhouse Manufacturing Co. 11304 S.W. Boones Ferry Rd., Portland OR 97219 |
| any[3] | any | 10′–any | 4′–16′ | | ✔ | ✔ | ✔ | ✔ | ✔ | | ✔ | 5,000[6] | 2–3 days | Sun Room Co. 322 E. Main St., Leola PA 17540 |
| 4[3] | 4′–16′ | 3′–any | 3′–18′ | ✔ | ✔ | ✔ | ✔ | ✔ | | ✔ | ✔ | 2,000[6] | 20–40 hours | Sun Room Designs Depot & First Sts., Youngwood PA 15697 |
| 2 | 6′–16′7″ | any | 2′8″–15′4″ | ✔ | | ✔ | ✔ | ✔ | | ✔ | ✔ | 2,500–15,000 | 24 hours[5] | Sunbilt Solar Products by Sussman 109-10 180th St., Jamaica NY 11433 |
| 3 | 7′6½″–8′½″ | 7′6″–any | 5′1½″–10′1½″ | ✔ | | | ✔ | ✔ | | | ✔ | 1,200–7,000 | 8–15 hours | Sunglo Solar Greenhouses 4441 26th Ave. W., Seattle WA 98199 |
| 1[3] | 7′2″–10′2″ | 5′–any | 8′6″–10′6″ | ✔ | | | ✔ | ✔ | ✔ | ✔ | ✔ | 3,500–15,000 | 48 hours | Sunlite Industries 3852 Hawkins N.E., Albuquerque NM 87109 |
| 1[3] | 7′–12′ | 4′–any | 4′–40′ | ✔ | | ✔ | | | | ✔ | ✔ | 20–40[4] | 2–4 days | Sunmaster Homes & Additions Box 1052, Alamosa CO 81101 |
| 4[3] | 4′7″–28′ | 3′4″–any | 1′8″–25′ | ✔ | | ✔ | ✔ | ✔ | | | ✔ | 1,000[6] | 12 mins. per sq. ft. of glass | Sunplace, Inc. 6601 Amberton Dr., Baltimore MD 21227 |
| 3[3] | 4′6″–14′ | any | 1′8″–20′ | ✔ | | ✔ | ✔ | ✔ | | ✔ | ✔ | 1,500[6] (7,500 avg.) | 2 days[5] | Sunshine Rooms Box 4627, Wichita KS 67204 |
| 2[3] | 7′10″–12′9″ | any | 6′–12′ | ✔ | ✔ | ✔ | ✔ | ✔ | | | ✔ | 1,395–50,000 | 1–14 days | Texas Greenhouse Co. 2425 White Settlement Rd., Fort Worth TX 76107 |
| 4 | 4′8⅛″–11′6¼″ | any | 1′8″–13′7⅝″ | | ✔ | ✔ | ✔ | ✔ | ✔ | ✔ | ✔ | 1,125[6] | 3 days | The Sun Co. Solar Design & Construction 14217 N.E. 200th St., Woodinville WA 98072 |
| 1 | 7′5¾″–10′5¾″ | 3′–any | 3′2¾″–15′2¾″– | ✔ | | ✔ | | ✔ | | ✔ | ✔ | 35[4] | 2–3 days | Vegetable Factory 71 Vanderbilt Ave., New York NY 10169 |

DRAWING BY BRENDA BOOTH

tes: [1]Not including free-standing greenhouses or commerical units; [2]for average-size room, not including site preparation or finishing; [3]variable roof ch on some models; [4]per square foot; [5]with two workers; [6]and up; [7]with three workers

faces, notes Gilmer. Look for weep channels as a standard feature (see drawing). "Gutters located only between the lights of glass on the upper surface of the rafters are not sufficient," says Gilmer. What you need are gutters around all four sides of every light of glass, on the inside of the room, he says. The gutters should overlap so that water cascades from one to the next as it travels to drainage holes.

● Style. Pick a design and roof angle that blend well with the rest of your house. Many companies offer models with a variable roof pitch, making it easier to mate the sunspace with the side of your house.

● Roofing. A clear roof admits more light, but the sunspace may overheat if you don't install shades or screens. An opaque roof minimizes overheating and can be insulated, but won't give you a view of the sky. Make sure the roof is engineered to easily support the snow and ice load you expect in winter. Check to see that the design complies with local building codes.

● Ventilation. The type of glazing and accessories you choose will determine how well you can control the temperature and humidity inside the room. "The biggest mistake we've seen is people who purchase a sunspace, looking for a good deal, and they end up with only one door and one window [built into the room]," says Overberger. "And they are going to *bake*."

● Cost. Check whether your state offers energy tax credits—some still do. Ask local realtors whether the addition will increase the resale price of your home. Even if it won't, the sunspace may help attract buyers. And if it's properly designed, it can benefit your home's energy budget.

The accompanying table lists some companies who make prefabricated sunspaces. Before you order a kit, write for more detailed information—*by Dawn Stover.*

# assembly: pro's tips

Do not stand on the glass during set in. Pros do it, but sometimes break through panes. If it's unavoidable, wear clean soft-soled shoes.

Once glass is in, a tedious process of weatherproofing—caulking and sealing—follows. Don't race or skimp: It's the key to final success.

Erect a knee wall with temporary braces before beginning the sunspace assembly.

It's important to lay the sill level and square. Our pros lay a bead of caulk between the knee wall and sill before tacking it temporarily.

This kit from CSI comes with pre-tenoned beams that fit precut mortises. As with most kits, each piece is numbered to coincide with steps in the instruction manual. Be sure to count all the pieces before you start assembly and lay them out in the order they'll be needed.

Don't expect your house to be plumb or level. You might have to shim out the wall plate to make sure it's parallel with sill.

Before anchoring the sill make sure it is positioned correctly by checking the plumb of rear posts with a level.

The Jancovics couldn't have asked for a more pastoral setting for their eastern Pennsylvania home. Their backyard slopes down to a babbling brook, and leafy oaks offer dappled shade. It's the perfect spot for a sunspace, they thought, except for one thing: Because the house sits on a hillock a second-story sunspace was the only option. This was no problem for contractor Bob Marx of Sun Rooms of Lehigh Valley (Bath, PA). He built an elevated platform to hold a model 9-15-58 sunspace from Creative Structures Inc. (1765 Walnut Lane, Quakertown, PA 18951). extending the understructure 15 feet to create a second-story deck. I covered the first day's work, asking questions so I could pass along tips to anyone thinking of erecting a similar kit—*by Naomi J. Freundlich. Photos by Robert Werber.*

Use a rubber mallet when setting posts to avoid damaging tenons. The mallet should also be used on all exposed surfaces to keep the redwood unscarred.

Have a utility knife on hand in case any of the joints are too tight and need to be shaved.

Use a bar clamp to draw rafters snug when attaching roof purlins and spacers. Pros toe in sheet-metal screws without pre-drilling.

It's extremely important to make a final check of square when the basic frame is complete, with rafters and front posts attached. Check with a carpenter's square and level, and measure accurately from opposite corners for identical dimensions. At this stage the sill can still be shifted to correct any problems. If the frame is not square, the glass will not go in.

Mahogany window units (mahogany is harder than redwood) come with the CSI kit and fit within the frame. Remove snap-in screens during assembly to avoid damage.

Note the bridge across the door frame for extra support. It is cut flush with the opening before the door is installed.

Crank window open before nailing in place. Use nails to attach windows to top framing to avoid splitting. The bottom is screwed in place.

Apply a continuous bead of black silicone caulk around all awning windows to form a waterproof seal. When caulking roof glass, keep it neat by masking edges.

Nailed-on spacers provide the rabbet in which the roof glass fits. Double-stick foil-backed butyl tape is pressed into place on edges of rafters and purlins before glass is lowered into the rabbets.

To keep the adhesive face clean, the foil is stripped back as the glass is lowered onto the tape.

# outfit your sun space

The newest addition to your household has finally arrived, shiny, new—and naked to the world. How do you dress it to protect it from the hot sun? Or keep it from getting too cold? What's the best way to keep it from getting too dirty, and to make sure it gets plenty of fresh air? This new arrival has special needs you may not have encountered before.

Of course, this "new arrival" is the almost-all-glass sunspace you've just added to your house. And it *does* have unusual requirements that demand the right accessories, depending on where you live—how hot or cold it gets—and how you'll use the new room. But if you outfit your sunspace with the right options, it will reward you with countless hours of "outdoor living" enjoyment.

A decade ago the sun room was used primarily as a greenhouse and, through solar gain, as an auxiliary heat source. As such, the concept of thermal mass and advanced technologies like phase-change materials had been of utmost importance. Times change, however.

"We see sun rooms used primarily as living spaces today," says Volker Schmidt, an engineer for Four Seasons, a large manufacturer of sunspaces. "So things like phase-change salts are rarely used because they are bulky and difficult to modulate. Solar gain and efficiency as a heat source don't carry the importance they used to."

"There are five basic things to consider when you accessorize a sun room intended as living space," says Dr. Harold Gray, director of the National Greenhouse Manufacturers Association: "Overheating in summer; retention of heat, especially at night during the winter; maintaining adequate ventilation and moisture levels; providing thermal mass for some solar gain as well as a carefree floor, especially if you are planning to house a lot of plants; and providing for supplementary heat in areas with cold winters." There are many products you might buy to deal with any of these situations, but first you have to define your needs.

**No-hands control**: Comfortex Corp.'s Smart Shades use remote-controlled solar-powered motors to power the tracked rail-and-drive operating system. They use Duette fabric to provide translucent shading in summer and thermal efficiency of between R-3 and R-4.

## You've got to wear shades

There are two approaches you might take to control the heat of the sun: Erecting solar shades or screens either inside or outside the sunspace glazing. Solar screens are made of a specially woven fiberglass or plastic mesh that the manufacturers claim blocks the sun's heat and glare with minimal interference with your view. The screens are commonly installed outside the glazing.

"By being mounted outside the sun space glazing, solar screens cut off the sun's heat *before* it enters the room," says Mark Edwards of Phifer Wire Products.

Solar shades, on the other hand, are special translucent sun blockers, sometimes made of reflective material, that normally are mounted *inside* the glazing. (One firm, Pioneer Roll Shutter Co., makes shades that are intended exclusively for exterior use, however.) The shades are designed especially to be used in the sunspace environment, and they usu-

**A ventilating fan** can be an important factor in keeping a sunspace from summertime overheating, but it must be weathertight and insulated for the wintertime. The TC 1000 ventilation system has an internal panel of foam insulation that is lifted up and out of the way for ventilating by a lifting motor, says Weather Energy Systems. It's then pulled down for a tight seal when the fan turns off.

ally transmit ample light, but are said to block the sun's heat energy by either reflecting or filtering the infrared radiation.

Protection against the summer sun, which travels at a high angle, is generally most effective on roof glazing and the upper areas of wall glazing. As an alternative to solar shades and screens, Accent Awnings makes a retractable awning that can be attached to the main house structure and extended over the sunspace roof only when needed. This protects the solarium during the hottest parts of the day without obstructing the view.

## Keep the heat

At the opposite end of the spectrum, you may be concerned with winter thermal protection. Depending on where you live and how your sunspace is sited, you might achieve ample solar gain during winter to keep the sunspace comfortable, with enough extra energy to supplement your house's heat. Even if you do, you'll probably need supplementary heat for overcast days and night entertaining. Four Seasons' Schmidt suggests hooking up with your existing heating system as a separate zone if possible, or using a non-venting gas furnace, electric baseboards, or an air-to-air heat exchanger if excess moisture is a problem in your sunspace.

Thermal shades, made of quilted or pleated fabric—usually with some kind of reflective backing—reduce heat loss through the sunspace glass. The shades generally run in a track under tension on the glazing frames to provide a tight seal and prevent sagging on curved or slanted areas. Most thermal shade systems offer a motorized option with remote control. Foam-filled shutters and louver panels like those from Boston Shutter & Door may be the best thermal protection in cold areas, but they are expensive and can be somewhat clumsy.

## Breath of fresh air

Exhaust, or ventilating, fans get rid of the hot, stale air that can accumulate in sun rooms during warm weather. Supply fans are used during the winter to move the warm air of the solarium into the main house when the sunspace is used as a heat source.

Ventilating fans may be mounted high at a gable end or in the roof of a sunspace and should be insulated in some way for winter. Supply fans are mounted between the house and the sunspace, and there should be two:

**With their wood-foam** sandwich construction, the Boston Shutter & Door louvers and shutters provide an insulating performance of R-7, says the company. Exteriors are laminated with white melamine for summertime reflectance; interiors are finished in birch or red oak.

One mounted high to provide heated air to the house and one mounted low to provide return air from the house to the sunspace.

"For any fan system to provide a positive gain to the house, the fan apperture must be closed at night," says Paul Raymer, president of Weather Energy Systems. "Otherwise more heat will be lost at night than will be gained during the day. And if the fans are controlled automatically, as with a thermostat, it's important that any aperture-closure system also be automatic so it will work when the homeowner is not home." Both ventilating and supply fans should be thermostatically controlled.

### From the floor up

Most sunspaces are built on a concrete slab (see "Sun-sational Sun Rooms" on page 32). Not only does this provide a good foundation, it also provides thermal mass that enables you to take advantage of the sun's energy in the winter.

"If you want to make the best use of thermal mass a dark-tile or brick floor is the way to go," says Robert Kleinhans, executive director of the Tile Council of America. "Not only is such a floor good for solar gain, but it is fade proof, durable, and waterproof, and requires little maintenance—important if you will have lots of plants in the sun room or if there will be a lot of indoor-outdoor traffic."

If you plan your sunspace carefully and choose your accessories to fulfill your needs, you'll add enjoyment and value to your house with a livable all-seasons room—*by Timothy O. Bakke.*

**MANUFACTURERS OF SUNSPACE ACCESSORIES**

**Sunshades and screens:** Accent Awnings, Box 777, Chester, PA 19016; Castec, Inc., 7531 Coldwater Canyon Ave., North Hollywood, CA 91605; Catalina Shading Systems, 230 E. Dyer Rd., Unit G, Santa Ana, CA 92707; JMS Mfg., 717B Fellowship Rd., Mount Laurel, NJ 08054; Phifer Wire Products, Box 1700, Tuscaloosa, AL 35403-1700; Pioneer Roll Shutter Co., 155 Glendale Ave., Sparks, NV 89431; Sol-R-Veil, 635 W. 23rd St., New York, NY 10011; Sun Control Products, 431 Fourth Ave. S.E., Rochester, MN, 55904; Verosol USA, 224 RIDC Park West Dr., Pittsburgh, PA 15275. **Insulating shades and shutters:** Appropriate Technology Corp., Box 975, Brattleboro, VT 05301-0975; Boston Shutter & Door, Box 888, Island Mill, Keene, NH 03431; Comfortex Corp., Box 728, Cohoes, NY 12047; Jaksna Energy Systems, 2450 Rosswood N.E., Rio Rancho, NM 87124. **Ventilating fans:** Vent-Axia, Box 2204, Woburn, MA 01888; Weather Energy Systems, Box 459, West Wareham, MA 02576. **Flooring:** American Olean Tile Co., 1000 Carnon Ave., Lansdale, PA 19446; Dal-Tile Corp., Box 17130, Dallas, TX 75217; Mid-State Tile, Box 1777-T, Lexington, NC 27293; Summitville Tiles, Summitville, OH 43962. **Phase-change material:** PSI Energy Systems, 1533-T Fenpark Dr., Fenton, MO 63026.

At the National Association of Home Builders show in Dallas last winter, I paused at the Four Seasons Solar Products booth, and Donald Staib, the company's national accounts manager, promptly beckoned me into a long sunspace flanked by a bank of heat lamps.

I passed into the first bay (glazed with double insulating glass, said the sign) and was overwhelmed by the heat. I scurried on to bay two (bronze-tinted double glass) and found an improvement to the ovenlike environment. Finally, in bay three the temperature was relatively comfortable. It was glazed with Heat Mirror, a triple sandwich with two sheets of glass and two air spaces surrounding a low-emissivity (heat reflecting) polyester film.

It was a graphic demonstration of how important the choice of glazing can be in a room that is mostly windows. And what a choice there is: not only the different glasses Four Seasons demonstrated, but several others as well. And many kinds of plastics. What glazing is best for your sunspace? That depends on climate, design and orientation of the room, and what you expect from it. Your choices also may be narrowed by your local building code—and your pocketbook. Once you understand the considerations, the data in the table on page 41 can help you choose.

## The great escape

Glazing has a reputation as a great leaker of heat. Here's why: While an ordinary 2 x 4 stud wall with batt insulation has an R-value (resistance to heat flow) of about 11, a single pane of ⅛-inch glass ranks a measly R-0.89. Add a second pane of glass with a ⅝-inch air space between the panes, and it creeps up to R-2—still low enough to lose heat like mad on a cold winter night.

Much of the heat that escapes will be radiant heat—the long-wave infrared radiation emitted by everything in the room. Stand near a window on a cold night, and you may feel chilly, even if the air temperature is warm. That's partly because you're radiating heat to the window. Glass is nearly opaque to most infrared, so it absorbs your body heat and reradiates it, mostly outside.

Low-emissivity double glazing (see sidebar: "Talking Glazing") has a higher R-value than standard double glazing because it reflects much of the radiant heat. With a ⅝-inch air space and a low-e coating on one of the two panes the R-value generally ranges

# get smart about glazing

## GLAZING CHOICES—BY THE NUMBERS

| Type | U-value[1] (winter) | R-value[2] (winter) | Shading coefficient[3] | Visible light trans. (%)[4] | UV trans. (%)[5] | Cost/comments |
|---|---|---|---|---|---|---|
| **Single glass** | | | | | | |
| Clear | 1.12 | 0.89 | 1.00 | 90 | 80 | Sunspaces are seldom made with single glass. |
| Tinted | 1.12 | 0.89 | 0.85 | 69 | 43 | |
| Reflective | 1.12 | 0.89 | 0.51 | 27 | 15 | |
| **Double glass** | | | | | | |
| Clear | 0.50 | 2.00 | 0.89 | 82 | 64 | Average cost for a sunspace with clear insulating tempered glass might be $25 per sq. ft. (psf) of glazing. Tinted glass should add around $1.80 psf to that price; reflective adds around $4.70 psf. |
| Tinted (bronze) | 0.50 | 2.00 | 0.73 | 63 | 34 | |
| Reflective (bronze) | 0.50 | 2.00 | 0.41 | 25 | 12 | |
| **Low-e glass[6]** | | | | | | |
| Clear | 0.31 | 3.20 | 0.76 | 72 | 49 | Low-e glass adds about $5 psf of glazing to the price of a sunspace (vs. clear insulating glass). |
| Tinted (bronze) | 0.31 | 3.20 | 0.61 | 55 | 31 | |
| **Heat Mirror[7] (two 5/16" spaces)** | | | | | | |
| 88 (with clear glass) | 0.26 | 3.85 | 0.70 | 71 | 34 | Heat Mirror glazing should add about $5.90 psf of glass to the price of a sunspace (vs. clear insulating glass). |
| 66 (with tinted glass) | 0.25 | 4.00 | 0.41 | 42 | 9 | |
| 44 (with reflective glass) | 0.25 | 4.00 | 0.16 | 12 | n.a.* | |
| **Laminated glass** | 1.08 | 0.93 | 0.82 | 79 | 1 | Laminated glass (annealed) is about three times the price of single tempered glass. |
| **Polycarbonate (¼")[8]** | | | | | | |
| Clear | 0.96 | 1.11 | 1.02 | 82 | 0 | Polycarbonate is more costly than single tempered glass. But curved eaves of it (a typical use) may be about half the price of curved eaves of tempered glass. |
| Tinted (gray/bronze) | 0.96 | 1.11 | 0.79 | 50 | 0 | |
| **Structured polycarbonate (8-mm)[8, 9]** | | | | | | |
| "Clear" | 0.64 | 1.78 | 0.96 | 82 | 0 | Structured polycarbonate costs more than single tempered glass, but much less than tempered insulating glass. |
| Tinted (gray/bronze) | 0.64 | 1.78 | 0.61 | 25 | 0 | |
| White | 0.64 | 1.78 | 0.53 | 20 | 0 | |
| **Acrylic (⅛")[8, 10]** | | | | | | |
| Clear | 1.06 | 0.94 | 0.98 | 92 | n.a. | Monolithic acrylics are 25–30% less than polycarbonates. Use only those appropriate for sunspace glazing. |
| Tinted (bronze) | 1.06 | 0.94 | 0.61 | 27 | n.a. | |
| **Structured acrylic (16-mm)[8, 10]** | | | | | | |
| "Clear" | 0.58 | 1.72 | 0.98 | 87 | n.a. | Structured acrylic may cost more than structured polycarbonate because a heavier gauge may be required. |
| Tinted (bronze) | 0.58 | 1.72 | 0.79 | 52 | n.a. | |
| White | 0.58 | 1.72 | 0.38 | 20 | n.a. | |
| **FRP** | | | | | | |
| Single "clear"[8] | 1.14 | 0.87 | 0.98 | 90.5 | 17 | Premium "clear" FRP is similar in cost to monolithic acrylic. It is used for horticultural greenhouses and hot-tub enclosures. Kalwall panels are $10–$20 psf (wholesale). |
| Kalwall panels[11] | 0.24 | 4.16 | 0.18 | 20 | 1 | |

Specifications assume ⅛" glass lites and ⅝" air spaces, unless otherwise noted. All values for tinted, reflective, and white glazing represent products commonly used in residential sunspaces, but all are available in a range of opacities. Data given for clear, tinted, reflective, laminated, and low-e glass are from PPG Ind. and represent typical production values for vertical glazing.

NOTES: [1]U-value is the heat-transfer rate through materials, measured in Btu/hr./sq.ft./deg. F temperature difference. Winter nighttime U-values are calculated assuming an outdoor temperature of 0°F, an indoor temperature of 70°, and a wind velocity of 15 mph. [2]R-value (resistance to heat flow) is the reciprocal of the U-value. [3]Shading coefficient compares the total solar heat gain through any other glazing with that through a single pane of ⅛" glass—which has a shading coefficient of 1. [4]Visible light transmission indicates the percentage of the visible spectrum that passes through the glazing. [5]UV (ultraviolet) transmission is given because the sun's shortwave UV energy fades fabrics. [6]Low-e glass data are for PPG's Sungate 100; other low-e products may differ. [7]Heat Mirror film comes in three types, as noted; all can be combined with different glass types. Data shown represent the common range of solar optical qualities available. [8]A range of thicknesses is used for sunspace glazing; also used for double glazing. Consult glazing or sunspace manufacturer for specifications. [9]Sold in 6-mm–16-mm thicknesses; 8-mm is used for curved glazing. Data represent GE Plastics' Thermoclear panels. [10]Data are for Exolite panels from Cyro Ind. [11]Available in many thicknesses and opacities; data given represent 2¾" size. *Not available

DRAWING BY BRENDA BOOTH

from 2.5 to 3.2, depending on the type of low-e coating. With Heat Mirror, the low-e film Four Seasons demonstrated, you can have triple-glazed windows that weigh no more than double windows, yet have an R-value of 3.8 to 4 (with two ⁵⁄₁₆-inch air spaces).

Low-e glazing has other advantages: Its interior surface stays warmer in winter. "When it's seventy degrees [F] inside and zero outside, low-e glass will have a room-side surface temperature of fifty-five degrees," says William Uhl Jr., residential construction marketing manager for PPG Industries. "Standard double glass would be forty-four degrees, and single glass would be fifteen degrees on the inside. With low-e glass the relative humidity in the room can be sixty percent under those conditions, and no condensate will form," Uhl adds. The higher surface temperature of the glass also makes the room more comfortable.

Low-e glazing is a benefit in summer too. It reduces radiant heat *gain* because it reflects heat radiated from outdoor surfaces.

But low-e glazing is more expensive than standard double glazing. Is it a good buy? All else being equal, the more extreme your climate, the better a buy it is likely to be. Andersen Corp. did a study of sunspaces in 16 cities across the country, and found that in all a properly designed sunspace could be more energy efficient than a standard room of the same size. With low-e double insulating glass that remained true, even when the sunspace faced north.

### How much of a good thing?
Heat loss is only part of the energy picture in a sunspace. You should also consider the amount of solar energy the glazing lets in. It is because of the solar gain that well-designed

sunspaces can be better energy performers than conventional rooms.

But the sun also can be the enemy in sunspaces: Overheating is a common complaint. The "shading coefficient" column on the table ranks the glazings according to the amount of solar energy they admit.

In general, the colder your climate and the more heat you intend to reap from the sun, the more you need to consider a glazing with a relatively high shading coefficient.

The hotter and sunnier your climate, the more important is a lower shading coefficient. "In southern locations tinted or reflective glass is very desirable," notes Dr. Harold Gray, executive director of the National Greenhouse Manufacturers Association. "Otherwise, your sunspace can become unbearable in summer." But beware of glazings with a low shading coefficient if you want to grow light-loving plants, Gray warns. "If you just want some green plants for decoration there's very little problem. But with some flowering and fruiting plants, watch out." He advises looking for a shading coefficient above 0.70 or 0.80 if such plants are in your plans.

One popular option is to choose a lower shading coefficient for overhead glazing and a higher number for vertical glazing. Thus in summer when the sun is high in the sky (striking the overhead glazing more directly), more of it will be blocked. But in winter when the sun hangs low, more energy will pass.

The "visible light transmission" column in the table gives the percentage of sunlight in the visible spectrum each glazing transmits, and thus indicates how bright the room will be. It also suggests how well you'll see out of your sunspace when the glazing is glass or the monolithic acrylic and polycarbonate sheets. But

with the structured-sheet plastics and fiberglass-reinforced plastics (FRP) that's not the whole picture. They may have good visible transmission, but the light is diffuse—great for many plants and for privacy, but not if you want a view.

### Glass vs. plastic
Plastic is much lighter than glass, and it can be bent on site to form curved sections. It is also much more impact resistant. GE Plastics says its Lexan polycarbonate sheets are 250 times stronger than glass. "If you have branches overhanging the sunspace, or vandalism is a problem, a glazing that resists breakage is worth considering," says Gray. "The structured-sheet plastics, especially the polycarbonates, are the most impact resistant," he adds.

Local building codes may have specific requirements for sloped or overhead glazing. If ordinary glass is used, a screen may have to be installed beneath to catch the shards if it should break. Codes generally allow laminated glass to be used without a screen, and some now permit tempered glass. Appropriate plastics are also permitted.

But plastic glazings scratch more readily than glass, they are flammable, some may yellow over time, and the monolithic sheets are flimsy, requiring closer spacing of the sunspace frame. The structured sheets don't provide a clear view. Plastics also have a high coefficient of thermal expansion, so seams are harder to seal. Special installation methods and materials must be used.

Whatever glazing you choose for your sunspace, you may find that thermal blinds and shading devices are necessary if you want it to be a comfortable living space—
*by V. Elaine Gilmore.*

---

## Talking glazing

**TINTED GLASS** transmits less solar energy than clear glass but absorbs more. Heat that is absorbed is radiated in all directions. Tinted and low-glazing are often combined into high-performance windows for warm climates.

**LAMINATED GLASS** sandwiches a tough plastic film of polyvinyl butyral resin between two sheets of glass. If it breaks, the film holds the shards.

**TEMPERED GLASS** has been heat treated to increase its strength. Most sunspace manufacturers who use glass provide tempered glass because of its improved safety.

**STRUCTURED PLASTIC SHEETS**—made of polycarbonate or acrylic—are

double-skinned assemblies with internal ribs a fraction of an inch apart. They combine structural rigidity and light weight.

**KALWALL PANELS** are two skins of fiberglass-reinforced plastic (FRP) with a ribbed internal structure and insulation (similar to angel hair for Christmas trees) between the skins.—*V. E. G.*

**LOW-E (EMISSIVITY) GLASS** has a micron-thin layer of metal or metal oxide on one side. The coating reflects much of the infrared radiation but readily transmits visible light.

**EMISSIVITY** refers to the heat-emitting (radiating) propensity of a surface. The emissivity number compares a given surface with a perfect radiator, called a blackbody (emissivity, 1). Ordinary window glass has a high emissivity, meaning

that it absorbs—then emits—most of the radiant heat that strikes it. With a low-e coating the glass reflects the heat instead. All else being equal, the lower the emissivity, the lower the U-value (thermal conductance—see notes below table).

**HEAT MIRROR,** a polyester film made by Southwall Technologies, has a low-e coating on one side. It is used as the center lite in triple, or even quadruple, glazing. Glass is used for the outside lites. The additional air spaces lower the U-value of the window.

**REFLECTIVE GLASS** has a mirrorlike metallic coating that reflects solar energy, including visible light. It is often used on office buildings and for overhead glazing.

# entry dress-up: front door

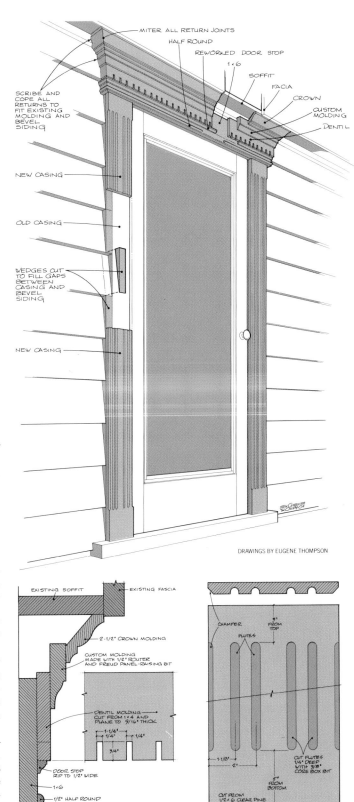

DRAWINGS BY EUGENE THOMPSON

**Labels (top illustration):**
MITER ALL RETURN JOINTS
HALF ROUND
REWORKED DOOR STOP
1×6
SOFFIT
FACIA
CROWN
CUSTOM MOLDING
DENTIL
SCRIBE AND COPE ALL RETURNS TO FIT EXISTING MOLDING AND BEVEL SIDING
NEW CASING
OLD CASING
WEDGES CUT TO FILL GAPS BETWEEN CASING AND BEVEL SIDING
NEW CASING

**Labels (lower left detail - DETAIL - CASING HEAD):**
EXISTING SOFFIT
EXISTING FASCIA
2-1/2" CROWN MOLDING
CUSTOM MOLDING MADE WITH 1/2" ROUTER AND FREUD PANEL-RAISING BIT
DENTIL MOLDING CUT FROM 1×4 AND PLANE TO 9/16" THICK
1-1/4"   1/4"   1/4"
3/4"
DOOR STOP RIP TO 1/2" WIDE
1×6
1/2" HALF ROUND

**Labels (lower right detail - DETAIL - CASING COLUMN):**
CHAMFER
3" FROM TOP
FLUTES
1-1/8"
2"
5" FROM BOTTOM
CUT FLUTES 1/4" DEEP WITH 3/8" CORE BOX BIT
CUT FROM 1/2×6 CLEAR PINE

H elp your home emerge from winter's blahs by giving it the quickest yet most effective face lift you can: Add drama and design to the frame around your front door. After all, the entry is the first thing your callers see.

I studied the style and proportions of my house before sketching up new casing that I could either make myself or create by combining stock moldings from the lumberyard. My design would adapt well to many other entries —even those without a soffit overhead. But one of the effects I like best is the way my new trim package fills that eight-inch gap on top by butting against the soffit, seeming to support it.

Sitting down to design your own casing can be intimidating at first, but these tips should help:

● Look at entry-door trims on well-designed homes in your area. Familiarize yourself with different trim styles, such as Federal, Georgian, and Greek Revival, by consulting books on architectural detail at your local library.

● Experiment on paper. Take a photo of your front door and have it enlarged to an 8x10 size. Tape tracing paper over the print and draw various designs around the door.

● Do sample assemblies with pieces of molding. Your new casing will consist of three basic parts—two pilasters (vertical strips that flank the door) and a head (the horizontal crosspiece at the top). It's easy to make the pilasters of a single board, but the head is usually built up from several different moldings.

Head for your lumberyard to check out its moldings— you'll probably find a dozen shapes that have possibilities. The larger crowns, coves, beds, battens, and stops—plus half and quarter rounds—are all worth looking at. If the yard doesn't have samples to lend you, offer to buy a couple of inches cut off each molding you want to play with. At home, set these short lengths on end and arrange them like blocks, building up full-size cross sections of various configurations until you find one that appeals to you. Then trace around each molding to get a profile like the sketch at right. If your design calls for a shape you can't buy, consider making your own—as I had to for my dentil and "panel-raising" moldings.

My actual trim work started with the pilasters—made from half-inch clear pine 5½ inches wide. I routed parallel

flutes then chamfered the edges. I stopped both flutes and chamfers about five inches from the bottom and three inches from the top.

After nailing up all trim, fill holes with an exterior wood putty, caulk all joints, prime the wood with an alkyd primer, and apply two coats of latex trim paint— *by A. J. Hand. Photos by the author.*

**After removal** of rotting sill, new sill was cut to fit and fastened down with screws, counterbored, and oak plugged.

**Pilasters are nailed** right over the old casing (left). Head moldings have mitered returns that butt up to the house.

# perfect paneling

PHOTOS COURTESY OF THE PLYWOOD PANELING COUNCIL; DESIGN BY RUSS ENGLISH

*Reprinted by permission of Homeowner magazine.*

**Before and after** photos above show how new-style paneling can give a lift to an out-of-date room. New wooden wainscot and decorator panels were applied directly over the old paneling. A picture molding and a plate rail provide attractive traditional details.

Now, as never before, prefinished wall paneling offers do-it-yourselfers a variety of stylish yet economical ways to perk up rooms. Today's paneling isn't what it used to be—dark and obviously artificial. The aesthetic has changed, and while deep, rich-looking veneers are still available in plywood paneling, lighter-colored natural and "pickled" finishes are now more prevalent. Milling details are more refined, and in addition to random and regular wide-board designs, there are wall panels reminiscent of beaded wainscot and other traditional styles. And some of the new paneling doesn't look like wood at all. "Decorator" wall panels with wallpaper-like finishes come in a variety of subtle patterns and textures. Used together or in combination with other materials, wood veneer and decorator paneling can be used to create both traditional and contemporary room styles.

Along with the new looks, wall

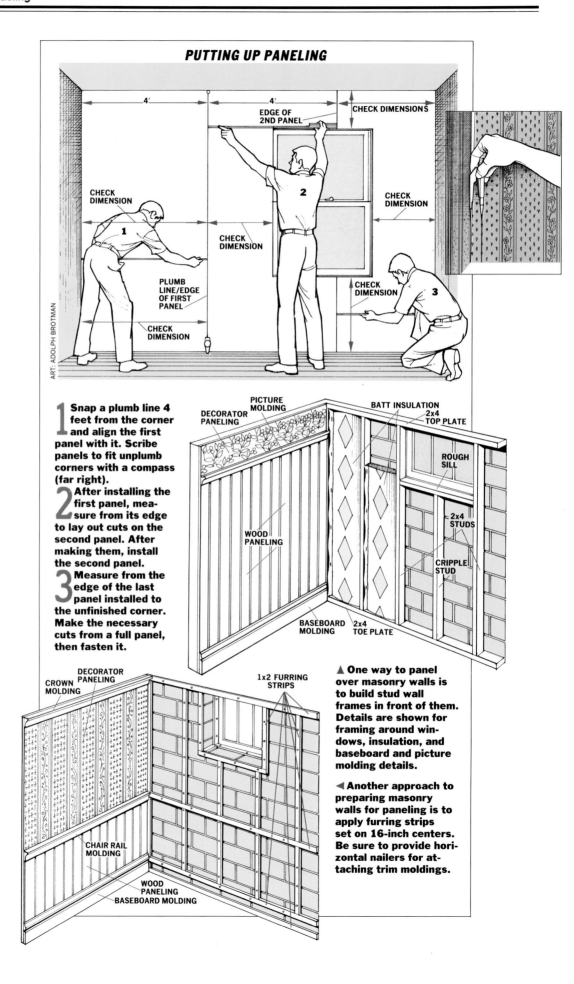

## PUTTING UP PANELING

ART: ADOLPH BROTMAN

4'   4'   CHECK DIMENSIONS

EDGE OF 2ND PANEL

CHECK DIMENSION

CHECK DIMENSION

CHECK DIMENSION

1

2

CHECK DIMENSION

PLUMB LINE/EDGE OF FIRST PANEL

CHECK DIMENSION

CHECK DIMENSION

3

**1** Snap a plumb line 4 feet from the corner and align the first panel with it. Scribe panels to fit unplumb corners with a compass (far right).

**2** After installing the first panel, measure from its edge to lay out cuts on the second panel. After making them, install the second panel.

**3** Measure from the edge of the last panel installed to the unfinished corner. Make the necessary cuts from a full panel, then fasten it.

PICTURE MOLDING

DECORATOR PANELING

BATT INSULATION

2x4 TOP PLATE

ROUGH SILL

WOOD PANELING

2x4 STUDS

CRIPPLE STUD

BASEBOARD MOLDING

2x4 TOE PLATE

▲ One way to panel over masonry walls is to build stud wall frames in front of them. Details are shown for framing around windows, insulation, and baseboard and picture molding details.

CROWN MOLDING

DECORATOR PANELING

1x2 FURRING STRIPS

◄ Another approach to preparing masonry walls for paneling is to apply furring strips set on 16-inch centers. Be sure to provide horizontal nailers for attaching trim moldings.

CHAIR RAIL MOLDING

WOOD PANELING

BASEBOARD MOLDING

paneling offers the same advantages it always has: It's economical at about 32 to 80 cents per square foot. It's an effective coverup for cracked, uneven walls, and once it's installed, paneling requires no finishing or maintenance other than an occasional bit of cleaning.

Putting up paneling requires only a few basic tools: a tape measure, a hammer, a portable circular saw, a chalk line, a level, a nail set and a compass. A portable saber saw is good for making cutouts for switches, outlets and window openings, in most cases, but these cuts can also be made with a sharp mat knife. A miter box and back saw are needed to cut trim moldings. You'll need a caulking gun and tubes of panel adhesive if you intend to glue the panels up, and also some panel nails, which have thin, ringed shanks and are available with heads painted to blend with paneling finishes.

Wall paneling comes in standard-size sheets: 4 x 8-, 4 x 10- and 4 x 12-foot panels are available, so it's possible to cover most walls from floor to ceiling with a single sheet. But full coverage isn't the only way to apply paneling. For example, you can use it on the lower part of a wall as a wainscot, or put up a border near the ceiling with decorator panels to create a subtle, traditional look. Seams between two dissimilar panels can be covered with chair-rail or picture molding for handsome visual transitions.

## Paneling prep

The method for preparing walls for paneling depends on their condition and whether there's an existing finish. Paneling can be applied over drywall, plaster and old paneling that's sound and flat. Baseboard moldings, door and window casings and any other trim must be removed, and jambs should be extended with wood strips so their edges will be flush with the face of the new paneling. It may also be necessary to reset switch and outlet boxes so they'll be flush with the new wall surface. Existing panels with a shiny finish should be sanded for better adhesion of panel adhesive.

Existing wall finishes that are loose should be renailed or taken down. If walls are wavy, furring strips should be applied on 16-inch centers and shimmed as necessary to create a flat, even base for nailing. Furring strips can also be applied to masonry walls to prepare them for panel application, and paneling can be nailed directly to wall studs set on 16-inch centers. Plywood paneling, which is more rigid and dimensionally stable than other types, is better for direct-stud applications and other cases where there is no existing wall finish to serve as a backing. It's a good idea to paint the ceiling and any other parts of the room that need it before installing the paneling.

Exterior stud walls and wall frames built in front of masonry walls can be insulated with batts. There should be a vapor barrier on the heated side of the wall. Rigid polystyrene insulation can be applied to masonry walls, but to meet fire codes, it must be covered with ½-inch drywall before paneling is applied.

## Putting up panels

Plan to apply the first panel in the most visible corner of the room. Check that corner to see if it's plumb, and if it is, measure from the corner along the floor, and make a pencil mark at exactly 4 feet. If the corner isn't plumb, make your mark at 4 feet ½-inch. Then suspend a chalk line tool from the ceiling, and align the pointer over the pencil mark. Snap the line onto the wall. Repeat the procedure in each corner. If the paneling won't go up to the ceiling, snap a level chalk line all the way around the room as a trimming guide.

Tack the first panel in place with its edge aligned perfectly with the chalk line on the wall. If the corner isn't square, set the legs of a compass about an inch apart. Guide one leg along the corner, and use the "pencil-leg" to mark the panel face. Detach the panel and cut along the scribed line. Then reattach the panel, fitting the cut edge snugly in the corner, and double-check the far edge for plumb. Once the first panel on each wall is set plumb, other panels can be butted in sequence.

Paneling can be fastened with a suitable mastic, paneling nails or both. Apply a squiggly line of adhesive around the perimeter about ½-inch from the edge and two beads lengthwise down the panel at points that correspond to the locations of wall studs (if it's a frame wall). Place the panel in position, and using a cloth-wrapped 2 x 4 to protect the panel face, whack it with a mallet to spread the adhesive. Then pull the panel loose from the wall to "air dry" the adhesive for a couple of minutes, and reposition the panel, pushing it in place. The panel should then stay where you put it, but if it doesn't, use paneling nails in unobtrusive places, such as the dark reveals that create the board pattern, or where trim will later be applied. You can either remove the nails when the adhesive sets, or set the heads and fill them with a dark-colored wax filler. If you choose not to use adhesive, drive nails into the studs or furring strips, spacing them no more than 24 inches apart.

When cutting around doors and windows, measure and cut exactly, using whole panels so that the panel pattern is uninterrupted. To lay out cutouts for doors, windows, switches and outlets, use the edge of the last installed panel, and the floor and ceiling for reference points. Measure from them, and make marks for the cuts on the face of a full panel. Always check doors and windows for plumb and level, and measure from the last panel edge to the cut line both top and bottom. If you're having a hard time visualizing a cut, hold the marked panel where it will fit to double-check.

Plywood panels are easy to cut with a sharp utility knife, a fine-toothed jig-saw blade or a smooth-cutting circular saw blade. To make long, straight cuts with a portable power saw, clamp a straightedge across the panel as a guide. Measure from the saw blade to the edge of the saw "shoe," and set the straightedge that distance from the cut line. Remember to adjust the position of the guide to compensate for the blade thickness (plus or minus ⅛-inch) to keep it on the "waste" side of the cutting line. When sawing across the grain, it's a good idea to score the cutting line with a mat knife to prevent splintering of the veneer.

## Finishing touches

Prefinished baseboard moldings, casings for doors and windows, and quarter-rounds are available to match most paneling. There are also inside- and outside-corner moldings for dressing off corners. Unfinished stock millwork, such as crown moldings and chair rails, can also be used to add detail and finish off paneled rooms. These can be prepainted or stained before installation, trimmed to fit, and the nail heads can be set, filled and touched up after the molding is nailed in place. To conceal the vertical seams between decorator panels, fill them with wall-board compound using a 1-inch putty knife. After it dries slightly, wipe the excess from the panel faces with a clean, damp sponge—*by Pete Prlaine.*

# makeovers with molding

While often used just to cover up joints between the bits and pieces our homes are made from, moldings can also unify and manipulate the way we perceive architectural proportions and add gracious details to ordinary spaces. Designing and installing moldings isn't difficult to master. On these pages, you'll find an introduction to both.

Wood moldings are an easy, inexpensive way to add details, decorative accents or a unifying theme to your home. The materials required are readily available: Just about every home center and building-supply outlet carries softwood moldings. There are also many molded and extruded plastic trim designs, which can be cut and fitted like wood, but reminiscent of old-fashioned plaster moldings, they're often larger and more detailed.

Stock moldings come in a wide variety of patterns and widths. (See the "Molding Sampler" on page 50.) If you're looking for the more exotic styles, mail-order firms offer hardwood, redwood and embossed moldings with decorative patterns.

As with all home-improvement projects, careful planning is essential for successful molding installation. Measure the areas where you plan to apply moldings, and work out scaled drawings on graph paper. They'll help you visualize the finished project and calculate material needs accurately.

Always overestimate the amount of material required. Molding is usually sold in 4-, 6-, 8-, 10- and 12-foot lengths. Always plan to buy lengths that will leave you with the least waste. There's always some waste in cutting, so add a few extra inches to your measurements.

It's easier to prime and paint new moldings before installing them. Of course you'll still have to do some touch-ups after nailing the moldings in place, but you'll be spared the task of masking the walls or using a shield to paint a clean edge. Before painting, lightly sand rough areas, and dust off the moldings with a damp cloth. Apply primer and at least one finish coat.

In most cases, 6d or 8d finish nails, which have compact heads, are your best bet for installing molding. For smaller moldings, like base shoes and small quarter rounds, use smaller finish nails or wire brads. Be careful not to mar the wood with your hammer

*Reprinted by permission of Homeowner magazine.*

**Dentil molding** and casing is used as window trim, and there's a crown at the ceiling. A chair rail tops the "wainscot," which is panelized with a picture frame.

as you work. Leave the nail heads protruding slightly, then use a nail set to sink them below the surface. Putty over the holes, then sand lightly and touch up the paint.

When applying long runs of molding, you may have to splice sections together. The most inconspicuous method is to cut the joining ends at a 45-degree angle, so they'll overlap to form a *scarf joint.* Apply wood glue to the mating surfaces, then nail the pieces in place. If the joints don't match perfectly, fill the gaps with a wood putty or spackle.

## Baseboards and crowns

*Baseboards* are applied where the bottom of a wall meets the floor. Base-

boards are often built up from several different stock moldings to create a larger, more detailed profile. (See "Classy Combinations" on page 00 for samples of baseboards and other built-up molding suggestions.) You might start with a standard, 6-inch-wide base molding, then add a quarter round or base shoe at the lower edge, and apply a fancy cap or casing along the top edge. Install the first component of a built-up molding all the way around the room, then go back and apply the additional pieces.

*Crown moldings* are set where the wall and the ceiling meet. They're "sprung"—set at a 45-degree angle to both the wall and ceiling. *Bed moldings* are similar to crowns and are sometimes used as a substitute. In a room with a high ceiling, an elaborate crown may be used to create a dignified, formal style. Lower ceilings can benefit from a more subtle approach. But even a strip of quarter round at the ceiling will add extra refinement.

## Horizontal wall moldings

*Chair, picture* and *plate rails* are among the easiest moldings to install. Traditionally, all are applied horizontally on walls. The original purpose of a chair rail was to prevent chairs from marring the wall finish. At one time, paintings were hung by wires from picture molding, eliminating the need to drive nails into plaster walls. Plate rails were once used to display collections of fine china, souvenir dishes and other bric-a-brac.

While all three can still serve in traditional roles, their function today is primarily decorative. Often they're used as transitional elements. For example, chair rails are sometimes used to cap wainscoting or to separate different finishes, such as paint and wallpaper. Or if a ceiling color is different from the wall finish, it can extend down the walls to meet the top of a plate or picture rail. Plate and

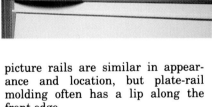

PHOTO: ROBERT PERRON

**At the top** of the page, graceful picture frame moldings are used to create wall panels between the chair rail and the crown molding.

**At the right,** a broad crown molding is used as a valance for a canopy over the four-poster bed.

**At the far right,** a custom stair-rail cap and mantel were shaped from hardwood stock.

picture rails are similar in appearance and location, but plate-rail molding often has a lip along the front edge.

## Window and door treatments

Many modern homes have plain *casings* around the windows and doors. They can be easily embellished by adding ornate molding strips on top of or along the edges of the existing trim. It's usually a good idea to coordinate casing and baseboard styles, since baseboards usually butt to door trim or to a *plinth block*—a plain, square block that serves as a transition between the two moldings.

If you want to start from scratch

with door and window casings, be careful not to mar the wall when prying off the old moldings. Loosen each piece by driving a thin chisel or pry bar under the molding. Be careful not to damage the underlying plaster or drywall; keep a piece of 1-inch scrap lumber handy to use as a protective surface to pry against. Once the old casings are off, pull out or hammer in all the nails left in the wall. You can then cut and install the new trim.

## Dressing up flush doors

You can make a plain flush door look like a traditional, raised-panel door by applying *quarter-round, half-round* or *panel molding* to its face in squares or rectangles. Plan to leave a 5- to 6-inch margin outside the "panels" at the door's top and sides;

---

## MOLDING SAMPLER

Trim moldings are made in many designs and sizes, and categorized by their traditional uses. Some of the many choices are shown below on a grid to indicate a range of relative sizes. Each square represents 1 square inch.

■ *Base moldings* are designed for installation where walls meet floors. Thicknesses range from ½ to ⅝ inch, stock widths from 2¼ to 5¼ inches.

■ *Base caps* are designed to be added to the top of base moldings. Thicknesses range from ¹¹⁄₁₆ to ¾ inch, widths from ¾ to 1⅜ inch.

■ *Base shoes* are designed to be added along the bottom of base moldings. Thicknesses range from ⁷⁄₁₆ to ½ inch, widths from ¹¹⁄₁₆ to ¾ inch.

■ *Casings* are designed for trimming doors and windows. Thicknesses range from ⁷⁄₁₆ to ¹¹⁄₁₆ inch, widths from 2¼ to 4¼ inches.

■ *Coves* are designed for trimming inside corners, such as where ceilings and walls meet. They can also be used to add detail to complex moldings. They're usually ⁹⁄₁₆ inch thick; widths range from ½ to 3¼ inches.

■ *Chair rails* are designed for horizontal installation on walls, generally 30 to 48 inches from the floor. Thicknesses range from ½ to 1¹⁄₁₆ inch, stock widths from 2¼ to 3 inches.

■ *Panel moldings* are designed for application to walls, doors and furniture to add detail or trim joints between panels. Thicknesses range from ⁹⁄₃₂ to ¹¹⁄₁₆ inch, widths from 1 to 2½ inches.

■ *Picture moldings* are designed for horizontal installation on the upper part of walls to support clips or hooks used to hang pictures. They're usually ¹¹⁄₁₆ inch thick and 1¾ inch wide.

■ *Quarter-round moldings* are designed to trim inside corners. Sizes range from ¼x¼ to 1¹⁄₁₆x1¹⁄₁₆ inch.

■ *Half-round moldings* are designed for flat installation on walls and panels and to add detail and depth to complex trims. Thicknesses range from ¼ to ⅜ inch, widths from ½ to 1 inch.

■ *Crowns* are designed to trim corners where ceilings meet walls. Thicknesses range from ⁹⁄₁₆ to ¹¹⁄₁₆ inch, widths from 1⅝ to 4⅝ inches.

■ *Astragals* are designed to be mounted as a stop at the center of double doors. They can also add depth and detail to complex moldings. Thicknesses range from ⁷⁄₁₆ to ¹¹⁄₁₆ inch, widths from ¾ to 1¾ inch.

■ *Glass beads* are designed to hold glass panes in a sash and are useful for adding extra detail to complex panel moldings. Thicknesses range from ½ to ⅜ inch, stock widths from ⁹⁄₁₆ to ⅜ inch.

■ *Wainscot caps* are designed to trim the top edge of wainscoting. Thicknesses range from ½ to ¾ inch., widths from ¾ to 1⅜ inch.

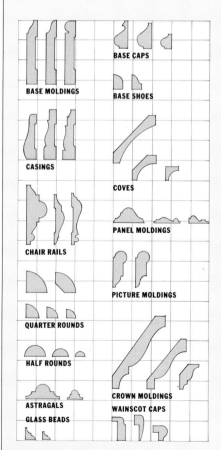

BASE CAPS
BASE MOLDINGS
BASE SHOES
CASINGS
COVES
PANEL MOLDINGS
CHAIR RAILS
PICTURE MOLDINGS
QUARTER ROUNDS
HALF ROUNDS
ASTRAGALS
CROWN MOLDINGS
GLASS BEADS
WAINSCOT CAPS

---

## CLASSY COMBINATIONS

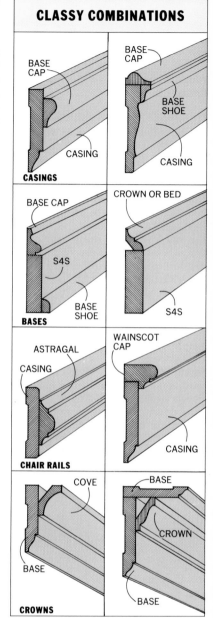

CASINGS
BASE CAP
CASING
BASE CAP
BASE SHOE
CASING

BASES
BASE CAP
S4S
BASE SHOE
CROWN OR BED
S4S

CHAIR RAILS
ASTRAGAL
CASING
WAINSCOT CAP
CASING

CROWNS
COVE
BASE
BASE
BASE
CROWN
BASE

**Wider, fancier casings,** baseboards, chair rails and crowns can be built up using stock moldings and *S4S* boards, which have a rectangular profile and are surfaced on four sides. Some examples of built-up moldings are shown above.

double the margin at the bottom. If the molding squares are small, you may want to glue and assemble them in a jig before applying them to the door.

## Picture frames

Picture framing is a classic application reminiscent of raised wall paneling. Molding is cut and nailed into rectangles, then nailed to the walls. Picture framing is often applied to wainscoting or the space above it. Another nice area for application is on the upper part of a wall, centered between a chair rail and a plate rail.

Although many moldings are named for their traditional roles, their uses today are nearly limitless. With a little imagination, careful planning and practice, you can create accents that catch the eye and enhance a room by adding detail, correcting awkward proportions and creating graceful transitions between all the architectural and decorative elements in it—*by John Birchard.*

## Cutting molding joints

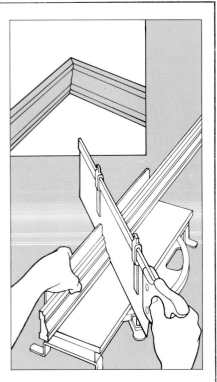

**A sharp, fine-toothed** back saw and a good-quality miter box are the most important tools for molding projects. A back saw has a thick reinforcement along the back to keep it stiff. A simple miter box is a three-sided wooden or plastic trough with slots at 45- and 90-degree angles.

An inexpensive miter box will deliver reasonable accuracy, but for finer workmanship and moldings that don't meet at right angles, choose an adjustable miter box. These usually have a clip or bearing system to hold the saw precisely. For very large jobs, look into renting or buying a power miter box, also known as a "chop saw."

Practice miter cuts on scrap pieces first (see the drawing at the right). Mark the cut on one edge of the work piece, usually the edge that goes against the back of the miter box. Line up the mark with the miter box guide slot so that the saw will cut just to the waste side of it. Hold the work firmly in place, and cut with smooth, light saw strokes.

For "sprung" moldings, like crowns

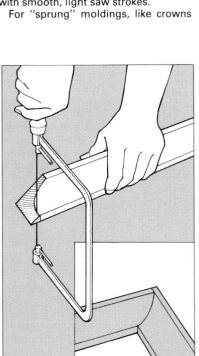

and beds—you may need to make a small jig to hold the molding at the correct angle while cutting the miter. This is the only accurate way to cut the compound angle needed.

Try to make your first cut as accurate as possible. It's better to cut a piece a little too long than a little too short, but it's also difficult to trim a small amount from an end. For greater accuracy when trimming ends, nail the molding to the miter box. For joints that meet at angles other than 90 degrees, the miter angle must bisect the angle of the joint. This is the only way to be sure all points of the molding meet evenly.

Coping joints is another approach for cutting moldings to meet at an inside corner. One piece is cut at 90 degrees, to fit flush with the end wall, while the mating piece is first mitered to 45 degrees, then sculpted to the countour of the molding face with a coping saw (see the drawing at the left). Again, practice coping on scrap material first, before trying it on expensive molding.

# putting in a powder room

Among major improvements, putting in an extra bath ranks high for adding convenience and value to a home. Many people believe it also ranks high for expense and difficulty, but that's not necessarily true. Powder rooms, also called "half baths," generally have just a lavatory, toilet and, occasionally, a shower, so space needs and fixture expenses are minimal. Plumbing costs can also be kept low with strategies that take advantage of existing water-supply and waste lines to keep runs to the new fixtures short.

*Reprinted by permission of Homeowner magazine.*

A new powder room can be a step-saver for family and guests alike when placed near a home's main living areas, and it can also help relieve the demand on other bathrooms when the family's trying to get out of the house in the morning. Whatever your reason for wanting to add a powder room, it shouldn't be too hard to find the space.

## Space requirements

A comfortable powder room with a toilet and lavatory can easily fit into a space measuring 12 to 16 square

PHOTO BY PAUL G. BESWICK

**This elegant** powder room, complete with a toilet, an ample-size lavatory and vanity, was installed in a 4 x 5-foot space. A toilet and sink can fit in as little as 12 square feet. With space-saving fixtures and ingenuity, you can fit a shower in a 24-square-foot area.

feet. To include a shower, 23 to 25 square feet would be the workable minimum. The space may be square or rectangular. Six powder-room layouts are shown in "Fitting Bath Fixtures Into Tight Spaces" on page 54, based on these approximate sizes.

For planning purposes, it's helpful to know the typical sizes of bath fixtures and the clearances needed to install and use them comfortably. There are many options in toilets. Variations in shape, mounting details, flushing systems and trap designs can affect the space that's needed for installation.

Most conventional toilet tanks measure 17 to 21 inches wide. A *one-piece* toilet with a round, rather than elongated bowl, and siphon-jet flushing action is one of the better options when space is limited. Toilets with this design usually measure just 24¾ inches from the back of the tank to the front of the rim, compared to 27½ to 29⅞ inches for other designs. A *close-coupled* tank and bowl with a *reverse trap* may take up as little as 22 inches from front to back, but reverse traps have a tendency to clog. Other space-saving options include tankless toilets, which rely on a special pressure valve to flush out the bowl, and toilets designed for corner installation. Consult a plumbing-fixture supplier for a more detailed summary of toilet options and sizes.

For comfort, there should be at least 24 inches clearance from the front of a toilet rim to any obstruction. There should be at least 28 inches between walls on either side of a toilet.

There are also many options for powder-room *lavatories*, or bathroom sinks. Wall-mounted lavatories generally take up the least space and are available as small as 12 x 14 inches. Small bar sinks can be adapted for use in a powder room, and corner sinks provide another space-saving option. In general, about 28 inches of

room is needed to stand and wash comfortably in front of a sink, and about 30 inches clearance is needed from side to side.

Standard shower enclosures measure 30 x 30 inches, but corner showers, which are readily available through bath-fixture suppliers, may be more adaptable to small spaces. Typically, corner units have two walls, each measuring 3 feet, and an angled front. The minimum clearance recommended in front of a shower enclosure is 28 x 28 inches.

## Choosing a location

To find the likeliest spots for putting in a powder room, draw a measured

**A sculptured custom vanity** with a Kohler sink (above) helps to save space in this powder-room design. The one-piece water-saving toilet, also from Kohler, both quiet and compact, is a smart choice for a powder room.

**The Neo-Angle Profile Shower** (far left) is another space-saver from Kohler. Its sleek modern design features an angled front oriented to the center of the space, for greater clearance.

**The compact Angle Hand Basin** from Porcher (center) is a wall-mount sink designed to fit into a corner. It has a 16-inch-deep, oval bowl.

**The Triangle Toilet** from Eljer (far left, bottom), designed for corner installation, is a popular choice for tight spaces.

**The Sonata** one-piece, acrylic shower enclosure from Kohler (lower left) can be built into a wall. It's a good design for half-baths that "borrow" their space from an adjoining room.

floor plan of your home, including exact dimensions for all rooms, hallways and closets. Account for the thickness of existing walls in your drawing. When the plan is finished, look for areas that fit the profile for total square footage and a workable shape for the fixtures you want to install. (See "5 Ways To Find The Space" on page 55 for a workable strategy.)

Consider rooms that are underused as prime candidates for powder rooms. In some cases, it may make sense to break through a hallway wall to "borrow" space from an adjacent room. Consider converting an underused closet to powder-room space. Appropriating some garage space is still another possibility. Whenever possible, try to limit the rearrangement of walls and doors to non-loadbearing partitions. Altering structural walls can be much more difficult and expensive.

If you can plan a new powder room so it is above, below or back-to-back with an existing bathroom, the cost and trouble of running the necessary piping will be kept to a minimum. Give preference to locations that are closest to a *soil stack*, which is a main waste pipe, and to existing water supply pipes and drain vents. Check your local building code to find out the maximum permissible distance from an existing vent stack to a toilet or lavatory.

Local codes also set standards for light and ventilation in bathrooms. You can usually meet the requirements if you can install the bath along an exterior wall of the house so that it can be fitted with a window. Most codes stipulate that bathroom windows be operable and have at least 3 square feet of glass. Meeting ventilation requirements is more of a problem when all the walls of a powder room are internal. When that's the case, consider installing an operable roof window with a shaft leading to the powder room or putting in a ventilation fan with a duct to the outdoors. Many combination light-fan fixtures are available through lighting supply outlets and will help you satisfy code requirements.

Also consider traffic patterns within the house when choosing a powder room location. Keeping them close to main living and entertainment areas will make them convenient for guests. Privacy is another concern—try to avoid having powder room doors open into the kitchen or dining room. Access from a hallway is usually best.

To enhance privacy further, consider installing a one-piece toilet with a siphon-flushing system. Although these fixtures are more expensive than other types of toilets, they're generally the quietest.

Another way to control noise is to

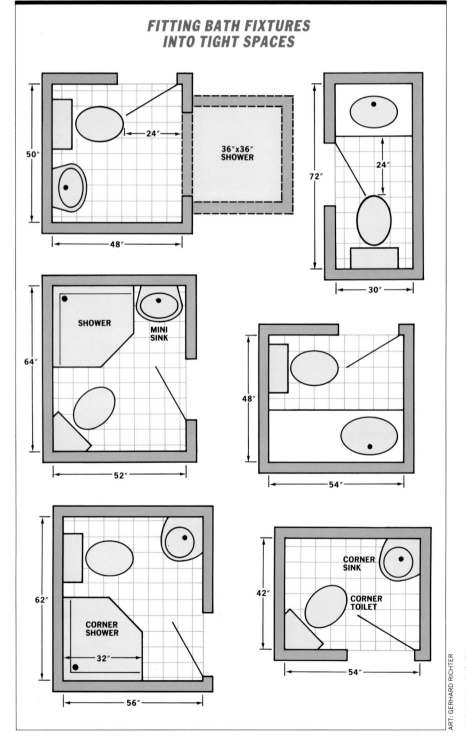

## FITTING BATH FIXTURES INTO TIGHT SPACES

36"x36" SHOWER

50"

24"

48"

72"

24"

30"

SHOWER

MINI SINK

64"

52"

48"

54"

62"

CORNER SHOWER

32"

56"

42"

CORNER SINK

CORNER TOILET

54"

ART: GERHARD RICHTER

**If you can find** an extra 12 to 24 square feet in your home, chances are you can fit everything you need for a powder room into it. The floor plans at the left show six ways to arrange fixtures in different sized spaces and shapes to maintain comfortable clearances within.

construct partition walls with 2 x 6 top and toe plates and 2 x 4 studs. In this system, the studs are set on 8-inch centers, with their edges set alternately on opposite edges of the plates. The studs aligned with one edge of the plates support the drywall on one side of the wall frame, and the studs aligned with the other edge carry the wall finish on the opposite side. This reduces vibration and, therefore, sound transmission. Batt insulation can also be woven among the staggered studs to create an even more effective noise-reducing baffle, and the walls can be finished with either one or two layers of perforated, sound-control gypsum wallboard.

All it takes to put a powder room into most houses is a bit of imagination and ingenuity. And since statistics show that homeowners who add a bath usually recover their costs and make a profit when they sell their homes, a powder room can be considered a good investment as well as a convenience—*by John Molnar.*

## 5 WAYS TO FIND THE SPACE

If you're looking for space for a new powder room in your house, maybe these model plans can help. The small drawing shows the first-floor plan for a house with two full baths. Green tints indicate potential powder-room spaces. In the larger plan of the same house, five different powder room layouts appear in the tinted areas. Here are the strategies for each:
**1.** Deepening a hall closet slightly yields space for a toilet and lavatory. **2.** Stealing some garage space and creating a new doorway in the hall makes it possible to install a toilet, corner sink and shower. **3.** Sacrificing den space and rearranging the hall closet creates space for a toilet and lav off the foyer. **4.** Space taken from the master bedroom's walk-in closet creates room for a toilet, lav and corner shower with access from the foyer. **5.** Space beneath the stairs can accommodate a toilet and lav.

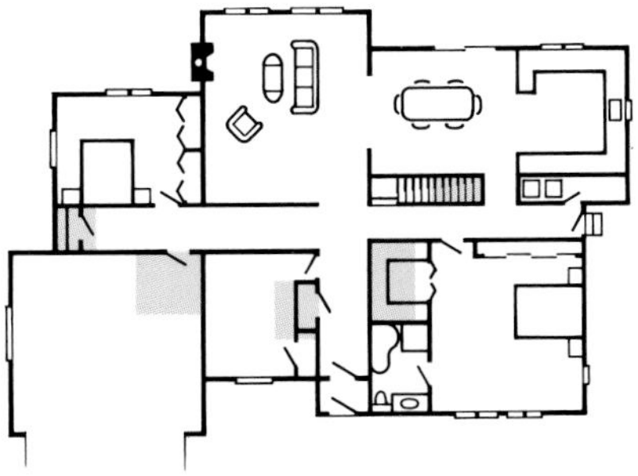

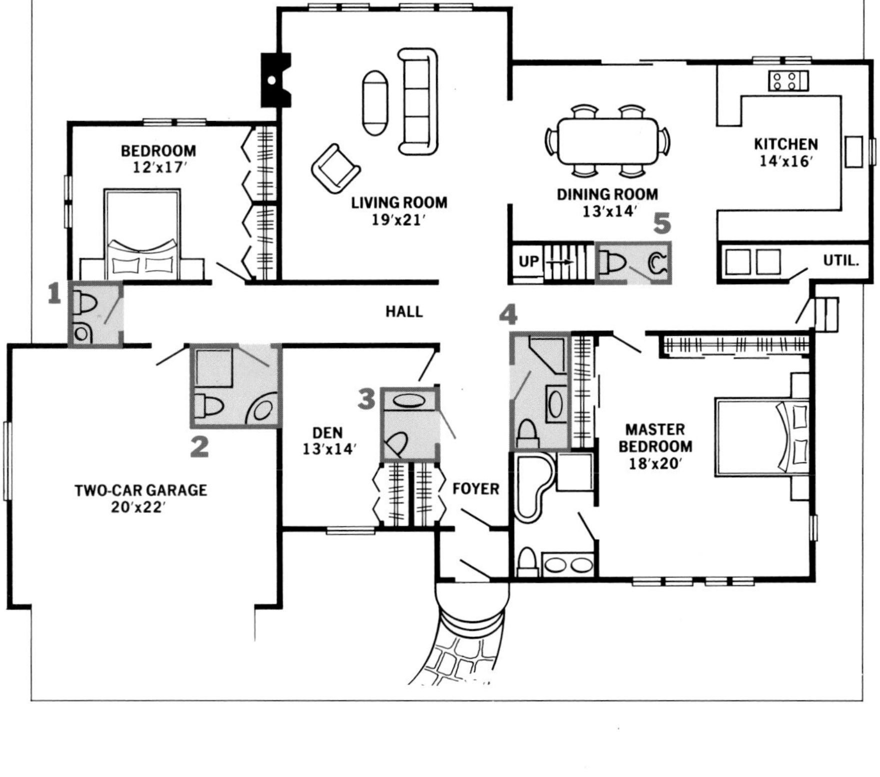

BEDROOM
12'x17'

LIVING ROOM
19'x21'

DINING ROOM
13'x14'

KITCHEN
14'x16'

UP

UTIL.

HALL

1

2

3

DEN
13'x14'

4

5

FOYER

MASTER
BEDROOM
18'x20'

TWO-CAR GARAGE
20'x22'

Layout at left shows typical ways to integrate these simple projects into a kitchen plan. Playhouse and drawer-tables are easily removed as kids grow.

# kitchen makeover: a working arrangement

PHOTOS BY CARL SHUMAN
AND ALLAN HOLM
DESIGNER: LOUISA COWAN,
ARMSTRONG DESIGN CENTER

**This family-oriented plan** includes space for needed implements and places for children to work and play. Built-ins include tables for kids with pull-out drawers (right) and a playhouse whose door becomes a seat (left).

There are kitchens that are purely functional and kitchens that serve a more universal purpose as meeting place, study area, first-aid station and message center all rolled into one. Serious cooks have the former; active households, especially those with young children, generally have the latter.

This kitchen, conceived by the Armstrong Design Center in Lancaster, Pennsylvania, addresses the needs of both groups. Wherever possible, storage areas have been built into otherwise unused or underutilized spaces, such as within overhead soffits, alongside end-wall cabinets, below existing counters and on walls.

*Reprinted by permission of Home Mechanix magazine.*

At the same time, the design includes elements that make the kitchen—which, on average, is the most-used room in a home—a true family gathering place.

All of the construction projects shown here and on the following pages are easily built and require little in materials or hardware. The designs can be adapted for many existing kitchen spaces. If you have a remodeling project or new home in mind, incorporate them into your plans. Flooring for this project is Armstrong's Century Solarium 12-by-12-inch tiles in the Crystal Garden pattern.

One of the most notable aspects of this kitchen is that certain items were included specifically for small children. A shallow cabinet at the end of the peninsula counter was transformed into a doll house, which will keep tots happy and busy within view of a parent working in the kitchen. The cabinet door cleverly folds open to become a child-sized seat.

Around the corner from the doll house, additional stool seating is provided for the junior set, along with miniature tables supported within specially arranged drawers. Existing or stock cabinet drawers are quickly adapted for the tables, which can be sized to fit within the drawers when not in use.

Even the shelf-like counter below the working counter at the rear wall serves as a convenient resting place for a child's cups and dishes. When constructing it, either install short (28- to 30-inch-tall) cabinets to accommodate the lower shelf-counter or add a second, higher counter above a standard counter at a comfortable working height.

Still another reason this kitchen is so accommodating within a small space is that its best features were designed into formerly unused wall, soffit and cabinet areas. A quick look around your own kitchen may turn up a number of equally underused spaces that could benefit from these economical and handsome built-ins—*by Michael Morris.*

**Decorative window grid creates a subtle pattern, may be continued across cabinets.**

**WINDOW TREATMENT**

1-1/8 x 1-1/8" PINE SQUARES
17" OR TO SUIT
90°
CROSS-LAP JOINTS (TYPICAL)
1" BRADS AND GLUE

**Soffit area between overhead cabinets is put to good use with hanging rack.**

**HANGING RACK**

1/2" DRYWALL
3/4" PLYWOOD
MOLDING TO SUIT
12"
1-1/4" LATTICE STRIP
28-1/2"
7-1/8"
3-9/16"
25"
3/4" PLYWOOD
3/4"-DIA. DOWEL

**Kids will enjoy** the hideaway house for play figures (above). When the kids stop playing with dolls, call it a "castle fortress" and repaint it. The playhouse door folds open into a seat. The cabinet can be converted easily for other uses, like storing tools and utensils (bottom left).

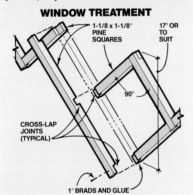

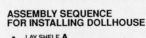

**ASSEMBLY SEQUENCE FOR INSTALLING DOLLHOUSE**

1. LAY SHELF, **A**, ON CABINET FLOOR

2. PLACE ROOF SECTIONS, **B** AND **C**, IN CABINET ATOP SHELF, **A**

3. RAISE SHELF, **A**, WITH ASSEMBLED ROOF AND POSITON SIDES, **D**

4. SLIP SHELVES, **E**, INTO DADOES IN SIDES. HOLD SHELVES IN POSITION AND SLIDE DIVIDER, **F**, INTO PLACE

5. REVERSE SEQUENCE TO DISASSEMBLE AND REMOVE DOLLHOUSE

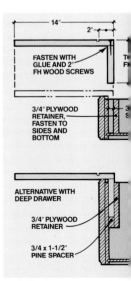

14"
2"
FASTEN WITH GLUE AND 2" FH WOOD SCREWS
3/4" PLYWOOD RETAINER, FASTEN TO SIDES AND BOTTOM
ALTERNATIVE WITH DEEP DRAWER
3/4" PLYWOOD RETAINER
3/4 x 1-1/2" PINE SPACER

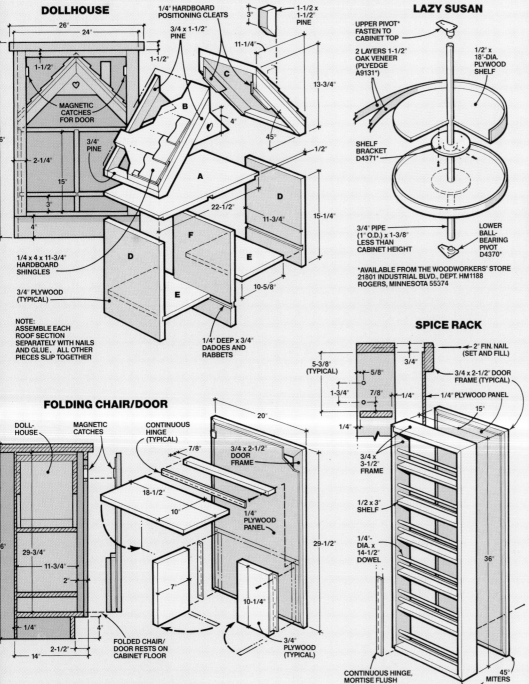

## DOLLHOUSE

- 26"
- 24"
- 1/4" HARDBOARD POSITIONING CLEATS
- 3/4 x 1-1/2" PINE
- 3"
- 1-1/2 x 1-1/2" PINE
- 11-1/4"
- 1-1/2"
- 13-3/4"
- 1-1/2"
- MAGNETIC CATCHES FOR DOOR
- C
- B
- 4"
- 45°
- 3/4" PINE
- 36"
- 2-1/4"
- 15"
- 3"
- 4"
- A
- 22-1/2"
- 1/2"
- 15-1/4"
- 11-3/4"
- D
- 1/4 x 4 x 11-3/4" HARDBOARD SHINGLES
- D
- F
- E
- 3/4" PLYWOOD (TYPICAL)
- E
- 10-5/8"
- 1/4" DEEP x 3/4" DADOES AND RABBETS

NOTE:
ASSEMBLE EACH ROOF SECTION SEPARATELY WITH NAILS AND GLUE. ALL OTHER PIECES SLIP TOGETHER

## LAZY SUSAN

- UPPER PIVOT* FASTEN TO CABINET TOP
- 2 LAYERS 1-1/2" OAK VENEER (PLYEDGE A9131*)
- 1/2" x 18"-DIA. PLYWOOD SHELF
- SHELF BRACKET D4371*
- 3/4" PIPE (1" O.D.) x 1-3/8" LESS THAN CABINET HEIGHT
- LOWER BALL-BEARING PIVOT D4370*

*AVAILABLE FROM THE WOODWORKERS' STORE 21801 INDUSTRIAL BLVD., DEPT. HM1188 ROGERS, MINNESOTA 55374

Stacked Lazy Susan makes full use of end-of-counter, corner or narrow cabinet spaces. Buy hardware and build your own for custom fit.

## FOLDING CHAIR/DOOR

- DOLL-HOUSE
- MAGNETIC CATCHES
- CONTINUOUS HINGE (TYPICAL)
- 7/8"
- 20"
- 3/4 x 2-1/2" DOOR FRAME
- 18-1/2"
- 10"
- 1/4" PLYWOOD PANEL
- 29-1/2"
- 36"
- 29-3/4"
- 11-3/4"
- 2"
- 7"
- 10-1/4"
- 1/4"
- 4"
- 2-1/2"
- 14"
- 3/4" PLYWOOD (TYPICAL)
- FOLDED CHAIR/ DOOR RESTS ON CABINET FLOOR

## SPICE RACK

- 5-3/8" (TYPICAL)
- 5/8"
- 3/4"
- 2" FIN. NAIL (SET AND FILL)
- 3/4 x 2-1/2" DOOR FRAME (TYPICAL)
- 1/4" PLYWOOD PANEL
- 1-3/4"
- 7/8"
- 1/4"
- 15"
- 1/4"
- 3/4 x 3-1/2" FRAME
- 1/2 x 3" SHELF
- 1/4"-DIA. x 14-1/2" DOWEL
- 36"
- 3/4" PLYWOOD (TYPICAL)
- CONTINUOUS HINGE, MORTISE FLUSH
- 45° MITERS

Swing-out spice cabinet adapts beautifully to otherwise unusable area at side of cabinet. Continuous hinge evenly distributes added weight.

## DRAWER/TABLE AND STOOL

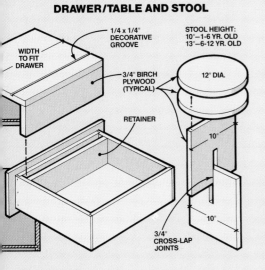

- 1/4 x 1/4" DECORATIVE GROOVE
- STOOL HEIGHT: 10"—1-6 YR. OLD 13"—6-12 YR. OLD
- WIDTH TO FIT DRAWER
- 3/4" BIRCH PLYWOOD (TYPICAL)
- 12" DIA.
- RETAINER
- 10"
- 10"
- 10"
- 3/4" CROSS-LAP JOINTS

## APPLIANCE GARAGE

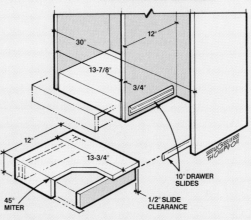

- 30"
- 12"
- 13-7/8"
- 3/4"
- 12"
- 13-3/4"
- 10" DRAWER SLIDES
- 1/2" SLIDE CLEARANCE
- 45° MITER

Heavy, bulky small appliances are stored out of the way, but are always accessible in these pullout "garages."

# creating closets

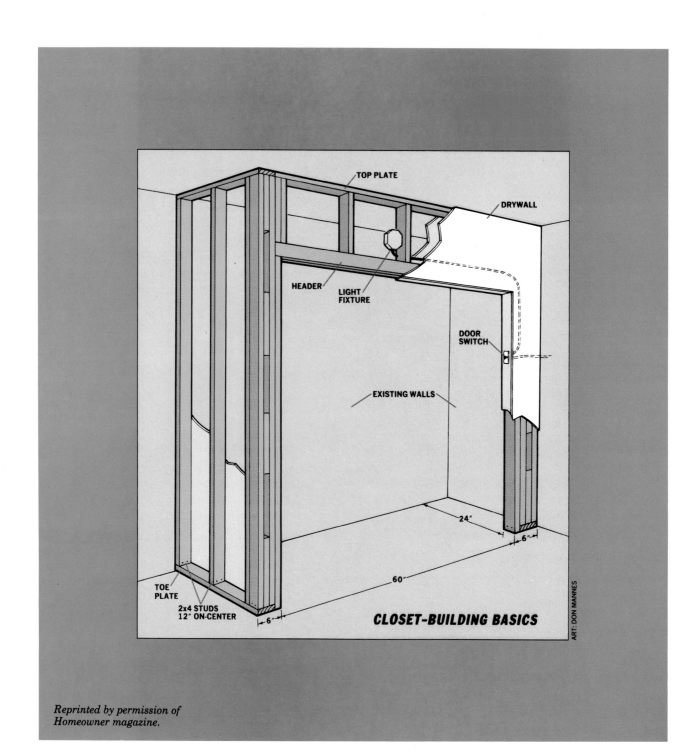

Labels in figure:
- TOP PLATE
- DRYWALL
- HEADER
- LIGHT FIXTURE
- DOOR SWITCH
- EXISTING WALLS
- TOE PLATE
- 2x4 STUDS 12" ON-CENTER
- 24"
- 6"
- 60"
- 6"

**CLOSET-BUILDING BASICS**

ART: DON MANNES

*Reprinted by permission of Homeowner magazine.*

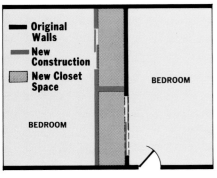

**Original Walls**

**New Construction**

**New Closet Space**

BEDROOM

BEDROOM

# making new closet space

**At the left,** new closets for adjoining bedrooms were created by framing a new partition in front of the common wall and dividing the closet space in half. A doorway in the new partition and another in the common wall allows access from both rooms.

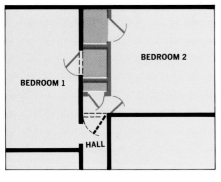

BEDROOM 2

BEDROOM 1

HALL

**Repositioning a doorway** at the end of a hall helped to create space for linen storage and two new bedroom closets in this plan. New partitions parallel and perpendicular to the common bedroom wall, plus cutting a new door opening, made it work.

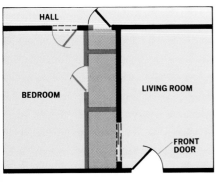

HALL

BEDROOM

LIVING ROOM

FRONT DOOR

**Cutting a new doorway** from the hall into the bedroom created a scheme for three new closets. Partition in the bedroom, built along its common wall with family room, created linen storage in the hall, a bedroom clothes closet and a new coat closet.

FAMILY ROOM

WINDOWS

**Stealing a bit** of floor space, defined by the short wall sections on either side of a pair of windows, created two abundant storage closets in this family room. Accordion doors need minimal clearance, helped to preserve the living space that remains.

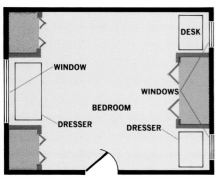

DESK

WINDOW

WINDOWS

BEDROOM

DRESSER

DRESSER

**Closets can be built** around windows and doors. In this plan two closets were built to flank a central window on one wall, creating a niche for a dresser, and a third closet was built between two windows, creating furniture niches on either side.

One thing many homes have in common, regardless of their style, age or size, is a shortage of convenient, accessible storage space. But if you can give up a little floor area, you can build in a lot of closet space without changing the basic structure of your home. Very often you can do all the necessary work yourself. The trick is in recognizing potential closet space when you see it.

## Planning the space

Before building anything, however, it's a good idea to take stock of your storage needs. If you want to add or enlarge a closet to relieve "clothes congestion," use the guidelines given on page 62 for the most efficient use of the available storage space. If you want to store away a variety of things, first make a list of what they are and assess how often you'll need to get to them. Pick convenient, close-at-hand spots for things needed daily or on some other routine basis. For long-term and seasonal storage space, look for out-of-the-way spaces in an attic or dry basement.

Assessing the size of things you want to store will also help you plan the optimal dimensions for a new closet. Keep in mind that bigger isn't necessarily better. For example, if a number of large, bulky items will be stored in a new closet, a depth of 4 or 5 feet might be most practical, if that much space is available. But a shallower design is usually better for a pantry closet where you need easy access to all the small cans, bottles and boxes that will be stored there. A new closet can also combine long- and short-term storage. For example, a 24-inch-deep closet is usually most efficient for clothes on hangers, but by making it 24 inches deeper, you can create room for sports gear, luggage and other items that you don't use every day.

If you're considering a walk-in closet, you'll need a minimum width of 5½ feet—2½ feet for the walk-in lane, 1 foot for shelves on one side and 2 feet for hanging clothes on the other. For a walk-in with clothes hanging on both sides, you need a minimum width of 6½ feet. The depth should be at least 4 or 5 feet to create an adequate "walk-in" lane. Remember, too, that the space needed to maneuver inside a walk-in closet is essentially wasted for storage purposes, but the convenient access to the stored items can make the trade-off worthwhile.

## guidelines for efficient storage

**Observing the old adage,** "A place for everything and everything in its place," will help you plan available storage spaces for maximum efficiency. To get the most out of your closet, keep the dimensions of the items to be stored in mind when you design the space.

In a clothes closet, for example, a single hanging rod should be placed about 12 inches from the parallel wall, 67 to 69 inches from the floor. For double rods, place the top one 76 to 84 inches from the floor and the bottom one between 36 and 42 inches above the floor. To prevent wrinkling, allow 1½ inches of space on the rod for each piece of clothing to be hung.

Plan the shelf widths and spacing according to the size of the items that will be stored on them. Use the following dimensions as a guide for the typical folded sizes of common articles of clothing and shoes.

| Blouse | 10"x13" |
| Nightie | 10"x19" |
| Pajamas | 8"x13" |
| Shirt | 8"x14" |
| Shoes | 9"x12" |
| Slip | 10"x11" |
| Socks | 4"x10" |
| Sweater | 11"x13" |

## Recognizing possibilities

Nothing helps you spot potential closet locations more than drawing a floor plan of your house. It will give you an overview of how spaces relate to one another and how things can be rearranged to make way for a new closet.

Keeping in mind the basic size and shape that's best for your storage purposes, check your floor plan for underused spaces along walls, in corners, even places where you now have furniture. Often rearranging furniture can open up a useful space. Use your imagination. A chimney that juts into a room may create space for closets on either one or both sides. Similarly, you could flank a centrally located bedroom window with closets and create a niche for a dresser by the window. The space between two windows may also present the opportunity to build a closet that bumps into a room. Sometimes it's possible to work a new closet into a relatively small space by designing it with a door system that needs minimal clearance to operate. (See some of the options in "Your Choice of Closet Doors.")

Take a close look at doorways and corners. If there's a 2-foot or longer run of wall between a door jamb and a corner of a room, you might be able to run a shallow closet along the adjacent wall, perpendicular to the door.

A doorway might also be in the way of an otherwise-good closet location. But don't let that stop you. A door can be shifted to open up the needed wall space. In non-loadbearing frame walls, it's fairly simple to take out an existing door frame and move it to another location.

In master bedrooms and other large rooms, consider building a new closet along an entire wall. Shortening the room's width or length by 24 to 30 inches may be a small sacrifice for gaining the advantages of a big closet.

The wall between two adjoining rooms is another place to consider adding two closets, one for each room. Say, for example, that you can spare 30 inches of floor space in the larger of two adjoining rooms. You would frame a new partition in that room, and divide the closet space with a short partition inside. Then you would install one set of closet doors opening into the large room, and cut a new doorway in the existing wall to make an opening into the smaller room (see the illustration on page 00). This approach creates new storage

## your choice of closet doors

**Choosing closet doors** that "fit" is important in more ways than one. Of course, they must fit the door opening, and they must also fit your home's decorating style. But the system you choose for mounting doors can be a factor in how the closet fits into the available space. There are a variety of options available for hinged and track-mounted door systems, and each opens up a range of storage possibilities.

**Standard Swinging Doors** are mounted with butt, pivot, Soss or European-style hinges. A single door may be mounted in openings up to 3 feet wide, but there must be ample clearance in front of the closet to allow the door to open fully. For openings wider than 3 feet, or to reduce the clearance needed in front of the closet, you can mount a pair of equal-width swinging doors.

**Sliding By-Pass Doors** are mounted with roller mechanisms that attach to the tops of doors, a top track and floor guides. They're a good choice for wide closets with minimum clearance in front since any number of doors can be mounted to close off the door opening and no swing space is needed. The potential drawback of sliding doors is that they allow access to only part of the closet space at a time.

**Bifold Doors** are mounted with a combination of hinges, a top track and

space in two rooms but requires a sacrifice of floor space in only one.

Long hallways with a wall at the end may offer a convenient location for adding a new closet. You can frame a doorway parallel to the end-wall to create a linen closet. Or, if one or more rooms are adjacent to the end of the hall, you can frame a partition and cut a doorway into the closet space from the room that needs it most.

## Avoiding problems

If your new closet plans call for

PHOTO COURTESY OF WOODFOLD-MARCO MFG. CO.

PHOTOS BY WING INDUSTRIES

**A factory-made** accordion door unit is used for a closet at top left.

**Bifold doors** are also a good solution for wide closets in tight spaces, such as the bathroom storage closet shown above. Louvered-panel doors offer ventilation and handsome styling.

**By-pass sliding doors,** which require no floor space to open, are shown at the left. Mirrors are a practical and popular dress-up for sliding doors, especially in bedroom.

guides. They're usually mounted in pairs of two or four door panels and offer a good solution for wide openings with relatively small clearance in front. In each pair, doors are hinged to one another, and when pulled at the center of each pair, the doors fold against one another. Bifold doors allow access to the entire closet, and require swing space equal to no more than a single door width (usually 12 to 24 inches).

**Accordion Doors** are available in factory-made units of wood or vinyl. They're mounted to the top jamb of a closet opening and are guided by an overhead track. Accordion doors are especially good for wide closets and require minimal front clearance to operate. The folded panels at the fixed end only partially block access to the closet when accordion doors are open.

**These mounting systems** are available as complete kits, doors included. You can also use standard interior doors, which are available in widths ranging from 1'6" to 3'0" and standard heights, including 6'0", 6'6", 6'8" and 7'0". Doors in these sizes are available in a variety of styles, including hollow-core flush doors with lauan, birch and hardboard veneers, solid-wood louvered doors and panel doors in many designs. Pre-fabricated mirror doors are also available, or you can have mirrors mounted on standard flush doors.

breaking through an existing wall, check for plumbing, wiring, ductwork or anything else that might complicate the project. While it's possible to reroute these "mechanicals," it's often easier to come up with an alternate plan that avoids changes of this kind. If a new closet project calls for skills you don't have, perhaps cutting a new closet doorway into a load-bearing wall, call in a pro.

## Closet construction

In most cases, adding new closets will involve dealing with non-load-bearing partitions, which are simple to build and alter. Closet walls usually consist of one or two short "stem" walls, which are made with 2x4 studs, top and toe plates, and a framed opening for the doorway in the "face" wall (see the illustration on page 60). An existing wall can usually serve as the back wall of a new closet. The new framing should be anchored to existing wall studs, ceiling and floor joists to provide structural stability.

The framing can be finished with wallboard or paneling, but before putting up wall finish on the inside of the closet, install any nailers or structural plates you may need between studs to support things like closet-rods and adjustable-shelving pilasters. Also, be sure to run the necessary wiring for closet lighting before finishing the walls. A common lighting arrangement includes a *door switch* that turns on the closet light whenever the door is opened. Planning for small details like this will help you get the most from your new closet space—*by Paul Barrett.*

# sideboard workbench

A recent "Superbench" was based on the *Popular Science* staff's idea of the ultimate workbench: A husky two-bench design made to flank a table saw or radial saw. One problem with the concept: It takes a lot of space. "But what about those of us who don't have that kind of shop space—or any shop space," said Executive Editor Richard L. Stepler, who calls a Manhattan loft his home. "Couldn't we design a workbench for people who live in apartments and condos or just don't have space for a shop? Couldn't we design a workbench that would double as a piece of furniture?"

Staff and consulting editors began the brainstorming process that must precede actual design: The bench should be contemporary in style and most likely spend its leisure time as a sideboard. For convenience, it must be quick to convert from workbench to furniture. And because bench-top tools cannot be permanently mounted on top, the bench would have to feature quick-mount bench-top tools and have lots of space inside to store tools and hardware.

Because it isn't likely you would undertake large jobs in a living-room or family-room setting, the bench was designed for light to moderate duty. While it's primarily a woodworking bench, we wanted the unit to be adaptable for hobbies, crafts, and repair projects that require a work surface and storage space.

We assumed that the builder of this bench would have limited space and tools to construct the unit, so we designed it without complicated joints and with easy assembly in mind. It can be made with portable tools.

For both the furniture top and the work surface beneath, I chose an attractive new material called Matte-wood. This versatile and tough material is made up of thin strips of oak glued together on edge.

While the workbench design is contemporary, it could be adapted to fit your personal needs, style, and space. Using different drawer pulls, staining the oak, using a different kind of wood or using trim moldings are just a few ideas. By eliminating the working top and permanently fastening the outer top, the project can function strictly as a sideboard. Or by eliminating the hinge-up outer top the design functions solely as a workbench.

If you want the convenience of storing all of your tools in the bench, multi-use tools are the best choice. A portable sander that clamps down to become a bench sander and a sabre-saw base that allows dual use of that tool are good options. When selecting bench-top tools, pick the smallest ones that will do your work. If you plan jobs that could soil the floor area, consider getting a painter's drop cloth, a tarp, or some heavy plastic film to protect the floor. Cut a 22-by-55-inch notch in it to fit around the bench base and tape or weight the edges.

Do not do painting, finishing, or stripping in a living area. Heavy jobs—like cutting large pieces of wood—are best done outside or by a lumber dealer. The lift-up bench top is fitted with a lock, which should be secured when the bench isn't in use. If there are children in the house, all doors and drawers also should be lockable.

Having a workbench in a living area also requires special attention to dust control and cleanup. A small shop vacuum is a must. When possible, select tools that either have vacuum exhaust ports or dust collector bags—*by Phil McCafferty. Photos by Mike Mitchell Photography.*

1. **Smaller bench-top tools** are mounted on base plates for quick attachment; rear of plate is held with lift-up pins; front, with clamp block. 2. Other tools store in compartments, which can be customized with shelves. A small shop vacuum is a must. 3. Attach ¾-inch-square strips around top of frame; stationary bench top is screwed to these through oversize holes. 4. Lockable drawers store many tools. Note that clearance must be cut in outer sides of end drawers for vise rods. 5. Holes to clear these rods are located and drilled in end panels by blocking up the vise assembly and marking locations prior to assembling ends of bench. 6. Vise can be used with bench dogs to clamp long pieces (as for sanding). Note center right the drop-leaf-style support that toggles the hinged lid in its upright position. Bottom photo shows array of tools bench can store. Hand tools mount inside lid with strip magnets or in positive-retention cases. For messy jobs, cover floor with a tarp notched to fit around base of bench as shown at right.

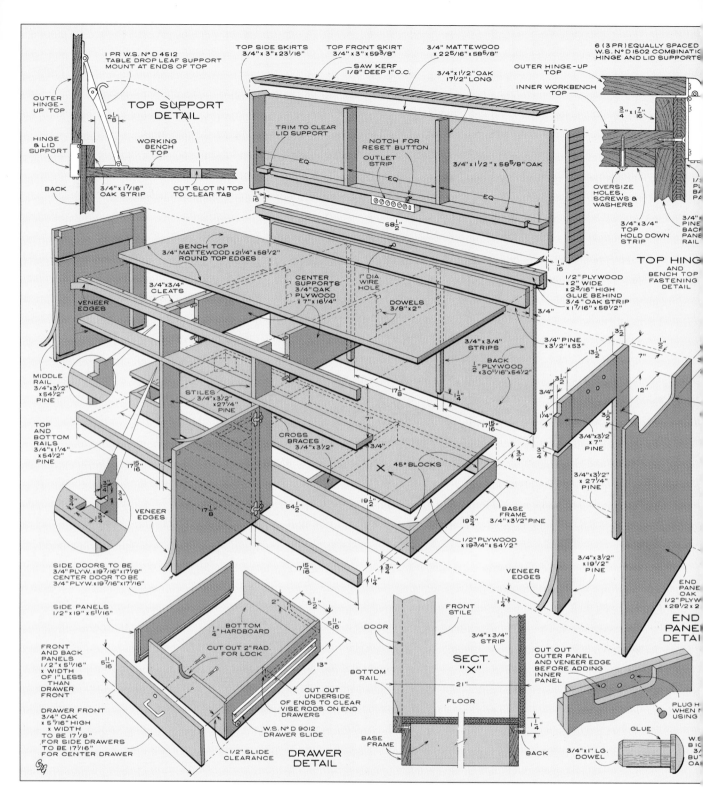

The bench is constructed from 1-inch lumber core oak plywood and 1-inch oak lumber where it will show, 1-inch fir plywood and 1-inch pine where it will not. If you prefer not to wait for a special order of Mattewood, you could substitute 1-inch lumber core oak plywood for the hinged top and 1-inch high-density hardboard for the working bench top. All joints are glued and screwed except the working top, which is only screwed on to allow it to be replaced if it should become damaged. The screw holes are oversize to let the top give a bit for climatic changes. Where they'll show, screw holes should be countersunk and plugged.

The first step is to assemble the base unit and prime paint. Attach the various pine strips to the end panels and to the back panel. Using a set of notched pine 1 × 4s (see detail) for the

vertical and horizontal rails, assemble the front. If the strips on the end, back, and front panels are spaced accurately, it's easy to assemble the project; but first make up the woodworking vise assembly (see detail) and mark the proper hole locations on the end panels.

Fasten the end panels to the base, followed by the back panel and then the front. Then install the 7-by-16¼-inch oak plywood pieces (marked center supports on the drawing) that tie the front and rear together and form the drawer openings.

Install the ¾-inch strips on top of the back panel where the working top will be attached to the frame. Slide the working top into the groove and fasten in place. Lay out and drill the various holes in the top for hold-downs and other accessories.

Cut the door and drawer fronts, allowing ⅙ inch on the cuts

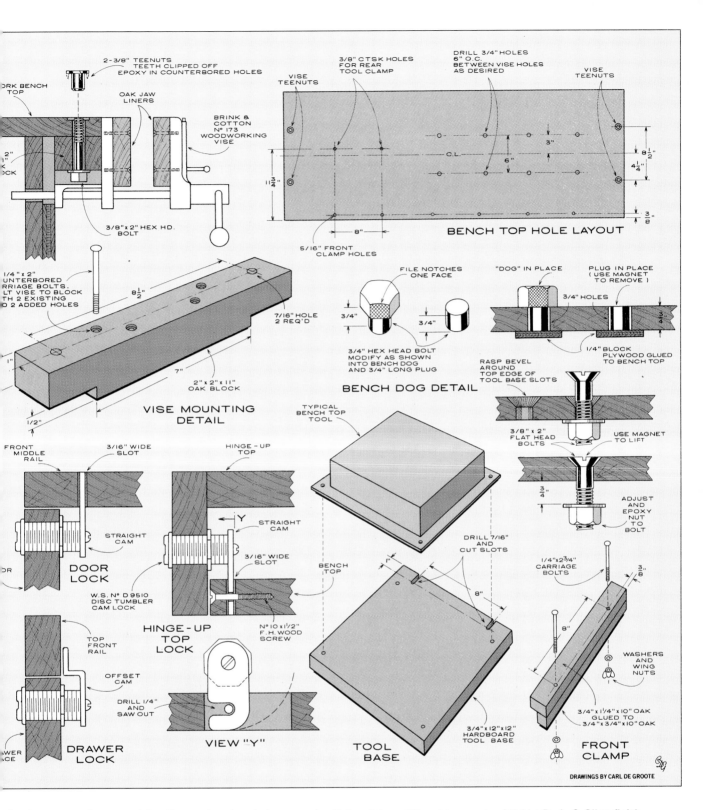

**2-3/8" TEENUTS** TEETH CLIPPED OFF EPOXY IN COUNTERBORED HOLES

ORK BENCH TOP

OAK JAW LINERS

BRINK & COTTON № 173 WOODWORKING VISE

3/8" x 2" HEX HD. BOLT

3/8" CTSK HOLES FOR REAR TOOL CLAMP

VISE TEENUTS

DRILL 3/4" HOLES 6" O.C. BETWEEN VISE HOLES AS DESIRED

VISE TEENUTS

C.L.

3"

6"

8½"

4¼"

11¾"

3/8"

8"

5/16" FRONT CLAMP HOLES

**BENCH TOP HOLE LAYOUT**

1/4" x 2" UNTERBORED RRIAGE BOLTS. LT VISE TO BLOCK TH 2 EXISTING D 2 ADDED HOLES

8½"

7/16" HOLE 2 REQ'D

7"

2" x 2" x 11" OAK BLOCK

1"

1/2"

**VISE MOUNTING DETAIL**

FILE NOTCHES ONE FACE

3/4"

3/4"

3/4" HEX HEAD BOLT MODIFY AS SHOWN INTO BENCH DOG AND 3/4" LONG PLUG

**BENCH DOG DETAIL**

"DOG" IN PLACE

PLUG IN PLACE ( USE MAGNET TO REMOVE )

3/4" HOLES

1/4" BLOCK PLYWOOD GLUED TO BENCH TOP

RASP BEVEL AROUND TOP EDGE OF TOOL BASE SLOTS

3/8" x 2" FLAT HEAD BOLTS

USE MAGNET TO LIFT

3/4"

ADJUST AND EPOXY NUT TO BOLT

FRONT MIDDLE RAIL

3/16" WIDE SLOT

HINGE – UP TOP

STRAIGHT CAM

TYPICAL BENCH TOP TOOL

STRAIGHT CAM

3/16" WIDE SLOT

**DOOR LOCK**

W.S. № D 9510 DISC TUMBLER CAM LOCK

BENCH TOP

DRILL 7/16" AND CUT SLOTS

1"

8"

1/4" x 2¾" CARRIAGE BOLTS

3/8"

8"

**HINGE – UP TOP LOCK**

TOP FRONT RAIL

№ 10 x 1½" F.H. WOOD SCREW

OFFSET CAM

DRILL 1/4" AND SAW OUT

**VIEW "Y"**

3/4" x 12" x 12" HARDBOARD TOOL BASE

**TOOL BASE**

WASHERS AND WING NUTS

3/4" x 1¼" x 10" OAK GLUED TO 3/4" x 3/4" x 10" OAK

**FRONT CLAMP**

WER CE

**DRAWER LOCK**

DRAWINGS BY CARL DE GROOTE

for clearance and veneer edging. Be sure to cut each drawer and door pair from the same piece so the grain will match.

Cut the hinged top panel, making it about 1/16 inch wider and 1/8 inch longer than the actual size of the working top for clearance. Cut, miter, and groove the top skirt end pieces and attach the magnetic strips (for holding tools) inside. Glue and screw the panel to the end skirts. Attach the front skirt with screws and glue.

It is easiest to finish the parts at this point. I used non-toxic

Dubno-Primer Oil and two coats of Kaldet-Resin & Oil to finish the project. Paint the base black and detail the grooves in the top skirt with black paint and a small brush or with a black permanent felt-tip marker.

Install the hinge-lid supports following the instructions that accompany the hardware. Install the drop-leaf supports and the top lock. The drop-leaf lid supports may require adjusting to hold the lid in exactly vertical position. You can consider adding shelves to suit your particular needs.

**SOURCES OF PRODUCTS USED IN THE SIDEBOARD WORKBENCH**

"W. S. No. XXX" items called out on the drawing refer to catalog items from The Woodworkers' Store, 21801 Industrial Blvd., Rogers, MN 55347; Mattewood: Trus Joist Corp., Box 60, Boise, ID 83707; 7" vise (#13PG): Woodcraft Supply, Box 4000,

Woburn, MA 01888; Dubno and Kaldet finishes: Livos, 614 Agua Fria St., Santa Fe, NM 87501; magnetic tool holders and outlet strip: Harbor Freight, 3491 Mission Oaks Blvd., Camarillo, CA 93011-6010.

# secretary shop

I had long been a tinkerer, and while living in the United States I always had a small shop. But when my wife and I moved to Switzerland, where there's an apartment shortage, we had to settle for a two-room flat. Crisis: No shop!

My solution was to build a piece of furniture that looks like a secretary desk when it's closed, but really is a workbench. It features:

- a stainless-steel work surface
- a built-in fluorescent light
- storage for my tools (including a small metal lathe)
- a metal vise

With this unit I can repair small appliances and build fairly complex projects without messing up our living room. And if a project gets interrupted, I can close the lid on it until the next chance I have to work on it.

Construction is mainly of inch-thick plywood. For the construction drawing, I've converted dimensions from metric. If stock is not available in similar dimensions in the United States, adjustments can be made. (If your unit is to be painted, as shown, consider using ¾-inch Medium Density Overlay plywood for all panels.)

The four legs are 2½-inch-square stock, joined by 5½-inch-wide aprons and a 1⅞-inch-wide rail at each side and across the back. The only rail across the front is the 1¼-inch-wide member below the drawer. The inch-wide "rail" below the two hinged doors is actually the edge of the plywood bottom. It is notched at all four corners to take the legs to which it is glued and toenailed. The 1⅝-inch-thick work top that is set on the top of the leg assembly (protruding 1½ inch at the front) was made of two ¹³⁄₁₆-inch-thick plywood panels glued together.

## Closing in the frame

For the effect of inset panels to close in the frame, I attached 1 x 1 cleats to the legs so that the plywood panels, when glued against them, would be recessed ¼ inch from the outside of the legs. The shelf inside the storage compartment is notched at all four corners to fit around not only the legs but also the cleats that position the closure panels. It rests on four lug-type shelf supports that fit into holes drilled in the legs. I made my shelf adjustable by drilling a series of these holes in each leg.

For the anchor for the swing-up lid, attach three plywood pieces to the back of the work top with glue and countersunk flathead screws driven up through the top plywood work top before it's glued to the sub-top. Note that this backboard won't interfere with long workpieces that must extend beyond each side of the workbench.

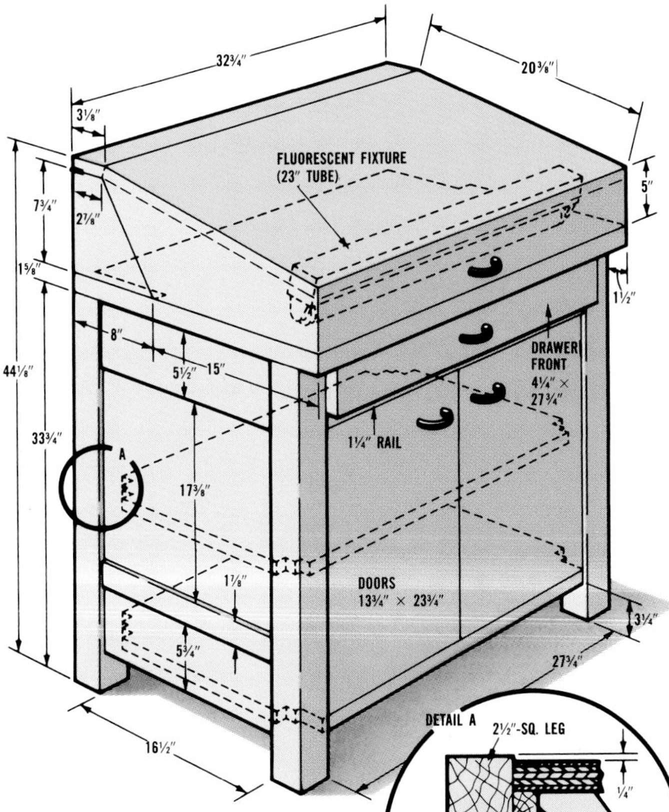
32¾"
20⅜"
3⅛"
FLUORESCENT FIXTURE
(23" TUBE)
7¾"
2⅞"
5"
1⅝"
1½"
8"
5½"
15"
44⅛"
DRAWER FRONT
4¼" × 27¾"
33¾"
1¼" RAIL
A
17⅜"
1⅞"
DOORS
13¾" × 23¾"
3¼"
5¾"
27¾"
16½"

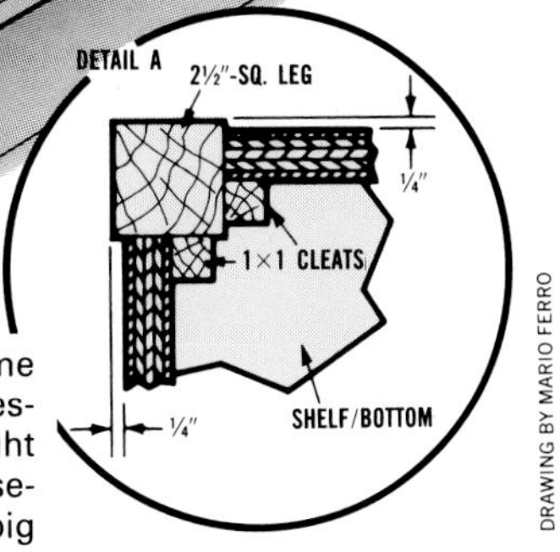
DETAIL A
2½"-SQ. LEG
¼"
1×1 CLEATS
SHELF/BOTTOM
¼"
DRAWING BY MARIO FERRO

**Plywood panels** inset between legs and horizontal frame members give the unit its furniture look. A 23-inch fluorescent tube is mounted inside the tapered lid to provide light for the work surface when the lid is raised and leaned securely against the wall (photo left). This leaves a gap big enough to hang a cordless vacuum on the back of the unit.

A metal shop cut a 22¼-by-32¾-inch piece of ¹⁄₁₆-inch stainless steel for a work surface. It's worth the expense because it's hard, won't rust, and easy to clean. I notched the rear edges to fit around the lid anchor using a hacksaw and file. You can attach the steel to the plywood by brushing a coat of contact cement on each. Be sure to use a wax paper slipsheet when applying because alignment is critical. After this has been slipped away, ensure a secure bond by tapping the entire surface with a rubber mallet.

Five pieces of plywood, assembled with finishing nails and glue, form the lid. A full-width piano hinge attaches it to the anchor. For appearance, it's important that the lid close snugly against the stainless-steel work surface. The beveled joint at the top of the lid is especially critical. No degree designation for it is given in the sketch because this is best obtained by assembling the large inclined panel to the tapered side pieces and "reading" the angle its square upper edge sets off the vertical (using a protractor or an adjustable bevel square) before cutting the cap piece to that bevel.

## Add doors and a drawer

The two plywood doors are mounted in the frame with full-height piano hinges and magnetic catches. The drawer is a simple box with four sides of ½-inch plywood and a ¼-inch plywood bottom. The front has an additional ½-inch piece glued on. The drawer slides on wooden cleats.

After filling all cracks and holes, apply an undercoat followed by a high-quality acrylic enamel. Mount pulls that will match other hardware in the room, and the disguise will be complete. There's a pull on each door, one centered on the drawer front, and one on the front of the lid, to ease raising. The weight of the unit—especially if it's placed on a carpeted floor—will anchor it firmly in place—*by Hans Wyssen.*

# beginner's bench

An ideal first project for your new home or apartment, this simple cabinet can be made with basic hand tools. Most parts are cut out of two and a half sheets of plywood—full four-by-eight sheets of both ½-and ¾-inch thicknesses, plus another four-by-four sheet of ¾-inch for the drawer fronts and door. *Popular Science* chose Medium Density Overlay (MDO) plywood with the smooth resin overlay on both faces because these surfaces

## PLANS AND VIDEO AVAILABLE

Because this is a beginner's bench—to be built without a workshop—expanded plans and a videotape demonstration of all assembly steps are offered. Even if you've never constructed anything before, these thorough instructions ensure success. For the plans only, send $2 to American Plywood Association, Box 11700, Tacoma, Wash. 98411. There are two video cassettes: one on basic woodworking techniques and one specifically on making this bench. They're $9.95 each (plus $2.95 for shipping) from InstructoVision, 36424 Ninth Ave. S.W., Federal Way, Wash. 98023.

take paint well. But if you want a cabinet in natural wood grain to match existing furniture, you might buy that half sheet in a cabinet-grade plywood so the door and drawer fronts would be in a wood grain.

If you choose regular plywood, it should be American Plywood Association-trademarked A-B or A-C. Or you might choose another type of structural panel, such as waferboard or particleboard. But whether you paint or go for a natural finish, you'll want to make an auxiliary work top out of tempered hardboard. You could cut this panel larger than the cabinet top so that cleats along its edges on the underside will snug it in place as you work. Without such a work top, of course, you'd soon mar the cabinet. The top can be removed and stored in a closet (or under a sofa) when you return to the cabinet mode.

This cabinet, with crisp modern pulls like those shown, will be at home in your living room, dining room, family room, or even a bedroom. Casters let you roll it wherever work can be best performed. It's a good idea to have locking levers on at least the two front casters to stabilize the workbench.

Though it's only two by three feet and about 33 inches high (depending on caster size), the unit offers four drawers and a compartment with shelves to store woodworking tools.

After laying out the plywood sheets as they're sketched, cut out all the panels. For ease of handling in a home without a workshop, have your lumberyard rip the full 3/4-inch sheet lengthwise and crosscut the 1/2-inch sheet—but note that these cuts should not be made on the center lines. (The 3/4-inch top should be 24 inches deep, and a center-line kerf would trim it to less.)

Cut dadoes across the right end panel and one face of the center partition, to take the central shelf. Cut rabbets across the bottoms of both end panels. Dado all drawer fronts. Because dadoes and rabbets are tedious to cut without power tools, you might want to rent a router or take these panels to a class for adults in a local school's woodworking shop.

Assemble all parts with glue and nails or screws. As an edge treatment, nail and glue 1/4-by-3/4-inch screen molding to front and ends, mitering the corners—*by Al Lees.*

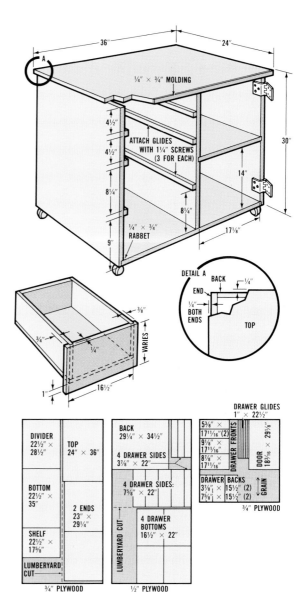

**When not in use,** beginner's work bench doubles as a handsome piece of furniture (photo left). Unit has an auxiliary work top that can be removed for storage.

# build a tenoning jig

The mortise-tenon joint is a classic wood connection used in furniture making, cabinetry, and other fine woodworking projects. But fashioning this joint without a special jig is difficult and dangerous. The reason: Although the mortise cavity can be readily cut on a drill press using mortising bits and chisels, tenon cheek cuts are most accurate when made with a table-saw blade. This is a hazardous procedure because tenons are usually cut at the end of narrow pieces of wood—chair and cabinet rails—that are hand held on end and moved along the rip fence. Rather than spending more than $200 on yet another accessory, my solution was to build a tenoning jig, tailoring it to my Delta UniSaw. With slight modifications, the jig will work as well on your table saw.

Most homemade tenoning jigs are designed to ride the rip fence; but the one I built is held firmly on the saw's table by twin "miter gauge bars" that fit into the slots flanking the saw blade. The result: All possible wobble is eliminated. This versatile jig can be used for both shoulder and cheek cuts and also for other chores like slotting dowels and cutting multiple pieces of similar length.

## Building the jig

Start by sawing the face to size and then form the groove for the slide. If you use the dovetail design, first form a groove that is 1½ inches wide and a fraction more than ¾ inch deep. Then slope the sides of the groove with a dovetail bit, working either on a drill press or with a portable router. You can skip the dovetailing procedure if you adopt the alternative method shown in the drawing. Here the face is made of three pieces, the front ones rabbeted for a slide that has matching rabbet cuts. Work carefully in either case because the slide must move smoothly and without wobble—it determines the accuracy of cut sizes.

Next form the bars so they will fit nicely and move smoothly in the table slots. After this it's best to position the bars in your table slots and then place the face over the bars so the distance from each end to the bars is the same. Then after accurately marking locations, form the dadoes that are required for the braces. Attach the braces with glue and No. 12 2¼-inch flathead screws and then place the subassembly so the braces are centered over the bars. Now you can attach the bars—but take 10 minutes

to do this five-minute job. It's critical that the angle between the face of the jig and the saw's table and the angle between the face and the side of the saw blade be 90 degrees. Add the rail and the see-through Lexan shield. The shield is there to keep sawdust or wood bits from flying in your face.

When fashioning the dovetail slide, note that the aluminum material listed for the cover is oversize. After the cover is attached to the wood slide with contact cement, the piece can be sized more accurately. You can form the ¼-by-7-inch slot that runs the length of the slide with a router. Alternatively, after cutting off one end, take a couple of passes with a saw blade to make the slot. Reattach the cutoff with glue. Be persnickety when beveling the edges of the slide to suit the dovetail or when rabbeting the slide if you choose the alternative method. This is another phase of the project where precision pays off because if the fit is off even just a little, the slide could jam.

The next step is to shape the slide head. Drill for and install the threaded insert and then add the guides, being sure they are centered about the insert and spaced to suit the hold-down. Attach the head to the slide so that its face will form a 90-degree angle with the saw's table.

The final step is the hold-down. Cut it to overall size and then shape it on a band saw or jigsaw, or with a hand saw. A handy way to improvise wing bolts is to grip the threaded rod between wood blocks in a vise and then use a prick punch to peen both the end of the rod and the inner circle of the wing nut until they are "welded" together.

## Using the jig

Essentially the jig is a carrier for unwieldy wood pieces. It allows you to secure workpieces and line them up in accurate positions and to move them past the saw blade with hands safely away from the cutting area. It's important to always use the hold-down; but if you find that this is impractical, remove it and utilize a clamp instead. The jig is designed for a maximum cut depth of two inches, which is adequate for tenoning work. It's a good idea to assign a particular saw blade for use with the jig to keep the kerf line uniform. A smooth-cutting carbide-tipped blade is recommended.

Always return the jig to its starting position after a cut

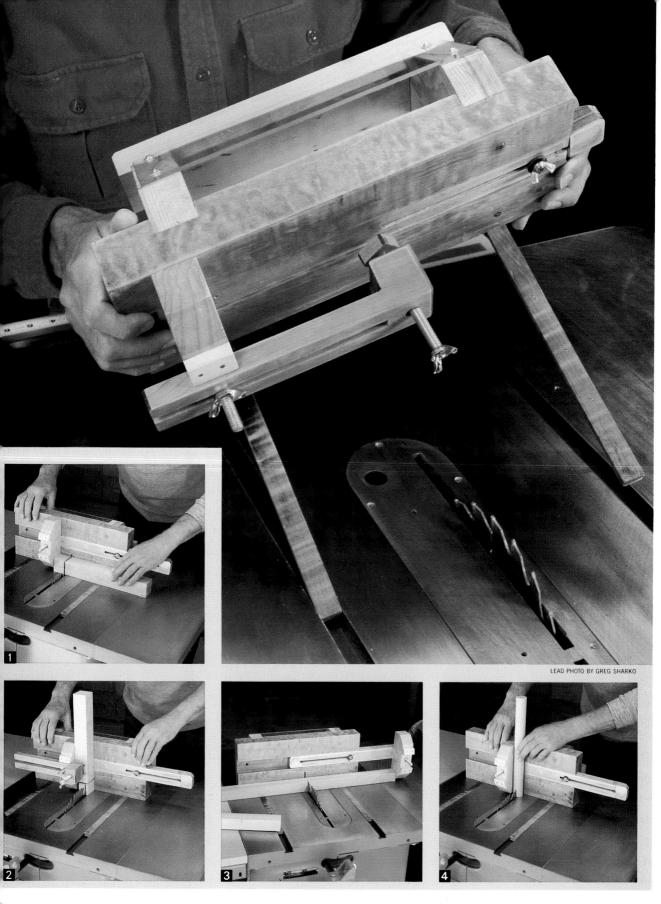

LEAD PHOTO BY GREG SHARKO

**The tenoning jig,** which fits securely in the table-top slots, can be used for shoulder (1) and cheek cuts. The distance between the slide head and the outside of the blade determines the tenon length. Use the hold-down (2) and always position the work so that cut-offs will not be caught between the slide head and the saw blade. The jig can also be handy for cutting multiple pieces of the same length (3). The distance from the slide head to a tooth on the facing side of the blade determines the length of the pieces. Sawing a slot in a round—needed, for example, when a chair rung is to be secured in a through or blind hole with a wedge is an operation that can easily be accomplished with this versatile jig (4).

and wait for the blade to stop before removing the work or cutoffs. Keep the table—especially the slots—and the jig clean. An occasional rubdown with paste wax in the slots, on the bars of the jig, and in the groove for the slide will ensure smooth operation. I find that with my tenon-ing jig the mortise-tenon joint has become a quick and elegant connection. The added features of safety and accuracy have made the jig one of the more important accessories for my table saw—*by R. J. De Cristoforo. Photos by the author.*

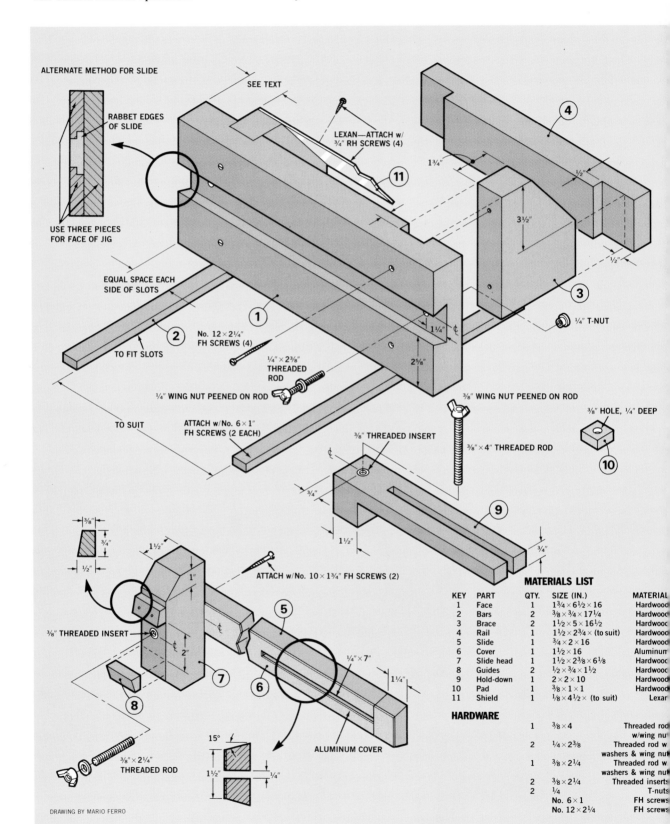

ALTERNATE METHOD FOR SLIDE

RABBET EDGES OF SLIDE

USE THREE PIECES FOR FACE OF JIG

EQUAL SPACE EACH SIDE OF SLOTS

TO FIT SLOTS

TO SUIT

SEE TEXT

LEXAN—ATTACH w/ ¾" RH SCREWS (4)

No. 12 × 2¼" FH SCREWS (4)

¼" × 2⅜" THREADED ROD

¼" WING NUT PEENED ON ROD

ATTACH w/No. 6 × 1" FH SCREWS (2 EACH)

⅜" THREADED INSERT

1¾"

3½"

2⅝"

1¼"

¼" T-NUT

⅜" WING NUT PEENED ON ROD

⅜" × 4" THREADED ROD

⅜" HOLE, ¼" DEEP

¾"

1½"

¾"

⅜"
¾"
½"

1½"
1"

2"

⅜" THREADED INSERT

ATTACH w/No. 10 × 1¾" FH SCREWS (2)

¼" × 7"

1¼"

⅜" × 2¼" THREADED ROD

15°

1½"     ¼"

ALUMINUM COVER

DRAWING BY MARIO FERRO

## MATERIALS LIST

| KEY | PART | QTY. | SIZE (IN.) | MATERIAL |
|-----|------|------|------------|----------|
| 1 | Face | 1 | 1¾ × 6½ × 16 | Hardwood |
| 2 | Bars | 2 | ⅜ × ¾ × 17¼ | Hardwood |
| 3 | Brace | 2 | 1½ × 5 × 16½ | Hardwood |
| 4 | Rail | 1 | 1½ × 2¾ × (to suit) | Hardwood |
| 5 | Slide | 1 | ¾ × 2 × 16 | Hardwood |
| 6 | Cover | 1 | 1½ × 16 | Aluminum |
| 7 | Slide head | 1 | 1½ × 2⅜ × 6⅛ | Hardwood |
| 8 | Guides | 2 | ½ × ¾ × 1½ | Hardwood |
| 9 | Hold-down | 1 | 2 × 2 × 10 | Hardwood |
| 10 | Pad | 1 | ⅜ × 1 × 1 | Hardwood |
| 11 | Shield | 1 | ⅛ × 4½ × (to suit) | Lexar |

## HARDWARE

| | | |
|---|---|---|
| 1 | ⅜ × 4 | Threaded rod w/wing nut |
| 2 | ¼ × 2⅜ | Threaded rod w washers & wing nut |
| 1 | ⅜ × 2¼ | Threaded rod w washers & wing nut |
| 2 | ⅜ × 2¼ | Threaded inserts |
| 2 | ¼ | T-nuts |
| | No. 6 × 1 | FH screws |
| | No. 12 × 2¼ | FH screws |

# mobile miter box

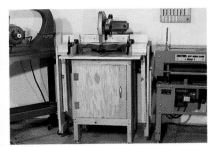

**For long work,** the mobile box's wings lift to provide nearly 8 feet of surface for work support. Work can be performed with one or both wings up, from either side of the table. When not in use (top photo), the drop leaves fold for compact storage. Wood bar-clamp fixtures (middle photo) are mounted to allow easy removal; their studs slip into sockets drilled in the clamp blocks. Stop blocks (photo above) are used to gauge duplicate miter-cut lengths. After the first miter is cut at one end, the stock is flipped end for end to butt up against the block.

I've always enjoyed working with a power miter box, and I got to like mine even better after using it to size, miter, and notch rafters for a backyard storage building. It was just the tool for the job. But I realized that the machine would be more practical, easier to use, and safer if I equipped it to provide considerably more support than the typical 18-inch-long tool table offers. Customizing the miter box soon became a project in its own right.

Because a miter box is a machine that should be bolted down wherever it is used, it was natural to think of mounting it permanently on its own mobile cabinet. That way it could readily be wheeled around to the next work location. With fold-down table extensions on either side, the unit could accommodate both small and larger pieces of work while occupying a minimum of floor space.

The cabinet I built offers much more than extra work support. Storage space for blades and accessories, removable clamps for work security, stop blocks for sawing similar pieces, and a guide for compound-angle cuts are all part of the design.

The cabinet's legs are notched to accept the front and back rails and are grooved on their inside edges to secure the panels and side rails. The side rails have tenoned ends and are grooved, like the legs, on their inside edges for the panels. Put the legs and front and back rails together as subassemblies and then connect them with the top side rails using glue and clamps. Slip in the panels, then add the bottom side rails, again using glue and clamps. It isn't necessary to glue the panels in place; they'll stay put without any help.

## Have wheels, will travel

The legs have casters for mobility, with a locking feature that's important for safety while sawing. One way to arrange the casters for maximum stability is to use fixed casters on the back legs and swiveling casters on the front legs. That way the machine won't have too much of a mind of its own when it's being wheeled to a new location.

Install the shelf cleats and the shelves before adding the back, which is simply surface mounted and secured with three-penny nails. The position of the top shelf is arbitrary and can be chosen to suit the items you wish to store. Be sure to recess the front edge of the shelf so there will be room for the perforated hardboard and tools stored on it when the door is closed.

It's best to install the door at the end of construction so it won't interfere with any work you'll have to do inside the cabinet. A sheet of perforated hardboard attached to the back of the door provides storage space for blades and other accessories that can be hung from hooks.

Cut the top to size, attach the trim pieces with glue and three-penny nails, and secure it to the rails with No. 10-by-1½-inch flathead screws. Assuming all the parts have been sanded, it's a good idea at this point to apply a couple of coats of sanding sealer, sanding lightly between coats and once more after the final one.

Bolt the saw in place so it is centered on the cabinet with the front edge of its base parallel to and 5¾ inches from the front edge of the cabinet's top. Before continuing, check to be sure the saw's components are in correct alignment. The table must be level. The angle between the surface of the table and the side of the blade must be 90 degrees. The angle between the fence and the blade at zero setting also must be 90 degrees. Any adjustment of miter settings can be attended to later.

Before cutting parts for the fixed table extensions, check the height of the saw's table against the dimensions that are supplied in the drawing and make any necessary changes to fit your saw. The extensions are assembled as units and then attached to the cabinet with No. 10-by-1½-inch flathead screws. The clamp blocks are notched to fit the base of the extension and are drilled to accommodate the studs on a pair of wood bar clamp fixtures. Hold the blocks in place with clamps after coating mating edges with glue.

Cut the tables to length and then form the ⁵⁄₁₆-inch-wide slot. Close the open ends with the ties, using glue and three-penny nails for the attach-

ment. The braces are duplicates, each piece having a ⁵⁄₁₆-by-6½-inch slot at one end. The last step here is to attach the tight pin hinges that allow the braces to swivel and the table to fold down.

The stops are straight pieces of wood that are drilled at one end so they can be reversed to accommodate either short or long pieces of work.

The guide for making compound-

angle cuts is simply a platform that is adjustable for distance between its front edge and the saw fence. It's meant to be used with the platform's edge running parallel to the fence.

The slots in the platform of the compound-angle guide should be located so they are centered over the clamp blocks. To locate the platform's guides accurately, secure the platform with the sheet-metal screws while it is butted against the saw's fence. The guides should allow the platform to move easily but without wobble.

The purpose of the platform is to allow a workpiece to be leaned against the fence at a repeatable angle. Making a routine 45-degree miter cut results in a compound angle with the slope determined by the angle between the work and the fence. If the slope angle is critical, you can determine the angle between the work and the fence with a T-bevel. Often, however, the slope angle doesn't have to be precise and actually can be judged visually. A picture frame would be a case in point: A few degrees one way or the other would not affect the project aesthetically or structurally, as long as all pieces are cut to the same angle.

Having a special setup for the power miter box doesn't relieve you of

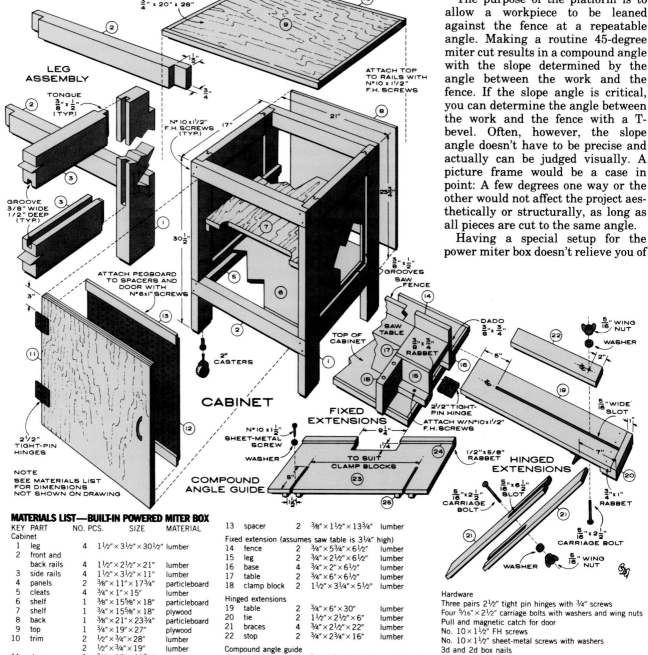

## MATERIALS LIST—BUILT-IN POWERED MITER BOX

| KEY | PART | NO. PCS. | SIZE | MATERIAL |
|---|---|---|---|---|
| **Cabinet** | | | | |
| 1 | leg | 4 | 1½″ × 3½″ × 30½″ | lumber |
| 2 | front and back rails | 4 | 1½″ × 2½″ × 21″ | lumber |
| 3 | side rails | 4 | 1½″ × 3½″ × 11″ | lumber |
| 4 | panels | 2 | ⅜″ × 11″ × 17¾″ | particleboard |
| 5 | cleats | 4 | ¾″ × 1″ × 15″ | lumber |
| 6 | shelf | 1 | ⅜″ × 15⅝″ × 18″ | particleboard |
| 7 | shelf | 1 | ¾″ × 15⅝″ × 18″ | plywood |
| 8 | back | 1 | ⅜″ × 21″ × 23¾″ | particleboard |
| 9 | top | 1 | ¾″ × 19″ × 27″ | plywood |
| 10 | trim | 2 | ½″ × ¾″ × 28″ | lumber |
| | | 2 | ½″ × ¾″ × 19″ | lumber |
| 11 | door | 1 | ¾″ × 18″ × 18¾″ | plywood |
| 12 | tool hanger | 1 | ¼″ × 13¾″ × 15″ | perforated hardboard |

| KEY | PART | NO. PCS. | SIZE | MATERIAL |
|---|---|---|---|---|
| 13 | spacer | 2 | ⅜″ × 1½″ × 13¾″ | lumber |
| **Fixed extension (assumes saw table is 3¼″ high)** | | | | |
| 14 | fence | 2 | ¾″ × 5¾″ × 6½″ | lumber |
| 15 | leg | 2 | ¾″ × 2½″ × 6½″ | lumber |
| 16 | base | 4 | ¾″ × 2″ × 6½″ | lumber |
| 17 | table | 2 | ¾″ × 6″ × 6½″ | lumber |
| 18 | clamp block | 2 | 1½″ × 3¼″ × 5½″ | lumber |
| **Hinged extensions** | | | | |
| 19 | table | 2 | ¾″ × 6″ × 30″ | lumber |
| 20 | tie | 2 | 1½″ × 2½″ × 6″ | lumber |
| 21 | braces | 4 | ¾″ × 2½″ × 22″ | lumber |
| 22 | stop | 2 | ¾″ × 2¾″ × 16″ | lumber |
| **Compound angle guide** | | | | |
| 23 | platform | 1 | ⅝″ × 9¾″ × 27¼″ | particleboard |
| 24 | ledges | 2 | ¾″ × 1″ × 9″ | lumber |
| 25 | guides | 4 | ½″ × ¾″ × 5½″ | lumber |

**Hardware**
Three pairs 2½″ tight pin hinges with ¾″ screws
Four ⁵⁄₁₆″ × 2½″ carriage bolts with washers and wing nuts
Pull and magnetic catch for door
No. 10 × 1½″ FH screws
No. 10 × 1½″ sheet-metal screws with washers
3d and 2d box nails
No. 6 × 1″ RH screws
Four casters (fixed type for rear legs, lockable swivels are best for front)

the responsibility of working safely. Always keep the guard in place and keep your free hand well away from the danger zone. Using one or both of the clamps helps you work more safely and accurately.

When cutting, allow the blade to fully stop before removing workpieces—no time is lost here if your machine has an electric brake. Wear safety goggles; and it doesn't hurt, es-

pecially during long use, to wear headphone-type hearing protectors.

Occasionally you may need to make a crosscut that is wider than the saw could ordinarily handle. This type of cut can be made by first taking a maximum-width cut, then turning the stock over and making a second pass to complete the cut.

A final pointer: Work with sharp blades. An all-steel combination

blade that is efficient for general sawing is the original equipment on many saws. But if you want ready-to-assemble results, consider a blade like the Teflon fluorocarbon-resins-coated model Freud, Inc., offers. With its unique tooth configuration, this blade delivers such burnished-looking cross and miter cuts that it has become a favorite choice for use with miter saws—*by R. J. De Cristoforo.*

# modify your miter box to cut duplicate lengths

I frame pictures—a lot of pictures. But when I finally treated myself to a power miter box I found I couldn't easily cut the identical pieces of molding that frames are made from; the lengths rarely come out the same. I needed a device that would mount on the saw and allow me to set a measurement to cut any number of pieces of equal length.

After thinking about what the ideal accessory would look like, I realized that a simple solution already existed: A three-foot combination square was just what I wanted. Then I checked the price for one at several tool suppliers and recoiled in horror. There had to be a cheaper solution. So I set about designing a square that would do the job at an affordable cost.

I already had one key item: A standard 12-inch combination square that I had bought at a garage sale for $2. I knew that if I could mate the head of the combination square with a three-foot metal ruler ($12), I would have my problem solved. Fitting the two parts together turned out to be easy.

To attach the head of the square to the ruler, I modified a ¼-inch bolt by grinding a notch into it with a length equal to the width of the ruler (see photo). Before I attached the ruler to the miter box, I cut off the first two inches of the ruler so the saw blade would clear it. Then I drilled two ¼-inch holes about four inches apart in the ruler. With the head of the square on the 15-inch line of the ruler, I loosely clamped the ruler onto the miter box. I adjusted the ruler so it was parallel to the bed of the box, with the head of the square exactly 15 inches from the blade.

I had to decide if I wanted to zero the ruler with the blade set at 90 or 45 degrees. I chose 45 degrees because that's the cut I most often make. (I have to add ½ inch to each measurement when I need to cut with the blade at 90 degrees. Similar additions are made when cutting at other angles).

After I had marked the locations of the holes on the box, I center-punched and then drilled two ¼-inch holes in the fence of the miter box. Then I attached the ruler to the fence with two ¼-inch bolts and wing nuts. The wing nuts allow me to remove the attachment quickly when I want to operate the saw without it.

My miter box modification is a success and a bargain. If you have a power miter box you might find this a handy attachment to make for yours —*by Steve Bryan.*

**Bolt a combination square** onto a power miter box and you've got a length gauge for making repetitive cuts (top). To handle longer lengths, replace the original 12-inch ruler with a three-footer. The close-up (above right) shows how the longer ruler mounts through two holes drilled in the back of the saw fence. The original attachment bolt is replaced with a ¼-inch bolt (above left) that is notched. This arrangement will allow the new ruler to slide through the head of the square.

# hardware for fast assembly

PHOTOS BY THOMAS M. JONES

**Knockdown,** or KD, fasteners are useful for putting together furniture that you want to take apart and reassemble. The photo at the left shows some of the wide assortment of KD fittings that are now available.

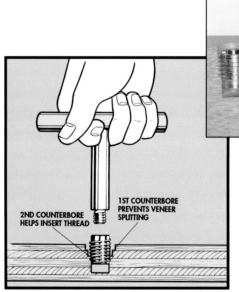

2ND COUNTERBORE HELPS INSERT THREAD

1ST COUNTERBORE PREVENTS VENEER SPLITTING

ART BY DON MANNES

**Threaded inserts** (above) provide permanent anchors for machine bolts used in wood joinery. To install a threaded insert, first bore a pilot hole slightly smaller than the insert diameter, then counterbore as shown in the illustration. Drive the anchor into the wood using an insertion tool with a threaded end.

**Cap nuts** (at left in photo) and T nuts (right) can both be used to join panels face to face using machine bolts. With either, first bore a hole, equal in diameter to the nut shank, in one of the mating pieces. Bore a hole slightly larger than the bolt shank in the second mating piece. T nuts have barbs to keep the nut from turning as the bolt is threaded in.

HM photos, Thomas H. Jones; HM art, Don Mannes

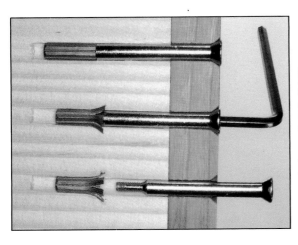

**Jaw Bolts** are used for joining a panel face to an edge. After boring a pilot hole, screw the bolt into the anchor and tap it in with a hammer. Turn the bolt several times to draw the bolt up and spread the top of the anchor so it bites into the wood. The bolt can be removed and re-threaded as needed.

**Trapez Fittings** (left) lock together with a machine screw. Some people prefer them to other plastic fittings, since the screw is easy to replace if it is lost.

**Joining Devices** (right) are interlocking plastic fasteners used to join panels at right angles. After attaching the components to the panel surfaces with screws, fit them together and secure the fittings with the slide-on cover plates.

**Furniture** Connectors (right) are a variation of the Joining Device, but instead of locking together with a cover plate, these fasteners are secured with a key.

In woodworking circles, knockdown furniture has a somewhat unsavory reputation. Justly or not, it is associated with bargain-basement, cookie-cutter design and is considered the last refuge of the truly unhandy. So why would anyone with the ability to build furniture want to use knockdown (KD) hardware in their own projects? The answer is, KD fasteners can be great problem solvers.

Knockdown fasteners are used primarily to join parts of projects that will be assembled and disassembled more than once. So if you move frequently and want to build furniture that's easy to pack up and take along, consider using KD hardware. Or if you want to build a piece that you can break down and ship economically to a relative or friend, KD fittings may be your best bet for joinery.

Knockdown hardware can also offer easy solutions for installing built-ins and wall units that are too large to move from your workshop fully assembled—just build modules in the shop and join the components on site using KD fittings. With many KD fasteners you need only a screwdriver or an Allen wrench to make the connections; in some cases you don't need any tools at all.

What all knockdown fasteners have in common is that they are designed to make it easy to put things together and take them apart. Among the various types are systems that rely on machine bolts and special nuts, or on threaded inserts, clamps and other devices that won't lose their holding power no matter how often the piece is assembled and disassembled. But many key differences exist among KD fittings.

For starters, each device is designed for a particular kind of joint. Some are meant for edge-to-face joints. You'd use one of these to join the sides to the bottom of a cabinet, for example, or the face frame to the front edges of the carcase.

Other KD fittings are useful for joining panels face to face. These can

**Blum KD Fittings** are useful for concealed edge-to-face joints. The metal bolt threads into a pilot hole bored in a panel edge with an ordinary drill bit. The plastic part of the fitting is mounted on the mating face in a recess bored with a Forstner bit. To join parts, first position the neck of the bolt in its plastic fitting and turn a screw to activate the locking cams.

**Minifix fasteners** are cam-type fittings that consist of a bolt and a disc with a slot along its edge. The disc turns, usually with a hex wrench or a screwdriver, so the slot can be positioned to receive the bolt and lock onto its neck. A standard Minifix fastener is shown at the right.

**The Blind Minifix** (left) is a variation of the standard version. While it's not as strong, it's very useful for edge-to-face joints when the bolt must be concealed.

**The Double** Minifix (left) has two bolts and can be used for edge-to-edge joints, either with a spacer, as shown, or without.

be used, for example, to join a side of one bookcase to another, or to assemble components that make up a wall unit.

A third type of KD fitting is designed for joining panels edge to edge. They are useful for installing two legs of a countertop in an L configuration, or for pulling two wall panels snugly together.

Another important difference among KD fasteners relates to the mechanical force inherent in the particular system. Some pull the parts they join together; others merely hold them in position. The pull-types, which include fasteners that work with machine bolts or cams, make for stronger joints.

When selecting KD fittings for a project, consider the type of materials you'll be joining. Be especially careful in your choice for edge-to-face and edge-to-edge joints. Fasteners that rely on screw-type threads and on expansion anchors generally work well in solid wood and in solid-core and veneer-core plywoods. But machine

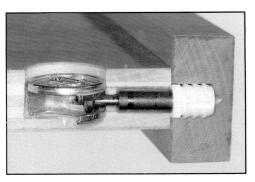

**The New KD** Fastener (left) is a large cam-type fitting used for face-to-edge joints when the bolt must be concealed.

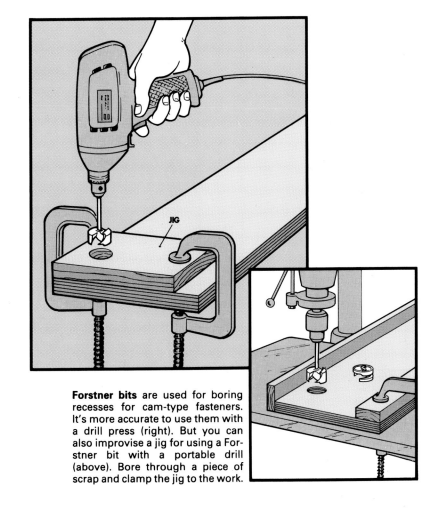

**The Tite-Joint** fitting (right) is designed for edge-to-edge joints. The bolt locks into two circular keepers and is tightened with a special wrench.

**The Joint Connector Bolt** (above) is an example of a KD fitting that utilizes a bolt and cross dowel. The fitting creates an extremely strong face-to-edge joint, and the cross-dowel head can be concealed inside a cabinet.

bolts with cross dowels and other types of face-mounted fasteners are better for particleboard.

Still another distinction among KD fasteners is the tools needed to install them. Many require only ordinary drill bits and maybe a screwdriver, wrench or hammer. But since accurate boring is generally more critical for successful installation of KD fittings than for other types of fasteners, it helps to work with a drill press. Some KD fasteners, particularly those with locking cams, require Forstner bits, which are designed for boring large-diameter, flat-bottomed recesses.

Finally, consider the finished appearance of the project when selecting KD fasteners. Some are more decorative than others, while many are easy to conceal on unseen surfaces of a project. Our photos show how 14 different KD fittings look and work. And the table on page 82 lists sources for each type, along with other useful information—
*by Thomas H. Jones.*

JIG

**Forstner bits** are used for boring recesses for cam-type fasteners. It's more accurate to use them with a drill press (right). But you can also improvise a jig for using a Forstner bit with a portable drill (above). Bore through a piece of scrap and clamp the jig to the work.

| Type | | Sources* | Joint | How It Works | Forstner Bit Size |
|---|---|---|---|---|---|
| Blum KD Fitting | | WW | Face-to-edge | Positions parts only | 25mm |
| Cap nut and machine bolt | | WW | Face-to-face | Draws parts together | Not needed |
| Furniture Connector | | CO | Face-to-edge | Positions parts only | Not needed |
| Jaw Bolt | | JM | Face-to-edge | Draws parts together | Not needed |
| Joining Device | | WW | Face-to-edge | Positions parts only | Not needed |
| Joint Connector Bolt | | WSNM, WW | Face-to-edge | Draws parts together | 10mm |
| Minifix (standard) | | WW | Face-to-edge | Draws parts together | 15mm |
| Minifix (blind) | | WW | Face-to-edge | Draws parts together | 15mm |
| Minifix (double) | | WW | Edge-to-edge, face-to-edge | Draws parts together | 15mm |
| New KD Fitting | | CO | Face-to-edge | Draws parts together | 7/8" |
| Threaded insert and machine bolt | | Home center, hardware store | Face-to-face, face-to-edge | Draws parts together | Not needed |
| Tite-Joint | | CO, WW | Edge-to-edge | Draws parts together | 7/8" |
| T-nut and machine bolt | | Home center, hardware store | Face-to-face | Draws parts together | Not needed |
| Trapez Fitting | | WW | Face-to-edge | Positions parts only | Not needed |

*Mail-order sources are abbreviated. Here's a key: CO=Constantine, 2050 Eastchester Rd., Bronx, NY 10461; JM=Jaw Manufacturing Co., Box 213, Reading, PA 19603; WW= The Woodworkers' Store, 21801 Industrial.Blvd., Rogers, MN 55374; WSNM=Woodworkers' Supply of New Mexico, 5604 Alameda Pl. N.E., Albuquerque, NM 87113

# special effects for decks

**An unusual shape,** a dramatic stair, built-in landscaping and an accent railing are combined in a unique, comfortable deck.

PHOTO: HEDRICH-BLESSING

*Reprinted by permission of Homeowner magazine.*

One of the things that makes decks so much fun to design and build is the simplicity of the structural system. Decks are usually put together with "dimension lumber"—2 x 4s, 2 x 6s and other standard sizes—with very few modifications except for cutting pieces to length.

But just because decks are structurally simple, it doesn't mean they can't reflect the sense of style and design coordination as do other parts of your home. In its overall design, a deck can be sized, shaped and detailed to be much more than a flat platform on a few posts. A well-designed deck does several things right: It accommodates intended uses (lounging, cooking, big or little parties); it fits with the house; it relates to the lay of the land and landscape features; it fits your budget well enough. And almost needless to say, a good deck design is the one you really like.

## Shape and size

Shape is a powerful design element. A square or rectangular deck of any size is simple and straightforward, but having one vast surface in a large deck might be monotonous. For a large deck, consider multiple levels or combinations of rectangles to give it more than four sides. A multi-level design also gives you a way to establish separate areas, such as for cooking, eating and lounging. A deck with curved or angled sides can escape the ordinary with a less formal look. Sometimes lot lines, trees or other circumstances require curves or angles, but they can also be an effective creative element, as in the deck shown above. When you're sketching out ideas, experiment with several shapes before you decide. Railings, screens and overhead shading structures can also be used to define spaces. Deck "furnishings," such as benches, tables and planters, can also be used for definition, whether they're built-in or freestanding. Stairways and ramps not only provide transitions from the house to the deck, between separate levels and between the deck and the yard, but they can also be important design elements.

Along with these major elements, the handling of smaller details can have a big impact on the look and feel of a deck. There are many options in joinery, decking patterns and trimwork. You'll likely pick up other good ideas from deck designers and builders and from books and magazines. The possibilities are many, but take them one at a time and you'll not be overwhelmed. Instead, you'll be on your way to creating a deck that's truly special, one that fulfills its potential for being a well-integrated, exciting and functional addition to your home.

### Choosing materials

Since the decking itself—the "flooring" applied on top of the basic structure—is the single largest visual element in most decks, it's a good place to start making design decisions. You can set the tone with the

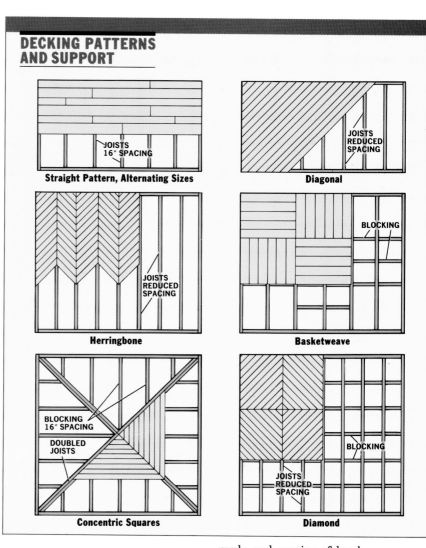

**DECKING PATTERNS AND SUPPORT**

Straight Pattern, Alternating Sizes
JOISTS 16" SPACING

Diagonal
JOISTS REDUCED SPACING

Herringbone
JOISTS REDUCED SPACING

Basketweave
BLOCKING

Concentric Squares
BLOCKING 16" SPACING
DOUBLED JOISTS

Diamond
BLOCKING
JOISTS REDUCED SPACING

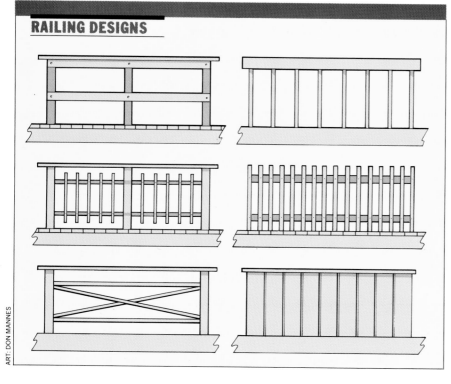

**RAILING DESIGNS**

ART: DON MANNES

grade and species of lumber you select, the size, pattern, and finish color you choose, and the way you handle joints and edges.

Because of their decay resistance, the common choices for decks are cedar, redwood and pressure-treated pine and fir. Pressure-treated lumber is the most economical. The type rated for "ground-contact" is best for all structural underpinnings of a deck (joists, posts, beams), no matter what type of wood is used for the decking, railings and other finished surfaces. Pressure-treated lumber rated for "weather exposure" can be used for decking. Right off the rack, pressure-treated lumber has a greenish cast, but it weathers to gray within a year.

As a rule, the pressure-treated lumber available at lumberyards is "construction grade," which means that it's likely to have knots, surface stains, checking and other imperfections that can detract from the overall appearance. If you want to use construction-grade lumber for decking, pick carefully through the lum-

**At the top,** luxuriantly planted boxes help to integrate an angular, multi-level deck with the surrounding landscape. Above, an open railing with a broad cap is used to provide a secure enclosure that doesn't block the view from a raised deck. At the left, a shading structure is used to define a lounging area on a large, multilevel deck.

ber rack to find the best pieces. You can also improve both the color and surface of defective boards by sanding them. (Always wear a dust mask when you work with pressure-treated wood.) But it's better to use pressure-treated lumber in Grade Nos. 1 and 2, which have a better appearance than construction grade. You usually have to ask your lumber dealer to order it specially.

Cedar has an orange-brown cast, and redwood is a deeper red. Both colors are naturally beautiful when

## BENCH DESIGNS

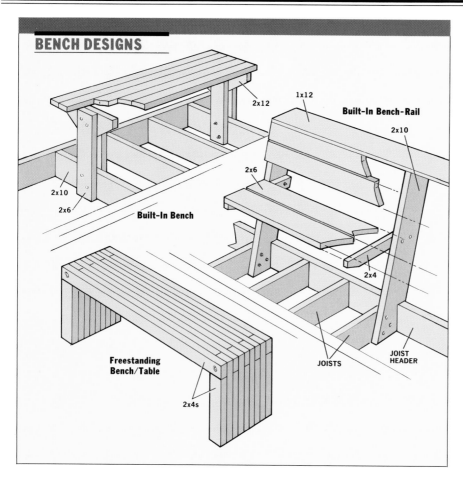

2x12

1x12

**Built-In Bench-Rail**

2x10

2x6

2x10

2x6

**Built-In Bench**

2x4

Freestanding
Bench/Table

JOISTS

JOIST
HEADER

2x4s

reduced so that the spans between joists are no more than 16 inches.

On multi-level decks, patterns can be varied to emphasize the sense of separate spaces. Using unrelated patterns on different levels of the same deck isn't recommended, however, because it can disrupt the unity of the overall design.

Along with decking patterns, there are a number of simple trim details that can be used to refine the look of a deck and conceal some of the structure (see "Fine Points," page 89). One is to allow the decking to extend (cantilever) beyond the structural frame. With 2-inch-thick boards, the decking can cantilever 6 to 8 inches without the need for additional support. Another approach is to fasten a trim band to the decking edges. By allowing the decking to cantilever and applying a wide band, you can conceal the support structure and create the impression that the deck is floating.

### Railing designs

For decks more than 36 inches from the ground, most building codes require a railing at least 36 inches high. Also, there are usually code specifications for the maximum opening between railing members, a

fresh, and both turn silver-gray when left untreated. With each, choose the better grades for good appearance.

There are many options for the size of decking boards and the patterns you can create with them (see "Decking Patterns and Support", on page 84). There are no limits to possible patterns other than the need to leave a slight gap between boards for drainage and to create an under-structure that will properly support the decking.

The simplest and most common pattern is to lay parallel 2 x 6 decking boards over joists spaced on 16-inch centers. In this scheme, the decking runs at right angles to the joists. Narrower boards (2 x 4s) in the same pattern can create a leaner, more refined look, or two different board widths can be alternated to add interest. Another way to enhance a simple pattern is to round-over or bevel the top edges of the decking.

A diagonal pattern adds interest and can make a deck seem larger. Herringbone, basketweave and other parquet patterns create interesting textures and reflect a higher level of craft than simpler patterns. Remember that for deck patterns running diagonal to joists, joist spacing must be

## PLANTER DESIGNS

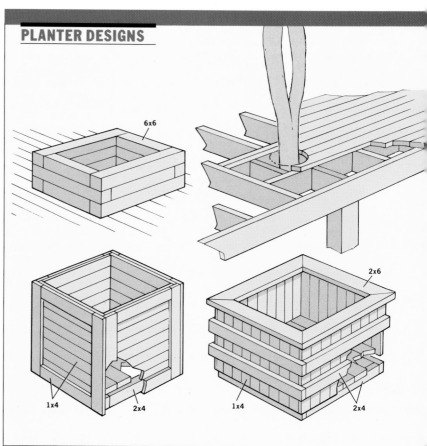

6x6

2x6

1x4

2x4

1x4

2x4

**Above, an exciting deck** for a difficult site was built with platforms at different levels. Special features include a hot tub, a swing, a deckside pond and dramatic lighting. Left, an intimate setting was created with a high privacy fence; the pattern is echoed in the planters and the built-in benches.

bers without a cap will encourage people on the deck to stand back.

Railing design can also affect the view from the deck. Keep it light if you want to look beyond while lounging in your chaise. On the other hand, a dense railing with wide vertical or horizontal boards can be used to block unwanted views and create privacy.

Keep in mind that the "line of sight" for people seated or standing on a deck is in the zone from 3 to 6 feet high. A high railing or "deck fence" in this zone will heighten the sense of enclosure. Also, solid railing panels should extend down to or

safety measure to prevent people from slipping through. (Look into codes in your area for specific requirements.) But along with meeting code requirements, it's also important to make good looks a priority. (A few approaches are shown in "Railing Designs" on page 84.)

The first thing to consider in designing a deck railing is the degree of enclosure you want. A light, open railing on a high deck might not provide enough sense of security. But a heavy, dense railing can lack grace. Railings with strong horizontal members emphasize the perimeter of the deck—they'll make a large deck seem bigger and a small deck seem even smaller. A railing with a broad cap rail will invite people to lean on it; a railing made up of slim vertical mem-

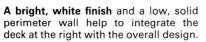

**A bright, white finish** and a low, solid perimeter wall help to integrate the deck at the right with the overall design.

## STAIR DESIGNS

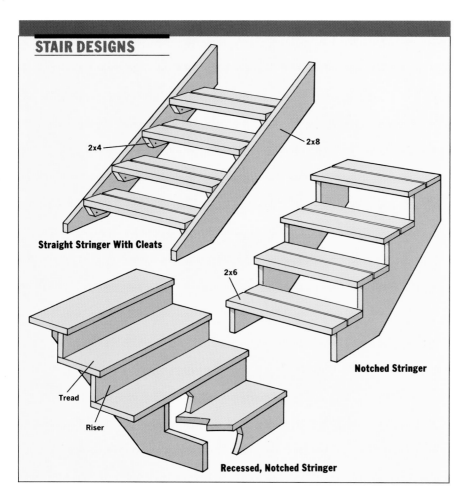

2x4

2x8

**Straight Stringer With Cleats**

2x6

**Tread**

**Riser**

**Notched Stringer**

**Recessed, Notched Stringer**

within an inch of the decking so the enclosure isn't "interrupted" by even a sliver of view.

Slim vertical railing members interfere less with the view from a deck than do horizontal rails. And it's the vertical members tied to the deck structure that give a railing most of its strength. Keep this in mind if strength, delicacy and views are concerns for your railing.

### Deck stairs

With attention to design, stairways can do more than simply connect a deck to the house and the grounds. For example, two or three wide steps rising from the yard to a low-level deck can provide a dramatic transition.

Longer stairways, on the other hand, seem easier to climb when they're narrower. Any stairway with three or more steps should have a handrail for safety, and this provides an opportunity to coordinate the stair design with the deck railings.

The relationship of tread width to riser height is a design element as well as a functional concern. A common ratio is 12-inch treads with 6-inch risers, which is also convenient since it's easy to make treads up with a pair of 2 x 6s. Or, you can build with wider treads and lower risers for a more graceful, slower climb.

It's not only physical dimensions that define the character of a stairway, it's also the way the stair is built. *Stringers* are the principal support for stair treads. They're usually built in one of two ways: Stringer boards can be notched in a saw-tooth pattern, in which case the treads rest on top of them. Or, cleats are attached to the stringer so that the treads rest between them (see "Stair Designs," on page 88). Choose the look that most appeals to you; both methods make for a strong stairway. Stairs built with cleated stringers almost never have solid risers, which means you can see through them when you're climbing up. (That could, however, be disconcerting on the way up to a high deck). Notched stringers may or may not have solid risers, but when they do, they seem more solid. Using notched stringers for a wide stairway, you can create an interest-

ing illusion by recessing them 12 inches or so from the ends of the tread's edge. The treads will seem to float in space, and if you use solid risers the same length as the treads, the stairway support will seem even more mysterious.

### Shading, benches and planters

After using size and shape, deck patterns, railings and stairs to create distinction, you can go still further with shading structures, benches and planters. When you choose to build any of these into a deck, you have a chance to coordinate the materials, patterns and finish details with other design elements for a unified, overall design.

Shading structures create a partially sheltered area within a deck. Usually, the roof is constructed with spaced slats, like a trellis, for partial blocking of direct sunlight. Sidewalls can be open or can have lattice or rails for more shading and a greater feeling of enclosure, while still allowing breezes to pass through. In some areas, putting in insect screening is a must for evening comfort in spring and summer.

Built-in benches establish inviting, casual places for relaxation and conversation, and can be used to define activity areas and traffic patterns. On low-level decks, benches are sometimes used instead of a railing. On higher decks, benches are often tied to the railing structure (see "Bench Designs" on page 86). It's worthwhile to note that since benches are usually built of the same sturdy materials as the deck itself, they don't require much maintenance or off-season storage as do other types of outdoor furniture.

Building-in benches means tying in the legs or seat supports to some part of the deck structure. A straight bench seat can be supported on simple trestles that are fastened to the joists or to blocking running between them. On the railing, you can fasten seat support members to the railing posts. If the railing is to serve double-duty as a back for a bench, it can be angled up to 30 degrees. For comfort, a bench seat should be 14 inches above the finished decking and at least 12 inches deep. Look for ways to coordinate benches with the over-all design by repeating patterns, proportions or detailing from some other part of the deck. For example, if the decking is finished with an edge band, you can add a similar band, in proportion to the size of the bench, to the seat. Or, if the handrail has rounded-over edges, you can treat the bench edges in the same way. You can even build free-standing benches and tables that echo the deck design by using the same or similar materials and joinery details.

## Planters

Plants and planters can relieve the monotony that sometimes results from using so much material of a single color, as is usually the case in deck construction. They also help to connect the deck with other parts of the yard. Planters can be used as focal points in the middle of a deck and as borders as an alternative to railings and benches. For ongrade decks, it's easy to create planters by leaving openings in the decking (see "Planter Designs," on page 86). In this way, you can either build the deck around existing plants and trees, or frame openings for new beds. Another approach suitable for raised decks is to build wooden boxes with trim details similar to ones used elsewhere. Or, you could make the planters from brick or stone.

If you use wood, choose either pressure-treated lumber rated for ground contact or clear heart redwood. Leave openings for drainage at the bottom of planter boxes, and consult a reference guide to ensure that the deck structure is strong enough to support the weight of the soil and plants (remember that plants gain weight as they grow).

## Fine finishes

All of the woods commonly used for decks weather naturally to silver-gray when left untreated. This usually takes about a year, but you can accelerate the weathering by applying a gray *weathering stain.*

If you want the decking to weather naturally, however, it's still important to treat it with a clear water repellent when it's new and once every couple of years afterwards. This prevents defects that can occur as untreated wood absorbs and releases water.

To maintain a "new wood" look, treat the decking once a year or so with an *oxalic acid* solution, which is available in most hardware stores and home centers. You just brush the solution on, let it work, then hose it off.

Semi-transparent stains can also be used to preserve the look of natural wood and maintain a uniform color. Many stains also contain water-repellents and mildewcides for added protection. Tinted and clear oils can give decking an appealing sheen.

With *floor* and *deck* paints, you can give a deck a uniform, opaque color treatment. There are many colors to choose from, from the whitest whites to brilliant shades of any other hue you might want. For a good-looking, long-lasting paint finish, sand all visible surfaces, and prime before applying two coats of the topcoat. Coat the underside, edges and end grain as well as the top surface to prevent peeling.

## A unified approach

With all the available design elements and all the possible approaches, there's a lot to think about when designing a deck. But deck building is an essentially simple undertaking, and so should be designing one. Take a unified approach in which similar materials, proportions and details are used throughout. And take the time to recognize opportunites for adding nice touches, the special effects that raise decks up from the ordinary and make them truly special—*by Michael Chotiner.*

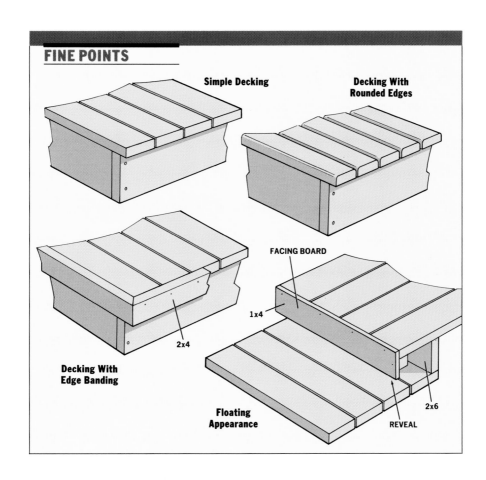

**FINE POINTS**

Simple Decking

Decking With Rounded Edges

Decking With Edge Banding

2x4

FACING BOARD

1x4

Floating Appearance

2x6

REVEAL

# two stepped decks

## spa deck

When Susie and Peter Stevenson first moved into their seaside home north of San Diego they knew that the side entry area needed work. Access was via a steep asphalt walkway that was slippery when wet. At its end rickety steps climbed to a cramped deck that only termites enjoyed.

"We also wanted to cover those eyesore utility meters at the lower corner," Susie tells me. "And I wanted to add some life by building in planter boxes. And if we could include a Jacuzzi, the kids would be ecstatic."

The final design covered all bases: Angled platforms turn the corner much more invitingly than the old blacktop ramp. And by hinging simple frames of redwood lattice, the meters were hidden, yet kept accessible for reading. Framing out this entry wall also provided concealed storage

for potting soil, brooms, and spa chemicals.

A spacious new deck running the length of the kitchen/dining-room wall adds useful space for entertaining, and the steps up to the spa deck create a lot of extra seating.

All construction was knotty garden-grade redwood (the Stevensons specified Construction Heart and Construction Common at the lumberyard). After building was underway, *Popular Science* discovered clever devices called Dec-Klips and had a batch of them shipped to the Stevensons. "We were so pleased with the results," Susie reports, "we almost wanted to tear out the deck boards we'd already face-nailed so we could start over with the Klips." As shown in the sketch below, they're simple devices that solve a multitude of

problems: They eliminate unsightly nail heads (and hammer dimples) from the deck surface and automatically space the boards for drainage as you go along. Because you nail into the *side* of each plank, there can be no nail popping later to snag bare feet.

And if you ever want to sand down the deck for refinishing, you won't have to set nail heads below the surface to keep them from ripping your sanding belt. "The Klips sped up our whole project," says Susie.

Fence construction was kept simple as well. Vertical 1 x 6 planks, with each joint covered with one-inch redwood lath for visual interest, were topped with lattice panels and a top rail. Each post was capped with a beveled square cut from a redwood 2 x 6 —*by Al Lees.*

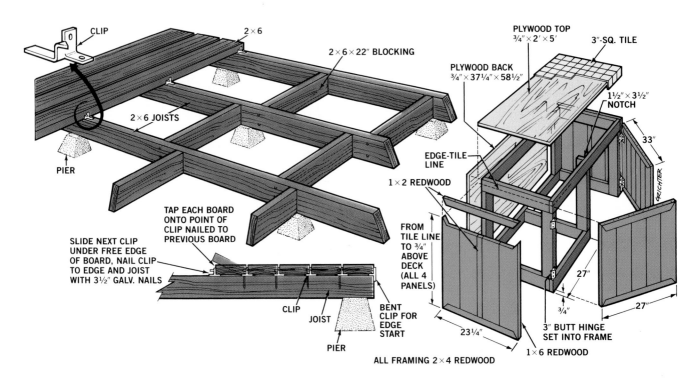

PHOTOS BY STEVEN F. MULLENSKY

**A flight of landings** (bottom right) swings around the back corner of the house to cover an old blacktop walkway. These stairs climb to an upper deck, which, at its far end, has two more steps up to a fenced alcove for the spa. Note in the top photo that the fence along the lower deck is topped with glass panels that serve as a windbreak without obscuring the ocean view. A buffet counter is attached to the house wall (photo and sketch left), sized to garage a rolling service cart. Other built-ins include a storage bin (above).

PHOTOS BY GEORGE LYONS

# pool deck

You enter this impressive pool area near Austin, Texas, through a gated brick archway tucked under a rustic cedar trellis that runs across the back of the house. The entire 1,600-square-foot area beyond is enclosed by a rambling wooden fence topped with redwood lattice that serves as a windbreak without impeding gentler breezes. The lattice is framed by 4 x 4 posts and 2 x 4 rails top and bottom. The fence consists of 1 x 6 redwood planks with a redwood 1 x 2 batten over each joint. Built against it are benches of various heights; sections of the top of the perimeter bench are hinged to give access to storage for pillows and sunning mats.

Sections of the best sunning deck (for early afternoon exposure) are also hinged so they can be raised as back rests. When not in use, the prop brace that holds each four-plank section at a comfortable angle is released and the sections drop flush with the deck surface.

The enclosed area under the foot of the fiberglass slide is a storage compartment for pool chemicals. It also houses a poolside phone, with the adjacent raised trapezoid (in the foreground of the large photo) providing a perch for taking calls with your back to the noise of the pool.

All deck planks are 2 x 6 redwood. Conventional decking over so large an area would have looked monotonous, so designer Stewart Neely stepped up odd-shaped sections and varied the direction of the planks. The designer was also challenged to preserve two existing sycamore trees. He located the conversation pit beneath one of them, taking advantage of its shade.

The substructure consists of 4 x 4 pressure-treated posts flanked by 2 x 6 beams and topped by a complex of joists and blocking that creates the various levels.

Back near the house, deck planks are nailed directly to sleepers laid (24 inches on center) across the existing brick patio. The big trellis is supported by 4 x 6 cedar posts; 2 x 6 rafters span the distance between two 2 x 6 ledgers—one lag-screwed to the house, the other fastened to the rear face of the 2 x 12 fascia board. There's only one center support post, so this fascia has only one joint, centered on this post.

Where raised deck areas meet the edge of the pool, the ends of the projecting planks are trimmed to the free-form shape with a sabre saw, and short lengths of 2 x 6 redwood are set in under the trimmed edge. Straight edges of these raised sections are faced with redwood planks, placed on edge.

To avoid corrosion that can stain the deck, be certain that all fasteners are hot-dipped galvanized or stainless steel. Because all levels will see barefoot activity, it's a good idea to round the top corners of all deck planks to minimize splintering. All surfaces should get a clear finish—*by Al Lees.*

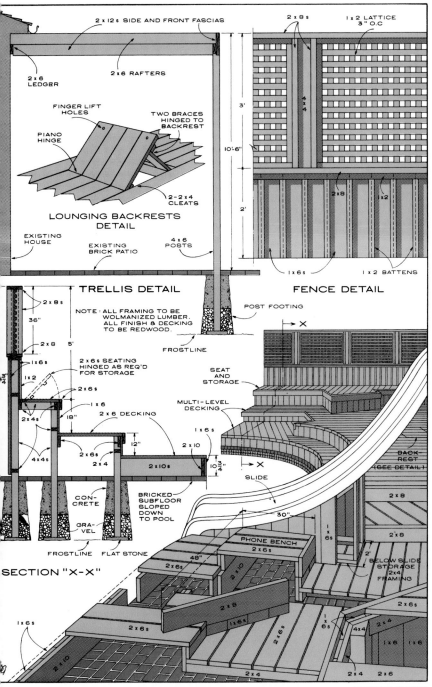

DRAWINGS BY CARL DE GROOTE

**Complex pattern** of levels creates a bleacher effect at far end of pool, with a variety of areas for sunning and seating. There's even a conversation pit—a lower area ringed with several levels of benches (at far left, under inset photo). Inset shows the reverse view: The rustic trellis along the back of the house, above the original brick patio. Note the access panel to pool gear in the foreground, with finger holes for easier entry.

# deck
# under glass

Problem: Tame a Southern California hillside for outdoor living yet preserve the panoramic view of the Pacific Ocean overlooking a golf course. Complicating the situation: Prevailing winds that could make sunning and alfresco dining on the deck windy propositions. The owners of the home, a 20-year-old Spanish-style tract house, also didn't want simply a basic square deck.

Solution: A dramatic, irregularly shaped multilevel redwood deck with a tempered glass railing that shields the deck from onshore breezes yet does not hide the view.

Designer Dana Nadeau of Capistrano Beach, California, took advantage of the apparent site drawbacks —an irregularly shaped lot as well as the steep terrain—to create a deck with several levels and irregular angles, avoiding the look of the basic square or rectangular deck.

## Defining levels

The deck's several levels are defined by differing orientations of the 2 x 6 redwood decking; this adds visual interest and defines deck areas, as well as aids in preventing tripping acci-

dents. The deck's lowest level, down two steps from the main section, is actually cantilevered over the hillside. The second section is built at ground level. A third, raised section wraps around the spa, which is also built on ground level.

The decking and all visible wood is redwood. The clear and select grades used are free or relatively free of knots and show streaks of lighter colored sapwood. The understructure of the deck is constructed of fir and pressure-treated fir.

The deck was built in segments, with the cantilevered section first. It's

**Glass railing** retains the view (below) yet provides shelter for the spa (above). Deck levels are defined by differing orientations of decking. Before view (facing page) reveals the steep hillside the deck reclaims.

supported on 4 x 4 posts set into 12-
inch-diameter concrete piers that are
dug 54 inches into the hillside. The
concrete piers were poured into Sono-
tube forms. The posts support 4 x 12
headers, which in turn support the 2
x 8 joists under the 2 x 6 deck surface.
Galvanized joist hangers reinforce
the construction. Cross bracing for
the support posts is also 2 x 6.

## Construction tips

The deck railings are 46 inches high.
Upright posts, double-lag-bolted to
the face of the deck, are dadoed to
hold tempered glass inserts and are
capped with 2 x 6 vertical-grain redwood. Shorter, alternating sections of
vertical redwood slats break the visual monotony of the glass and help
to define the deck areas.

The ground-level section of the

**Though it** appears to
float from above,
deck is firmly an-
chored to the hill-
side when seen from
below (top). Con-
crete footings 12
inches in diameter
support 4 × 4 posts.
Cross bracing mem-
bers are 2 × 6s. Ver-
tical supports for
glass are double-
lag-bolted to deck
edge (left). Posts are
dadoed for glass
inserts, as are 2 × 6
top caps (below).

deck is supported on 4 x 4 pressure-
treated joists, which rest on top of
concrete piers. A third, raised section
built around two sides of the Sund-
ance acrylic spa hides the plumbing
and electric service, as well as provides easy access to the whirlpool.
The spa, which has its own redwood
surround, was simply set in place and
the deck was built around it. A redwood lattice privacy screen completes
this section of the deck.

All exposed redwood is finished
with Watco oil-based semi-transparent stain—*by Richard L. Stepler.*

# deck doctors

**Foam says this deck cleaner** is working. Once you spray it onto the deck and work it in with a broom, rinse with water.

Nature is ruthless. An unattended house will eventually rot and collapse; a car that is not cared for will rust and decay; even elegant statuary and magnificent cathedrals are etched, worn smooth, and compromised by the effects of weathering.

The same holds true for the deck in your backyard. Unless you are unusually diligent, there will come a time when the effects of mold, mildew, and ultraviolet radiation will make your deck look worse for wear, and your elegant addition will become a weather-beaten blemish.

Until a few years ago there was not much you could do to keep your deck fresh looking, short of sanding it down or drenching it with a chlorine bleach or acid solution. Trouble was, sanding took a tremendous amount of effort—and often required resetting nailheads. Acids and bleach are toxic materials. They also give a deck a washed-out look. Enter wood renewers.

Wood renewers made especially for decks started surfacing four or five years ago. The first ones were acid- or bleach-based, but newer formulas kill mold and clean off gray tarnish to re-

**MANUFACTURERS OF DECK RENEWERS**
Darworth Co., 50 Tower Lane, Avon, CT 06001; **The Flood Co.**, Box 399, Hudson, OH 44236; **Koppers Co.**, 436 Seventh Ave., Pittsburgh, PA 15219; **Macklanburg-Duncan**, Box 25188, Oklahoma City, OK 73125-0188; **Osmose Wood Products**, Drawer O, Griffin, GA 30224; **United Gilsonite Laboratories**, Box 70, Scranton, PA 18501.

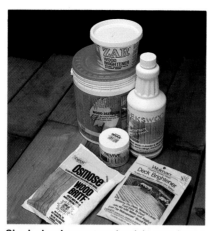

**Six deck rejuvenators** banish gray better than Grecian Formula: Zar Wood Brightener, Weather Warrior Wood Restorer, Flood Dekswood, Cuprinol Revive, Osmose Wood Brite (left foreground), Wolman Deck Brightener.

veal fresh-looking wood without using acids or chlorine bleach. Of the half-dozen wood-renewing products now on the market, four are powders that are mixed with water; one is a concentrated solution that is diluted before use; and one is a liquid that's used full strength. I spoke with several experts in the field to find out how and why wood weathers, how exactly the restorers work, what they are made of, what differences there are between them, and what you can do to keep your deck looking good once you have cleaned it.

## Protecting your investment

"You've spent $3,000 to $5,000 on a deck," says Richard Tripodi, vice president of marketing for Darworth Co., "and now, three or four years later, it looks weather-beaten and is fast becoming an eyesore. What do you do?"

That was a major concern homeowners expressed to Darworth, the manufacturer of Cuprinol wood preservatives and stains, in a consumer survey taken a few years ago. "Nobody, including our company, thought too hard about maintenance before," Tripodi says. "Everyone was so hung up on new deck building that nobody was paying attention to what you do, say, three years down the road."

What precisely happens to wood exposed to the elements? According to Alan Ross, who holds a Ph.D. in organic chemistry and is technical director of protection products for Koppers Co., manufacturer of Wolman Deck Brightener, three things affect decks: Dirt settles on, gets ground into, and gets spilled on the wood; mildew and other organisms grow on the wood's surface, darkening it; and ultraviolet radiation breaks down the surface cellulose cells, making them go gray. Any product that is going to rejuvenate weathered wood effectively must attack these three problem areas.

"Historically, the most common substance used to clean wood has been a sodium hypochlorite or calcium hypochlorite material like household bleach," Ross says. "Those materials will remove mildew, but they leave behind degraded cellulose cells and give the wood a washed-out appearance. Also, they are toxic to plants.

"Another common material is oxalic acid, which is particularly good at dissolving tannin resins. It's effective on redwood, which is notorious for tannin secretion," Ross continues. "Oxalic acid does not really do anything for mildew or dirt. What it does remove are dark tannin stains."

One of the first of the wood restorers was Dekswood, a concentrated liquid from The Flood Co. that is based on a solution of detergents and 10 percent oxalic acid. I tried it on a small area of weathered redwood, spraying it on, rubbing it in with a stiff brush, then rinsing it off. It cleaned the redwood well. A newer product, also a liquid, is Macklanburg-Duncan's Weather Warrior, a solution based on the chlorine bleach sodium hypochlorite and cupric hydroxide, an acid. I was not able to use Weather Warrior, but some of its label warnings include "May discolor clothing," "Avoid contact with plants," and "Wear gloves."

The newest wood-rejuvenating products, the first of which appeared last season, are the four powders, Wolman Deck Brightener, Cuprinol Revive Deck Cleaner, Zar Wood Brightener, and Osmose Wood Brite. They are all based on the active ingredient sodium percarbonate. (You'll see other names on the labels, like disodium peroxydicarbonate, percarbonate of soda, and sodium carbonate peroxyhydrate. According to Ross, they are different chemical names for the same substance.)

"Sodium percarbonate is used in some denture cleaners, and is similar to what detergent people call non-chlorine bleach, or oxygen bleach," Ross says. "It relies on oxygen rather than chlorine to do the cleaning, and is not as caustic or reactive with colored materials like fabrics—or wood pigment."

In fact, the difference between a so-dium percarbonate-based cleaner and a sodium hypochlorite-based one can be likened to the difference between an all-fabric bleach and a chlorine bleach: One enhances color while the other bleaches color out.

"After the powder is mixed and sprayed or mopped onto the deck," Ross tells me, "the sodium percarbonate foams and breaks down into two chemicals, hydrogen peroxide and sodium carbonate. The hydrogen peroxide softens and helps remove the upper gray cell layers of the wood; sodium carbonate, which is perhaps better known as soda ash and is found in baking powder, baking soda, and soaps, acts as a cleaner. After you let the solution stand on the wood for about 10 minutes, you go over the deck with a stiff-bristle broom, then rinse it off with water. The effect is not unlike what you'd get if you were to plane the wood to get an extremely fine veneer off its surface."

Although the powders all contain some form of sodium carbonate, there are subtle differences among them, primarily in some of their cleaning agents. For example, John Molski, United Gilsonite Laboratories' technical director, told me Zar Wood Brightener uses sodium metasilicate and sodium perborate, along with sodium sesquicarbonate, as cleaners. "We did about two years of testing, using exposure panels as well as actual weathered decks, to come up with the right combination of cleaning power and safe use."

## Keeping up appearances

Now that you've cleaned your deck, how do you keep it looking good?

"Depending on the effect you want," Darworth's Tripodi says, "you can use a semi-transparent stain and wood preservative or a clear wood sealer. A stained finish will give you just about any color you want. A solid stain is not recommended, however, because you won't see much of the wood's grain and the finish will wear noticeably in high-traffic areas. A semi-transparent stain will enhance the grain effect, and the finish will probably last for two or three years. A clear sealer will not last as long as a stained finish. It should be reapplied annually. A water-based clear sealer is easy to apply: You can just spray it on with a garden sprayer."

No matter what you do, you won't completely eliminate the ravages of time. But with a little care and the right equipment, you can soften its blow and keep your deck beautiful— *by Timothy O. Bakke.*

# fancy fences

A long with possibly making good neighbors, fences do other good things—mark boundaries, provide security and privacy, keep children and pets in and uninvited visitors out. Fences create a unified setting—much the way a frame adds focus to a painting. But function isn't everything. Like frames around paintings, fences can be plain or fancy, or something in between.

It's no big secret that fencing is easy to make, even for a woodworking beginner. Take a look at the four designs in this story. They look nice at completion, but not because they're complex. Each has only a few basic parts that are made with off-the-rack lumber and a few simple methods. The most demanding tasks are mass production of the sections and accurate, sturdy installation.

## Tools and materials

The keys to a successful, durable fence are using quality materials, following established installation procedures and periodic maintenance. Use pressure-treated lumber or naturally decay-resistant wood, like cedar or redwood—they weather well if left

**As an adjunct** to a backyard deck, this tall fence (above) serves the need for privacy and a taste for fresh breezes. The angle of the louvers blocks views onto the deck from the outside, but the spaces between them permit airflow. Designed by architect William B. Remick, AIA, the fence is built of redwood, which is highly decay-resistant and has a rich natural color. The drawing at the left shows all the important construction details of the fence, plus the structural tie-ins for the deck frame.

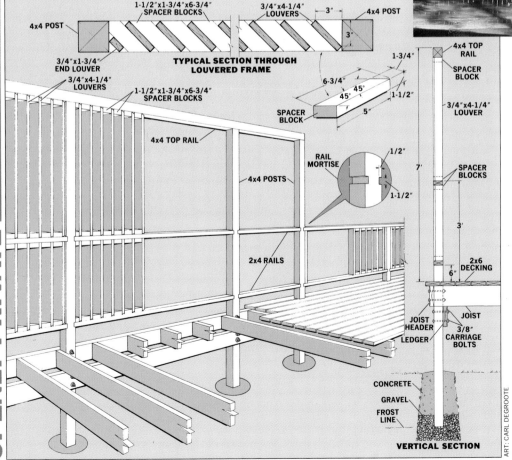

OPENLY PRIVATE

1-1/2"x1-3/4"x6-3/4" SPACER BLOCKS
3/4"x4-1/4" LOUVERS
3"
4x4 POST
4x4 POST
3"
3/4"x1-3/4" END LOUVER

**TYPICAL SECTION THROUGH LOUVERED FRAME**

3/4"x4-1/4" LOUVERS
1-1/2"x1-3/4"x6-3/4" SPACER BLOCKS
4x4 TOP RAIL
4x4 POSTS
2x4 RAILS

6-3/4"
45°
45°
45°
1-1/2"
5"
SPACER BLOCK

RAIL MORTISE
1/2"
1-1/2"

1-3/4"
4x4 TOP RAIL
SPACER BLOCK
3/4"x4-1/4" LOUVER
7'
SPACER BLOCKS
3'
2x6 DECKING
6"
JOIST HEADER
LEDGER
JOIST
3/8" CARRIAGE BOLTS

CONCRETE
GRAVEL
FROST LINE

**VERTICAL SECTION**

*Reprinted by permission of Homeowner magazine.*

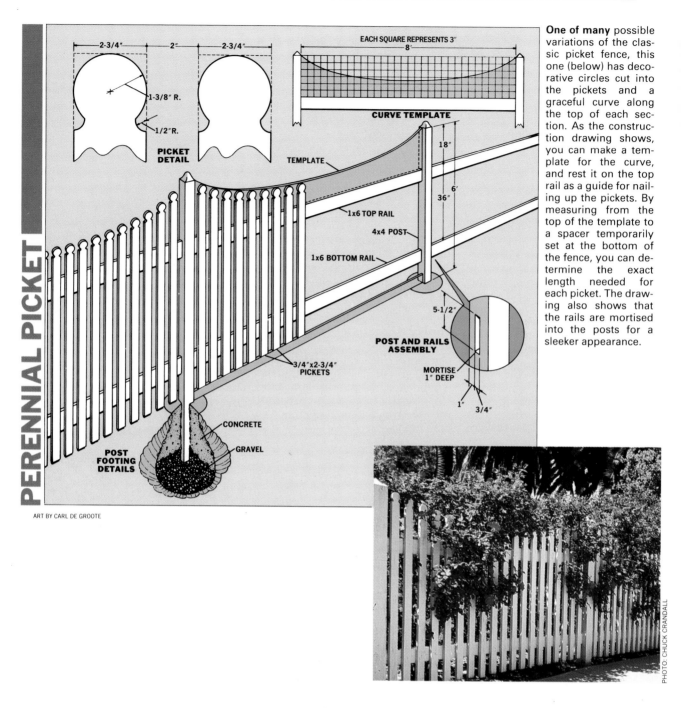

**PERENNIAL PICKET**

EACH SQUARE REPRESENTS 3"

2-3/4" · 2" · 2-3/4"

1-3/8" R.

1/2" R.

**PICKET DETAIL**

**CURVE TEMPLATE**

TEMPLATE

18"

6'

36"

1x6 TOP RAIL

4x4 POST

1x6 BOTTOM RAIL

5-1/2"

3/4"x2-3/4" PICKETS

**POST AND RAILS ASSEMBLY**

MORTISE 1" DEEP

1"

3/4"

CONCRETE

GRAVEL

**POST FOOTING DETAILS**

ART BY CARL DE GROOTE

**One of many** possible variations of the classic picket fence, this one (below) has decorative circles cut into the pickets and a graceful curve along the top of each section. As the construction drawing shows, you can make a template for the curve, and rest it on the top rail as a guide for nailing up the pickets. By measuring from the top of the template to a spacer temporarily set at the bottom of the fence, you can determine the exact length needed for each picket. The drawing also shows that the rails are mortised into the posts for a sleeker appearance.

PHOTO: CHUCK CRANDALL

untreated, or can be painted or stained.

To fasten the fence parts, use galvanized nails and screws. Ordinary nails will rust and leave unsightly stains on the wood.

For maximum strength and durability, fence posts should be set in or bolted to concrete footings. You can save time and effort by using premix concrete—you'll need about one bag per post. You'll also need gravel to line the bottom of post holes to promote drainage.

The basic tools for building fences are a hammer, a crosscut saw, a pair of sawbucks, a line level and a carpenter's level. You'll also need a drill, a spade, a power sander, a nail set and a combination square. While you may already have these tools, a posthole digger and a sledge hammer are also essential to building a fence, and both can be rented.

### Planning on paper

First, take a tour of your yard and make a scale plan drawing of it. Take the major yard features into account, including large rocks, trees, slopes and anything else that might present an obstacle. Let your own needs and

the lay of the land determine how the fence should run. You might decide it doesn't have to run down that steep incline or enclose quite so much space. The idea is to spot potential problems and set sensible limits for the project.

Work out a few plans on paper before committing yourself to any particular scheme. Remember to plan in detail for gates and other types of passages that might be needed. You'll want to make them wide enough for easy passage, but not difficult to build or hard to operate. Gates usually open into the yard, so check for bushes, flowerbed borders and other impediments. When you know exactly what you want, you're ready to take the plan to your yard.

## Taking measurements

Use a tape measure to determine precise distances along the fence lines. You must first mark the exact spot for each fence post. Set the spans between posts according to the strength rating for the size rails you're using. Eight- and 10-foot spans are common because they not only coincide with the strength of the dimension lumber in the sizes you're likely to use, but also because they match standard lumber lengths and minimize waste.

Use stakes and string to mark out the post locations, making sure lines are straight and corners are square, or set at the desired angles. Place stakes for the gate posts and other in-ground structural members.

Note all distances and other critical details on your rough plan. Double-check your calculations. It's simple at this point to move stakes and strings and erase lines on your drawing, but changing things after sections are made and posts are set can add a lot of work.

Once everything is in order, prepare a final drawing on graph paper, including all measurements. This drawing should ensure that you don't have any spans that boards or rails can't cover. With your final plan, you can put together a shopping list of all the materials you'll need.

## Starting to build

Actual construction starts with digging the post holes at the sites marked off with stakes and strings.

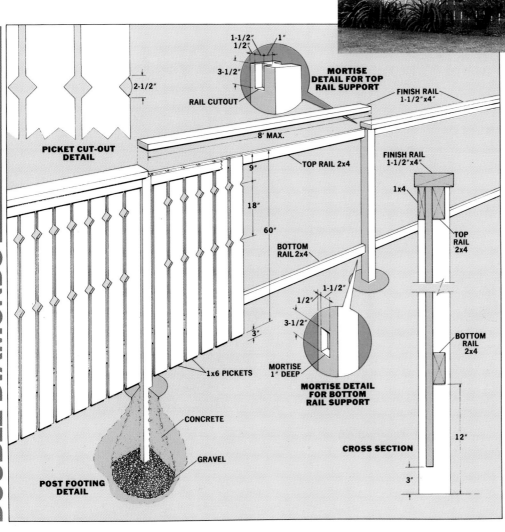

PHOTO: CHUCK CRANDALL

**Diamond-shaped** cutouts and narrow reveals between boards are used to lighten and decorate the face of a privacy fence (above). The broad cap rail strengthens the fence and protects the end grain of the slats and posts from the weather. This is especially important since the mortise joints for the rails at the post tops would tend to trap water.

**DOUBLE DIAMONDS**

**PICKET CUT-OUT DETAIL**

1-1/2"  1"
1/2"
3-1/2"
**RAIL CUTOUT**
2-1/2"

**MORTISE DETAIL FOR TOP RAIL SUPPORT**

**FINISH RAIL 1-1/2"x4"**

8' MAX.

**TOP RAIL 2x4**

9"

18"

60"

**BOTTOM RAIL 2x4**

**FINISH RAIL 1-1/2"x4"**

1x4

**TOP RAIL 2x4**

1-1/2"
1/2"
3-1/2"

**MORTISE 1" DEEP**

**MORTISE DETAIL FOR BOTTOM RAIL SUPPORT**

3"

**1x6 PICKETS**

**CONCRETE**

**GRAVEL**

**POST FOOTING DETAIL**

**BOTTOM RAIL 2x4**

**CROSS SECTION**

12"

3"

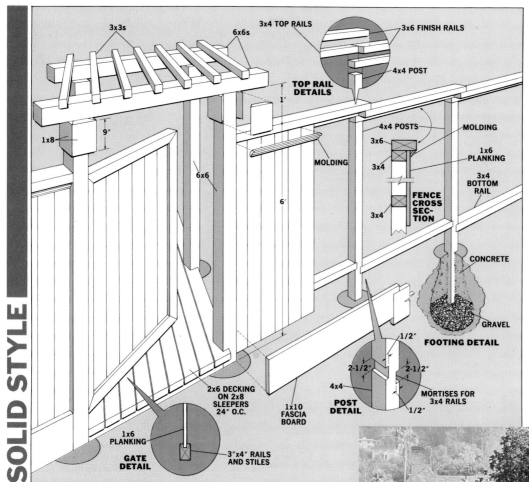

## SOLID STYLE

**3x3s**

**6x6s**

**3x4 TOP RAILS**

**3x6 FINISH RAILS**

**4x4 POST**

**TOP RAIL DETAILS**

1'

9"

**1x8**

**6x6**

6'

**MOLDING**

**MOLDING**

**4x4 POSTS**

3x6

3x4

**MOLDING**

**1x6 PLANKING**

**3x4 BOTTOM RAIL**

3x4

**FENCE CROSS SEC- TION**

3x4

**CONCRETE**

**GRAVEL**

**FOOTING DETAIL**

1/2"

2-1/2"

2-1/2"

4x4

1/2"

**MORTISES FOR 3x4 RAILS**

**POST DETAIL**

**2x6 DECKING ON 2x8 SLEEPERS 24" O.C.**

**1x10 FASCIA BOARD**

**1x6 PLANKING**

**GATE DETAIL**

**3"x4" RAILS AND STILES**

**This solid redwood** fence (below) offers absolute privacy but also has some nice decorative details including panel moldings and pillars with simple capitals supporting the arbor over the gate. The stepped treatment of the cap rail and baseboard of each fence section shows a good solution for erecting a fence on a sloping site. The solid baseboard can help keep pets inside the yard.

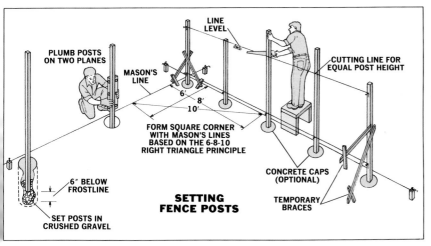

PLUMB POSTS ON TWO PLANES

MASON'S LINE

LINE LEVEL

CUTTING LINE FOR EQUAL POST HEIGHT

6'
8'
10'

FORM SQUARE CORNER WITH MASON'S LINES BASED ON THE 6-8-10 RIGHT TRIANGLE PRINCIPLE

CONCRETE CAPS (OPTIONAL)

TEMPORARY BRACES

6" BELOW FROSTLINE

SET POSTS IN CRUSHED GRAVEL

**SETTING FENCE POSTS**

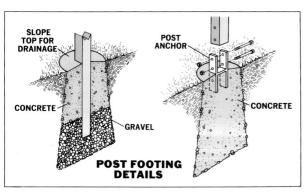

SLOPE TOP FOR DRAINAGE

POST ANCHOR

CONCRETE

GRAVEL

CONCRETE

**POST FOOTING DETAILS**

**The initial step** in building a fence of any style is setting the posts. The drawing above shows basic methods for laying out, plumbing and setting fence posts. Two variations for concrete fence post footings are shown at the left. Let the concrete cure before continuing.

In frost-prone regions, dig at least 6 inches deeper than the frost line. As a rule of thumb, about one-third of the total post height should be set below ground for strength. The holes should be only a few inches wider than the posts. Leave enough room to pour concrete around the posts once they've been set in the holes. The earth around the concrete should be firm for support.

## Setting the posts

Once you've dug all the post holes, place a shovel or two of gravel at the bottom of each. Insert a post cut to rough length in each hole—soak the cut ends of each post in a wood preservative approved for ground-contact.

One-by-one, plumb each post (see the drawing at the top of page 103). The easiest way to do this is to fasten a couple of temporary braces to each post and place a carpenter's level on one side of the post. Adjust the post until the level's bubble indicator is centered between the gauge lines, then set one of the temporary braces in the ground to hold it in place. Then, move the level to an adjacent side of the post and repeat the very same procedure.

When the post has been plumbed and braced on the second plane, recheck the plumb of the first side. Follow the same procedure for each post, and when you think they're all set correctly, sight down the row from one of the ends. Readjust any posts that don't seem to line up.

When you're certain that all the posts are correctly placed, plumbed and in alignment, mix the concrete and pour it into the post holes. Gently tamp the top of each footing smooth, and form a slight dome that will shed water. Let the concrete set for about a week before imposing any stress on the posts. After that you can cut the posts to the finished length, using stringlines and a line level as a guide.

## Setting up a fence factory

The panel elements on fences, that is, the assemblies that go in between the posts, are usually repetitious in pattern and size. This is a good thing to keep in mind when it's time to order lumber for the fence. You'll want to buy lengths that either match or are multiples of the lengths of the finished pieces. This will minimize waste.

It's usually possible to set up some systems for mass-producing fence

parts and even partially assembling them. You can set up a temporary factory in your garage or workshop for efficiency.

For example, instead of cutting and shaping fence pickets one at a time, cut all the lumber for pickets to length first, then cut out the decorative shapes in two separate operations. You can even organize the marking and cutting of picket lengths for efficiency: Instead of measuring for each length with a rule, you can cut one prototype and use it as a marking gauge for all your lumber. Have a helper hand you the marked lumber and stack the cut lengths so you can concentrate on cutting.

If the finished assembly will be light enough for you to carry and fit between the posts, you can nail the pickets onto rails cut a little longer than the span between posts. Instead of measuring and marking the position for each picket on the rails, you may want to use pre-cut spacer blocks so you can simply lay the pickets on the rails and fasten them on. Once you have the exact measurement between posts for a particular panel, you can cut the rails to the correct length and fasten them to the posts.

When a site is not level, it may limit the amount of precutting and pre-assembly you can do for the job. In these cases, you may need to devise schemes for compensating for slopes and uneven terrain. The point is to organize repetitious tasks as best you can to make completing them faster and more accurate.

## Finishing touches

Once assembly is complete, set all the nail heads, fill the holes and sand all the rough spots. All of the lumber types suitable for fences (redwood, cedar and pressure-treated wood) will weather to a silver-gray if left untreated, and if that's the look you want, apply only a clear water-repellent to prevent moisture-related defects from developing. To accelerate the appearance of weathered wood, apply wood bleach to the fence.

Paints and stains also offer options for protecting and decorating fences. Both short-term and over the long run, semi-transparent or opaque stains may be the easier choice for coloring fences because you don't have to prime the wood before staining, and stains don't peel as paint can. If you prefer paint, first seal knots with a shellac-based primer, and then prime all surfaces with a paint compatible with the topcoat—*by Tim Snider.*

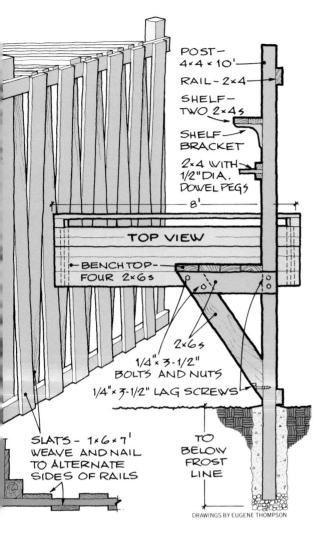

POST—
4×4×10'

RAIL— 2×4

SHELF—
TWO 2×4s

SHELF—
BRACKET

2×4 WITH
1/2" DIA.
DOWEL PEGS

8'

**TOP VIEW**

BENCH TOP—
FOUR 2×6s

2×6s

1/4"× 3-1/2"
BOLTS AND NUTS

1/4"× 3-1/2" LAG SCREWS

SLATS — 1×6×7'
WEAVE AND NAIL
TO ALTERNATE
SIDES OF RAILS

TO
BELOW
FROST
LINE

DRAWINGS BY EUGENE THOMPSON

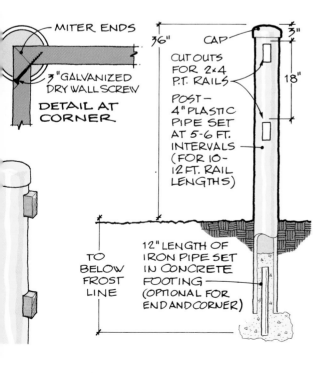

MITER ENDS

36"    CAP    3"

CUT OUTS
FOR 2×4
P.T. RAILS

18"

POST—
4" PLASTIC
PIPE SET
AT 5-6 FT.
INTERVALS
(FOR 10-
12 FT. RAIL
LENGTHS)

3" GALVANIZED
DRY WALL SCREW

**DETAIL AT
CORNER**

TO
BELOW
FROST
LINE

12" LENGTH OF
IRON PIPE SET
IN CONCRETE
FOOTING
(OPTIONAL FOR
END AND CORNER)

# two
# novel fences

## woven wood

My "patio" was a small barren slab outside my windswept back door. So around two sides of it I erected a woven-wood privacy screen that's also a windbreak (though the slits between the slats let through a pleasant breeze and also create an attractive shadow pattern). I used the inside patio corner of the fence to support a combination potting bench, workbench, and fish-cleaning table.

All lumber is pressure-treated to resist insects and decay, and I've let it weather naturally. The 4 x 4 posts are set in concrete; three of them will support a corner that's eight feet per side. (My seven-foot-tall fence has withstood 80-mph winds.) If you need a longer fence, add center posts.

Dig holes to below the frost line, or a minimum of two feet. Place a few egg-size rocks in the bottom of the hole for drainage. Drop in a 4 x 4, wedging it in place with a few rocks and using a level to make sure it's plumb. Shovel in concrete to within six inches of ground level. Repeat for each post, making sure they're aligned and parallel. Let the concrete set several days before you back-fill the holes.

Connect posts by nailing 2 x 4s between them. Nail the bottom rail at least an inch above ground level, then use a 1 x 6 slat to locate the top rail. Slats should precisely lap the two rails. Pre-start all nails, two inches from each end, driving them into opposite faces. Snugging the first slat against the corner post, drop the bottom of the slat on the opposite side of the bottom rail, then drive the two top nails. Now drive the two bottom nails from the other side. Repeat with the next slat, but reverse the rail sides. Butt the slats and check plumb every three boards. When you reach the end post you may need to trim a board length-wise to fill the gap—*by Judy Campbell.*

## pipe posts

The posts for this long-lasting, easy-to-erect property-line fence are lengths of plastic sewer pipe. They'll never rot, and their color is built in, so they'll never need painting. The 2 x 4 rails can be redwood or pressure-treated lumber stained any color you want. The crowning touch: Terminating caps glued on the top of each post after the fence is assembled. You can buy these caps (and the adhesive) from the plumbing supplier who sells you the pipe.

The only tricky part of the project is cutting the slots through which the rails pass. Rail ends butt inside the posts. The cutouts must be centered on lines drawn down opposite sides of each post, 180 degrees apart (except for a corner post, where the center lines should be at 90 degrees). Stand one rail upright on a sheet of cardboard and trace around its butt. Cut on these lines to create the template that you then center on each post's vertical lines. Drill a half-inch hole inside one corner of the marked outline, insert the blade of a sabre saw, and cut out the rectangular opening.

If you need an especially solid post (as at a corner), you can anchor it in concrete as shown—*by Conn J. Nast.*

# give your house a breather

A aahhh. It's the end of the day; you're reclining in your simulated leather Barcalounger smoking a big stogie, slippers resting on the acrylic pile carpet; your faithful dog lying at your side. In the attached garage, your car cools down after the commute home. And your wife is preparing a garlicky concoction that soon has the room smelling like Anthony's Italian Kitchen. But before you take a swig of beer, think for a moment about what you don't see: Indoor air pollution.

Synthetic materials, household chemicals, poorly vented stoves, attached garages, animals, and even excess moisture are all sources of indoor air pollution. Formaldehyde, nitrogen dioxide, particulates, and carbon monoxide are the most common. Radon, a radioactive, cancer-causing gas emanating from the soil beneath a house, is a particularly worrisome culprit.

Tightly built homes save energy, but the reduction in ventilation measured in air changes per hour (ACH) can exacerbate an existing problem. The best solution for indoor air pollution is to remove the source. But if that's too expensive (tearing out formaldehyde-gassing particle board), or impossible (eliminating the cigar smoker), mechanical ventilation could be the answer. And if you live in a colder climate, a ventilator that recovers heat from the house exhaust —a heat recovery ventilator, or HRV —would be an even better choice. HRVs have been around for several years, but new models with higher efficiencies and more features warrant another look.

The principle of an HRV is simple. One fan pulls in cold fresh air while another is blowing out warm stale house air. The actual heat exchanger, the core of the unit, picks up the heat from the exhaust and transfers it to the incoming stream. Optimally, the two streams will not mix. There are several different types of exchanger cores (see drawings): plate type, rotary wheel, and a core made from heat pipes are the most common.

Most HRVs come with removable air filters, and some have optional electronic air cleaners to also keep outdoor pollutants from entering the house. Window or wall-mounted HRVs are available for single rooms

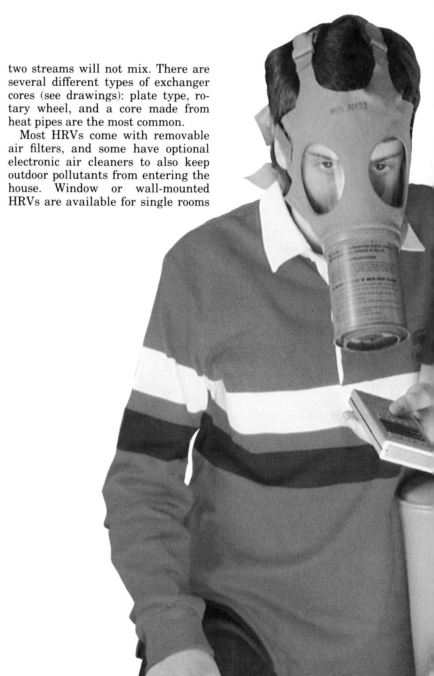

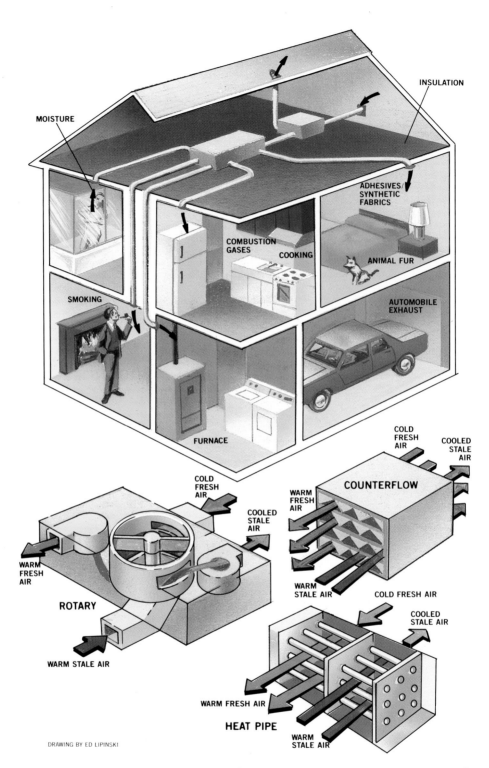

MOISTURE

INSULATION

ADHESIVES/
SYNTHETIC
FABRICS

COMBUSTION
GASES

COOKING

ANIMAL FUR

SMOKING

AUTOMOBILE
EXHAUST

FURNACE

ROTARY

COLD
FRESH
AIR

COOLED
STALE
AIR

WARM
FRESH
AIR

WARM STALE AIR

COLD
FRESH
AIR

COOLED
STALE
AIR

COUNTERFLOW

WARM
FRESH
AIR

WARM
STALE AIR

COLD FRESH AIR

COOLED
STALE
AIR

HEAT PIPE

WARM FRESH AIR

WARM
STALE
AIR

DRAWING BY ED LIPINSKI

or apartments, but the most effective —and expensive—systems require their own ductwork.

The ventilators work best when they run at a continuous low setting, but in most units the fans can be turned on to high speed to ventilate problem areas.

The big news in HRVs is that the products are improving. Colin Mc-Gugan should know. He is the super-visor for HRV testing at the Ontario Research Foundation in Mississauga, Ontario. The laboratory performs a standard test that certifies Canadian HRVs for use in a government low-energy housing program called R-2000.

"Manufacturers have improved their fans so that they can move more air. They've tightened up the cores so there's less cross leakage. And in some cases they've increased their heat-recovery efficiency," says Mc-Gugan. This recovery efficiency can be loosely defined as the ratio of the heat recovered to the total heat that could be recovered by a "perfect" ex-changer.

For example, if the cold incoming stream is 30 degrees F, the exiting stream is 70 degrees, and the air sup-ply from the exchanger is 60 degrees,

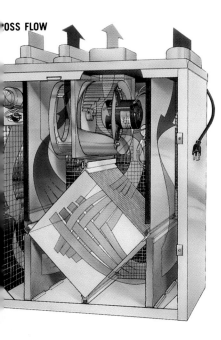

**OSS FLOW**

**The sources** of indoor air pollution include building materials, cleaning products, improperly vented combustion appliances, and attached garages. A whole-house heat-recovery ventilator is typically located in a basement or attic. One fan brings stale air from bathrooms and kitchens through ductwork to the exchanger core where, in winter, it gives up heat to incoming fresh air. The warm fresh air is sent through the house as ventilation and the cool stale stream is exhausted. In cooling season the opposite takes place.

Heat exchangers employ several core types. With a flat-plate core, multiple plates separate tiny air channels of supply and exhaust air streams. The streams can either run parallel in opposite directions—counter flow—or perpendicular to each other—cross flow. In a rotary core, a porous plastic wheel revolves slowly from the warm airstream to the cold airstream, picking up heat from one and delivering it to the other. An optional desiccant-coated wheel also transfers moisture from the warm to the cool stream. In a heat-pipe core, as warm air runs past one end of the pipe, the refrigerant vaporizes and moves to the other end of the pipe. As the cold stream passes by this end, the refrigerant condenses and gives up its latent heat. The condensed refrigerant then wicks back and the cycle repeats itself.

the exchanger's efficiency is 75 percent of the theoretical maximum (30 degrees of a possible 40 were transferred). The Canadian standard for heat-recovery efficiency is more complicated, taking into account electrical energy consumed by fans and defrost. Called the "sensible recovery efficiency" (see table), this will decrease in colder climates. Increasing

the surface area for heat exchange by using a double core is one way to improve efficiency.

Another important improvement in today's HRVs is defrost capability—especially important for areas where temperatures frequently drop below zero. In cold weather the heat-transfer surface can dip below the dew point of the exhaust stream, causing moisture to condense out. When the moisture freezes, ice can block the exhaust vent, vastly lowering the HRV's efficiency.

According to William J. Fisk, a staff scientist at Lawrence Berkeley Laboratory who led early research on ventilation and indoor air quality control, five years ago most units either had no defrost mechanism or used an energy-hungry electric preheat to warm incoming air upstream from the exchanger. Now many units employ defrost mechanisms that automatically shut off cold supply air for several minutes and recirculate warm house air through the core.

Heat-recovery ventilators are not for every home—sometimes a more direct approach to pollution reduction is cheaper and more effective. Properly venting heating and cooking appliances as well as an attached garage could reduce high levels of carbon monoxide, nitrogen dioxide, and particulates. Getting rid of household chemicals (cleaning fluids, paint thinners, and pesticides) could reduce organic chemical concentrations. Booklets on identifying and reducing household pollutants are available from the American Lung Association.

An HRV is most effective in a "tight" house: one that receives minimal infiltration, 0.5 ACH. In a leakier home airflow is diverted from the heat exchanger and defeats the energy-recovery process. If you live in a temperate climate, opening some windows might also be enough ventilation. But Fisk says, "When you have a combination of a severely cold climate and relatively high energy prices, an HRV looks attractive." He adds, "Some leaky homes with specific pollution problems—a moderately elevated concentration of radon or formaldehyde—would also benefit from an HRV."

Pasqual Franco had such a problem. He found an elevated radon concentration in his basement. Franco's 20-year-old Connecticut home is weatherized, but was built before the era of tight homes. He installed an HRV to continually flush the air out of his 45-by-45-foot basement, and

with it went the dangerous radon reading. "I had radon readings of over four picocuries [per liter of air, the level at which the EPA recommends remedial action]," says Franco, "but after I installed this heat exchanger the level dropped to only 1.1." A word of caution: If you've got radon above 15 pci/liter, an HRV is not for you. Fisk's computer modeling has shown that a severe radon problem will not be remedied by dilution with an HRV.

Radon is one reason homeowners install HRVs. But in Canada, at least, excess humidity seems to be the most common problem. In tight houses condensation builds up and can't leave the house via cracks and leaks. Says Craig Henderson, a sales manager for Nutech Energy Systems in London, Ontario: "I've seen homes that actually sweat." The moisture can cause mold and mildew growth, and it can rot the structure and soak the insulation. For this reason, as well as general comfort, Canadian Energy Mines and Resources strongly recommends an air-to-air heat exchanger in all R-2000 certified homes.

But to rid a home of excess moisture the HRV must have a "sensible heat" core—one that doesn't transfer moisture (latent heat). Flat-plate cores and heat-pipe cores exhaust the moisture in the stale air. But rotary wheel exchangers can have permeable membranes and recover moisture with the heat. The rotary wheels are advantageous in a cold, dry home as well as for use with an air conditioner.

"In the cooling season a lot of the heat-exchange load is moisture and sensible cores don't remove this," says McGugan. With a rotary exchanger, moisture is removed from incoming air and transferred to the exhaust.

## Comparing performance

Choosing the right HRV for your home isn't simple. A heat exchanger's capacity is rated at cubic feet per minute (cfm). So to find the right unit to provide a given ACH, you must know your house's volume in cubic feet.

Virtually all units made in Canada have been independently tested and certified for R-2000 use. The resulting performance figures, including efficiency at a range of air volumes, pressure, and temperature, allow the consumer to make an educated choice. In the United States, the Home Ventilating Institute (HVI) has put together a standard—almost

# HRV MANUFACTURERS

| | Model | Type | Core type | Net airflow[1] (cfm) | M.L. (%) | Efficiency[2] SRE(%) 32°F | (%) -13°F | Max. power consumption | Sugg. retail ($U.S.)[3] |
|---|---|---|---|---|---|---|---|---|---|
| Air Changer Marketing 1297 Industrial Rd. Cambridge, Ontario N3H 4T8 | DRA150 | ducted | counter flow | 104 | 76 | 76 | 57 | 84 W | 595 |
| | DRA275 | ducted | counter flow | 231 | 78 | 78 | 56 | 260 W | 945 |
| AirXchange, Inc. 401 V.F.W. Dr. Rockland MA 02370 | 502 | ducted | rotary | 142 | 75–80 | 77 | 43 | 145 W | 495 |
| | 570D | ducted | rotary | 65 | 75–80 | n.a.[4] | n.a. | 45–55 W | 376 |
| | 570 | wall mounted | rotary | 70 | 75–80 | n.a. | n.a. | 45–55 W | 360 |
| Altech Energy 7009 Raywood Rd. Madison WI 53713 | NewAire HE-1800C | ceiling mounted | cross flow | 70 | 73 | n.a. | n.a. | 55 W | 400 |
| | NewAire HE-2500 | ducted | cross flow | 110 | 78 | n.a. | n.a. | 120 W | 535 |
| | NewAire HE-5000 | ducted | cross flow | 210 | 78 | n.a. | n.a. | 240 W | 795 |
| American Aldes Ventilation Corp. 4539 Northgate Ct. Sarastota FL 34234-4864 | VMP-H 3/5 | ducted | counter flow | 90/140 | 70 | n.a. | n.a. | 145 W | 980[5] |
| | VMP-H 4/8 | ducted | counter flow | 130/180 | 70 | n.a. | n.a. | 170 W | 995[5] |
| | VMP2I 6/7 | ducted | counter flow | 150 | 70 | n.a. | n.a. | 140 W | 1,496[5] |
| BossAire 1321 Tyler St. N.E. Minneapolis MN 55413 | BX-125 | ducted | cross flow | 125 | 80 | n.a. | n.a. | 160 W | 772 |
| | BX-150 | ducted | cross flow | 184@0.4 | 80 | n.a. | n.a. | 220 W | 880 |
| | BX-250 | ducted | cross flow | 279@0.5 | 80 | n.a. | n.a. | 250 W | 1,211 |
| | BX-350 | ducted | cross flow | 377@0.5 | 80 | n.a. | n.a. | 314 W | 1,498 |
| Conservation Energy Systems 3310 Millar Ave. Saskatoon Saskatchewan 575769 | VanEE 1000 | ducted | cross flow | 129 | n.a. | 55 | 49 | 1.2 amps | 450 |
| | VanEE 2000 | ducted | cross flow | 216 | n.a. | 70 | 60 | 2.05 amps | 550 |
| | VanEE 2000+ | ducted | double cross flow | 237 | n.a. | 83 | 57 | 2.05 amps | 1,150 |
| Des Champs Laboratories Box 440   17 Farinella Dr. East Hanover NJ 07963 | E-Z-Vent 210 | ducted | counter flow | 115/150 | 75 | n.a. | n.a. | 0.8 amps | 700 |
| | EZV-220 | ducted | counter flow | 180/240 | 73 | n.a. | n.a. | 1.5 amps | 760 |
| | EZV-240 | ducted | counter flow | 325/430 | 72 | n.a. | n.a. | 3.0 amps | 920 |
| | EZV-310 | ducted | counter flow | 110/145 | 85 | n.a. | n.a. | 0.8 amps | 770 |
| | EZV-320 | ducted | counter flow | 165/220 | 84 | 67 | 70 | 1.5 amps | 840 |
| | EZV-340 | ducted | counter flow | 310/415 | 83 | n.a. | n.a. | 3.0 amps | 1,010 |
| Enermatrix, Inc. Box 466 Fargo ND 58107 | EMX-10 | ducted | unbalanced cross flow | 96 | 50 | n.a. | n.a. | 2.0 amps | 399 |
| | EMX-15 | ducted | cross flow | 90 | n.a. | n.a. | n.a. | 1.5 amps | 429 |
| | EMX-20 | ducted | cross flow | 113 | n.a. | n.a. | n.a. | 2.8 amps | 479 |
| | EMX-25 | ducted | cross flow | 250 | 71–84 | n.a. | n.a. | 2.42 amps | 899 |
| Environment Air Ltd. Box 459 Bouctouche New Brunswick EOAIGO | ENV-W60 | wall or window mounted | heat pipe | 60 | 65–80 | n.a. | n.a. | 40 W | 460 |
| | ENV-K5 | ducted | heat pipe | 125 | 60–80 | n.a. | n.a. | 180 W | 630 |
| | ENV-K6 | ducted | heat pipe | 190 | 60–80 | 63 | 63 | 180 W | 795 |
| | ENV-K8 | ducted | heat pipe | 290 | 60–80 | n.a. | n.a. | 240 W | 1,100 |
| | ENV-K10 | ducted | heat pipe | 590 | 60–80 | n.a. | n.a. | 388 W | 1,480 |
| Les Industries Douvent Ltéé. 1375 Boul. Charest Ouest (Suite 6) Quebec PQ G1N 2E7 | Fan-X-Changer WR-2S | ducted | capillary wheel | 210 | 50 | n.a. | n.a. | 1.2 amps | 480 |
| Nutech Energy Systems 124 Newbold Ct. London Ontario N6E 1Z7 | Lifebreath 100DEF | ducted | cross flow | 64 | 80 | 64 | 58 | 136 amps | 850 |
| | Lifebreath 200STD | ducted | cross flow | 182 | n.a. | 80 | 77 | 100 W | 995 |
| | Lifebreath 200MAX | ducted | cross flow | 193 | n.a. | 70 | 69 | 114 W | 800 |
| | Lifebreath 300 DCS | ducted | double cross flow | 220 | n.a. | 79 | 75 | 234 W | 1,295 |
| | Lifebreath 195 DCS | ducted | double cross flow | 182 | n.a. | 80 | 77 | 161 W | 1,195 |
| QDT. Ltd. 1000 Singleton Blvd. Dallas TX 75212-5214 | SAE-150 | ducted | heat pipe | 150 | 70 | n.a. | n.a. | 125 W | 599 |
| Raydot Inc. 145 Jackson Ave. Cokato MN 55321 | Raydot | ducted | counter flow | 225 | 73–82 | n.a. | n.a. | 135 W | 890 |
| The Star Heat Exchanger Corp. B109-1772 Broadway St. Port Coquitlam British Columbia V3C 2M8 | Nova | wall or window mounted | counter flow | 70 | 60 | n.a. | n.a. | 34 W | 307 |
| | 165 | ducted | counter flow | 160 | 80 | n.a. | n.a. | 66 W | 570 |
| | 200 | ducted | interface tube counter flow Interface flow | 180 | 80 | 79 | 67 | 66 W | 652 |
| | 300 | ducted | counter flow | 240 | 80 | 79 | 67 | 132 W | 826 |
| Vent-Aire Engineering Development, Inc. 4850 Northpark Dr. Colorado Springs CO 80907 | ECS 10 | ducted | counter flow | 100 | 65 | n.a. | n.a. | 58 W | 354 |
| | ECS 20 | ducted | counter flow | 220 | 75 | n.a. | n.a. | 168 W | 884 |
| XchangeAir Corp. Box 1565 Fargo ND 58103 | BDR-95 | ducted | cross flow | 80 | 80 | n.a. | n.a. | 122 W | 540 |
| | BDR-210 | ducted | cross flow | 135 | 80 | n.a. | n.a. | 250 W | 740 |
| | BDR-315 | ducted | cross flow | 255 | 80 | n.a. | n.a. | 250 W | 975 |

Notes: [1]Net airflow is given at 0.3 in. (a standard measure of static pressure), except where indicated. Dual listings are for lo/hi airflows; [2]manufacturer's listed (M.L.) efficiency is not confirmed by independent tests. Sensible recovery efficiency (SRE) is an independent result from tests performed at the Ontario Research Foundation at a net airflow of 117 cfm; [3]suggested retail price usually includes core, housing, two fans, filters, and basic controls. Ductwork and insulation are extra; [4]not available; [5]price includes most accessories.

identical to the Canadian test—but so far few manufacturers have had their units tested. That leaves the consumer dependent on manufacturers' claims of efficiency.

In practice, heat exchangers seem to perform below expected efficiency. A recent study by Battelle's Pacific Northwest Laboratories in Richland, Washington, of 38 energy-efficient homes found exchangers averaging 52 percent efficiency.

Many reports of poor heat-recovery efficiency and air delivery far below manufacturers claims are the result of improper installation, according to Nick Des Champs, president of Des Champs Laboratories (makers of E-Z-Vent units) in East Hanover, New Jersey. "If the ductwork is installed improperly, there can be such a high pressure loss through the ducts that no air flows," he says. The installation problem is also being addressed by the HVI, which in conjunction with the Bonneville Power Authority is implementing an installation training program to help beef up field HRV performance—
*by Naomi J. Freundlich.*

# dry-laid paving

A few years ago, I decided to build paved borders around the vegetable and flower beds in my yard. With the beds separated from the lawn it was easier to mow grass along the edges. I also installed paved strips under my fences to control weeds where my mower couldn't reach. I laid the paving blocks, or

**Richard Carothers'** side-yard design (left) has matching steps. Seen above is an example of the interlocking pavers available in various shapes, colors, and load-bearing ratings. Because of their shape, these Uni Paving Stones can't tip or twist.

## Mortarless paving

**1** Lay patio blocks in place before permanently setting headers, to ensure adequate spacing. Square all corners.

**2** Screeding board must fit inside headers and have depth guides nailed at each end. Sand should raise paver tops slightly above headers—allow at least ½ in. for settling. After screeding, wet sand.

**3** With pavers in place, use a broom or the back of a rake to spread sand into the joints.

**4** Spray the surface with a fine mist of water. Let dry, then sweep in more sand, and gently spray again.

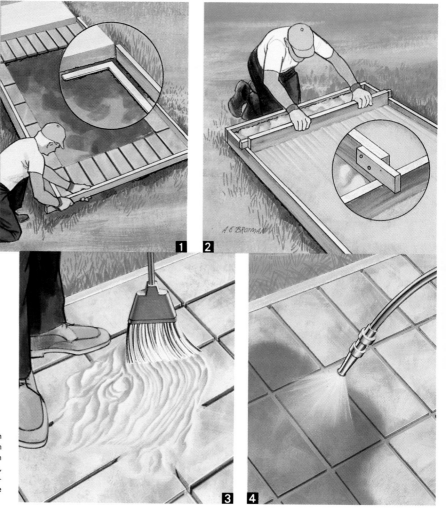

**FOR MORE INFORMATION**
The author's ring-bound handbook on rammed-earth technology, first offered to *Popular Science* readers in 1982, is still available at the same price. $11.50, from Rammed Earth Works, Blue Mountain Rd., Wilseyville, CA 95257. A new videotape on the history and principles of rammed-earth building is $25 from the same source.

pavers, in place on a sand bed. That freed me from the tedious job of making forms, mixing and pouring concrete, and waiting for the pavement to harden.

Pavers can also be used to create stepping stones, walkways, and small terraces. They'll easily support people and loaded wheelbarrows. The blocks come in a variety of sizes, shapes, and colors, so you can customize your design.

Except for the concrete discs sold as stepping stones and a few novelty shapes, pavers are usually rectangles measured in multiples of four—up to 24 by 24 inches. The original paver, the clay brick, is 4 by 8 inches. Bricks of other materials—concrete, adobe, and cinder—are often called blocks. But because "block" suggests a building material, blocks used underfoot have come to be called pavers. Some dealers refer to the 8-by-8-inch and 8-by-16-inch units (which are actually shorter in both dimensions, to accommodate mortar) as "patio

blocks"; other concrete pavers are called "tiles." Concrete tiles are fine for paving, but fired clay tiles aren't recommended. They're fragile, and slippery when wet.

The technique for laying any of these pavers is basically the same: Prepare a surface, preferably leveled sand. If you use soil, make sure it's loose and free of pebbles. To maintain grade, set up a grid of headers, usually 2 x 4s (see drawings). Allow a drop of at least ⅛ inch per foot for drainage.

Add sand—at least 2½ inches if you're using 2 x 4 headers. A cubic foot of sand makes a 3-inch pad in a 4-foot-square grid. (An 80-pound bag holds about ¾ of a cubic foot.)

Screed, or smooth, the sand. Then wet it and gently place pavers in position. With small pavers use plywood to spread your weight as you work. Minor variations in spacing won't be too noticeable in the finished job, but variations in elevation will. Correct errors by tapping pavers with

a rubber mallet or levering with a small wrecking bar. After the pavers are laid, sand swept into the joints acts somewhat like mortar.

To control weeds, you may want to use a plastic weed blocker beneath the pavers. Or if you lay the pavers on soil, you can plant thyme, moss, or dwarf mint in the joints. You may even want to save strips of sod to place between blocks.

Your best buys are 8-by-16-inch concrete pavers—about 65 cents apiece. For a few cents more you should be able to get them in terra cotta or dark gray.

For a fancier but more expensive look, try patterned blocks like the Uni Paving Stones (see photo). They're vibrated into position with a flat plate compactor machine, which rents for about $15 an hour. The stones are made by Uni-Group U.S.A., 4362 Northlake Blvd., Palm Beach Gardens, FL 33410—
*by John Robinson. Photos by the author.*

# dirt-cheap dirt floor

PHOTO BY DANIEL D'AGOSTINI

My family and I live in a beautiful earth home with a handsome earth floor. It may sound unbelievable, but as a successful builder of rammed-earth houses, I'd been trying for a while to expand the use of earth to finished flooring. After much experimentation, I've finally found a suitable mix of soil and cement to do the job.

Why bother? Well, a soil-based floor is softer and more comfortable than a conventional concrete slab, and if you lay it yourself, it's less expensive. As a bonus, it can be stamped to look like rustic tiling that has an earthy color. Finally, a soil-cement floor is a natural for passive solar heating and a perfect medium for a hydronic radiant slab (see sidebar).

Soil-cement is softer underfoot because it is less dense than concrete. Unlike the aggregate used in concrete, soil expands significantly when it's wet. As a soil-cement slab dries and the soil particles lose water, they

shrink, and millions of tiny air pockets develop. These air pockets essentially make the floor a little spongy.

I speak from experience because my family and I have lived in houses with concrete floors and ones with soil-cement floors. Soil-cement is warmer, softer, more forgiving, and just as easy to maintain as concrete. An extra bonus: Dishes rarely break when they hit an earth floor.

Over the years, my firm has tried more than a dozen variations on the earth-floor theme. We've experimented with a range of moisture contents and methods of application. I now feel confident in passing on the secrets of what my firm calls Terratile—a cast-in-place soil-cement tile.

## Starting the subgrade

Terratile can be poured over just about any surface and to any thickness. Our preference is a one-inch-thick Terratile topping poured over a well-compacted four-inch base of rammed earth.

It's best to wait until most construction work is done before putting down Terratile. The tiles need protection from the elements when curing. So we do all of the subgrade work as soon as the foundation is finished and save the rest for later.

To prepare for a slab floor inside a perimeter foundation, you must first install all underground utility-lines —plumbing supply and waste lines and electrical and other service conduits. The ground should be flat, fairly level, and firmly packed. Spread two or more inches of sand or pea gravel over the ground as a capillary break, then lay a six-mil polyethylene vapor barrier over the entire floor area as extra protection against wicking. On top of the barrier spread about three inches of rammed-earth mix; then tamp it down until it's firm and sounds solid. The height of this portion of the subgrade should be about three inches below the desired finished floor level. At this stage we stop working on the floor and proceed with the roof and the other framing. A little water sprayed on the packed-earth floor every so often will help settle it and keep it from becoming dusty.

When we come back to work on the floor, it's time to lay the piping for a hydronic radiant slab. If that's not part of the plan for the house we're building, we need only bring the level of the base up to within one inch of the desired floor level and tamp it firm. Then we're ready for the topping.

### The right mix

Structural concrete is a carefully controlled mixture of sand, gravel, Portland cement, and water. Its strengths and limits are well-documented. Soil-cement, on the other hand, is a not so carefully controlled mixture of soil, Portland cement, and water. The strengths and limits of soil-cement are highly variable, just as soil itself is variable. A coarse, gravelly soil might yield soil-cement that is almost as strong and dense as concrete, while a heavy clay soil will, when mixed with cement and water, yield a material only slightly stronger than a dirt clod.

What we're looking for in a Terratile floor is a balance between the durability of concrete and the low density of soil-cement. There are a couple of other factors, such as workability and setup time, but most importantly, we want the surface to be durable. To be used as a finished floor it has to be able to stand up to a lively game of musical chairs. It takes a sandy soil and at least 12 percent cement to get that kind of toughness.

Some soils are sandy enough to work well for soil-cement just as they are, but most of the soil we come across here in the Sierra foothills is heavy clay—we call it "Calaveras Red." It makes just about the best rammed-earth walls in the state, but it needs the addition of 60 percent sand before it's right for Terratile. On the other hand, in some parts of the San Joaquin Valley, southwest of my home in Wilseyville, California, the

soil might require only about 25 or 30 percent sand to make a good mix. No matter what the native soil, though, we almost always add a little bit of sand because it makes the wet mix much more workable.

When using Calaveras Red, we mix three parts sand, two parts soil, and one part cement. In your part of the country the ratio might be different. If your soil is sandy, use only two parts sand. Either way, add one part cement to the other five.

To prepare for mixing a big batch of Terratile, we first have masonry sand delivered and dumped into a pile on our work area. Then we screen (through half-inch hardware cloth) a few yards of native soil into another adjacent pile. We set up our small electric mixer within arm's reach of the two piles (make sure enough sacks of cement are stacked nearby) and get a five-gallon bucket and a charged water hose with a shut-off on the end. The bucket is for measuring the water we add.

Enough water should be added to give the mix the consistency of soft ice cream. Usually that's about one gallon of water per shovelful of cement. A full batch (one wheelbarrow full) in our three-cubic-foot mixer is nine shovels of sand, six shovels of soil, three shovels of cement, and three gallons of water. It takes about seven or eight minutes to mix that quantity thoroughly. A good operator on the mix pile can pump out a yard in about two hours—just the right pace for the person spreading the mix on the floor.

### Keeping a level slab

When it's poured thin, as we prefer,

Terratile is best worked in small batches. That way you can stamp the tiles as you go, and you don't have to worry about getting too far ahead of yourself. The thin Terratile takes an initial set and is ready for stamping after only 30 minutes because the earth base draws water out of the wet mix long before the cement starts to hydrate. A good-size crew for pouring Terratile is three people, one to mix and deliver, one to spread, and one to stamp.

It's difficult to keep the floor flat and of uniform thickness when working with only wheelbarrow-sized batches. To maintain level, we use string lines, a four-foot level, a three-foot finishing trowel (called a darby), and a 24-inch steel trowel. Even with these tools and a lot of skill, it's still tricky to keep the floor really flat. In fact one of the characteristics of Terratile is a certain unevenness, which in the end contributes to the handmade look.

Start pouring in the far corner of the room. Spread the mix out using a

**A hydronic radiant floor** is created (right) by laying down plastic tubing and holding it in place with earth before the soil-cement is poured (see sidebar). In photos far right top and bottom, three stages of soil-cement installation are shown. Mixture has been poured over a compact base (foreground) and is being troweled smooth. Once it begins to firm, it is cut into tiles with concrete stamping tools. After tiles have cured and shrunk apart, they can be grouted (bottom right).

steel trowel, first working the mix up against the edge of the building where you've marked your pencil or chalk level lines. Spread the mix in a band just over two feet wide, parallel to the far wall. One wheelbarrow full will cover 8 to 10 square feet. By the time you've covered the width of the room, the batch should be ready to stamp. (I'll get to stamping in a minute.) After you've spread the first band, you can no longer work from the clear mark on the foundation. Here's where you'll need the four-foot level. Dump a batch of mix; spread it around and up against the first band you poured; work the old and the new together at the edges to get good intermixing; then level out from the mark on the foundation to make sure you're not climbing or dropping. We use the darby to keep the interfaces flat.

You can use a string line pulled taut across the room to check the level every so often; but if you were careful to get the subgrade flat and level, the thickness of the Terratile itself should be a good indicator of how you're doing. Keep up the pouring and spreading until you've finished the room or until you're ready for a break. When you take a break, do it after you've completed a band. That way, when you come back to work, you can cut back to the last stamp line and the seam between old and new will be in a grout line.

The process of stamping Terratile is similar to that of cutting cookies out of rolled dough. The stamping tools cut so deeply through the thin slab that as the mixture dries and contracts, the tiles shrink away from each other. So after drying and shrinking, the floor actually becomes a composite of individual soil-cement tiles. And if you choose to, you can remove a few Terratiles and replace them with color-glazed ceramic tiles to add accent. You can also pour some extra Terratile on a piece of plywood

or particleboard and make some tiles for detail work—perhaps a Terratile baseboard. One of the reasons I like this process so much is that it creates individual tiles, not a slab that is embossed to look like something it isn't.

## Stamp as you go

To stamp the tiles we use either hard plastic stamping tools manufactured by Goldblatt Tool Co. (Kansas City, MO), or for smaller projects, hand-cut beveled boards. The stamping tools are best (see photos) because they provide a platform to stand on as you work. At $50 each, however, they can be expensive if you're only pouring a small area. The major problem with using beveled board is that you must stamp each band before you pour out the next one, which in some cases forces you to wait a few minutes while a band sets up enough to stamp. With the plastic tools, as soon as a band has set sufficiently to handle your weight, you can begin stamping.

Timing is critical. If the slab is too wet, the grout lines flow back together when the tools are pulled out. If the slab is too dry, the cutting blades on the tools will crack the edges of the tiles.

When we can, we use lines snapped into the wet slab with taut strings as guides for the stamping. Make marks two feet from the edge of the slab at both ends, draw a string tight over the marks, then lift and snap it. The line it makes in the wet slab is your guide for placing the tools.

Pouring a Terratile floor takes patience. We try to tackle no more than four hundred square feet a day, which gives us time to keep checking back on our work to make sure the tiles are flat and the grout lines clean. In fact the floor turns out best if you have enough time to re-trowel each band after it's been stamped and had a few minutes to set up. By carefully troweling across the stamped tiles, you can knock the curls off the edges and

level the transition from one tile to another.

## Giving it the grout

Soil-cement takes longer to cure than concrete. Even at one inch thick, it will be three or four days before you should walk on it. To be safe, wait at least two weeks before grouting. The reason for the wait is that soil-cement continues to shrink as the water evaporates. If you grout before the tiles have finished shrinking, cracks will develop in the grout lines.

When the Terratile is dry and ready to grout, the color will be uniform and much lighter than when wet. For grouting we use 30-mesh sand and Portland cement in a four-to-one ratio, mixed wet. Start in the far corner and spread the grout mixture over the entire area with a rubber grouting float. Work the grout into the lines, then drag the float toward you at a 45-degree angle to the lines.

Make a pass over the area with a large wet sponge to smooth out the grout lines and clean off the tops of the tiles. Watch carefully that you don't pull grout out of the lines. Repeat the above two steps until you've completed the floor, then return to the beginning and carefully wipe off each tile one at a time with a damp sponge, keeping the water in your bucket clean. The tiles are easy to clean because the porous soil-cement sucks the water out of the thin grout so quickly, the cement doesn't stick.

## Finally the finish

For outdoor use Terratile can be left unsealed. But if you want it to look its best, a few coats of wax can't be beat. Buffing with a heavy-duty floor polisher works the wax into the porous soil-cement to seal it and create a smooth finish. The tile may require two or even three coats before it's sealed. A final coat of wax will make it shine—*by David Eastone.*

# While you're at it, why not pour a hydronic radiant floor?

Circulating warm water through a soil-cement floor, whether the water is warmed by the sun or by fossil fuels, creates a comfortable environment. The heat is low, where your body wants it, but no noisy blowers and bulky air ducts are required. And now, with readily available flexible polybutylene tubing, the major drawback to radiant slabs—cracked pipes under the slab—has been eliminated.

To start, purchase a 1,000-foot roll of ½-inch polybutylene tubing. To keep heat evenly distributed, you'll want several different zones, each using no more than 250 feet

of run. Determine where you want your manifold (a centrally located closet is preferable) so that you can begin and end all runs there. Set up a temporary batter board to tie off the ends of the tubing until after the floor pour. For each room lay out the tubing using 12-inch spacing. Be careful not to run the tubing under any future framed wall. You can even run the tubing to places you want the warming first, for example, along the sides of your bed or next to the shower.

Start at the manifold and roll out the tubing along the path you've mapped. Have your

partner follow behind, piling soil mix on top of the tubing to hold it in place as you roll it out. Don't spare the mix, because you'll be using it before long to raise the floor level in preparation for the Terratile.

Roll out the tubing for each zone in this same manner and then spread the rest of the soil mix—enough to just cover the tubing. The tubing should be close to the slab, but not actually in it. Rake, level, and hand tamp the mix until it's firm. Spray the floor lightly with water to help settle it and to moisten the subgrade before you pour the Terratile.— *D. E.*

# laminated wood floors

Now more than ever, appearances can be deceiving. Solid-surface manufactured counter tops look and feel for all the world like natural marble or another stone. Pressed hardboard siding convincingly impersonates real lap siding. Concrete retaining-wall blocks are a double for rough-hewn granite. What's more, these products are not just studies in appearance. In most cases they equal—and sometimes can better—the performance of their natural counterparts.

The same is now true for wood flooring. Many wood floors I've seen recently could easily pass for solid wood. But in the new flooring, which is laminated and prefinished, beauty is only skin—or at least ⅛ inch—deep. The flooring is basically cross-laminated plywood with a top layer of high-quality hardwood.

This alternative to conventional wood flooring is a relative newcomer to the United States. Much of the laminated flooring available in the United States is imported from Europe, where it has been common for years and has gained a reputation as a reliable—and in many cases preferred—wood flooring material. It

can be glued down or "floated" over a foam underlayment, approaching an ease of installation that almost any homeowner can master (see "Float a Fancy Floor"). The only problem with it has been that anyone familiar with solid wood flooring could identify it quickly because of its piecemeal, patterned appearance compared with the randomness of a true solid plank or strip wood floor. Now there are products made in the United States that are said to have overcome that handicap. I spoke with representatives from large flooring suppliers to find out more about prefinished laminated wood floors and what they mean to the homeowner who wants to install one.

## Plywood floors

Take a piece of plywood, glue on a thick hardwood veneer, and finish the surface with a hard, stain-resistant ultraviolet-light-cured urethane finish. Now glue the plywood to the existing floor or lay it over a ⅛-inch blanket of closed-cell polyethylene foam. That, in simplified terms, is what you get with a laminated wood floor. Any homeowner can have a wood floor over any subfloor—often

even below grade—in just about any room in the house.

Of course, for years homeowners have been able to enjoy a wood floor where strip or plank flooring wasn't practical by using glue-down solid-wood parquet flooring. However, parquet, which is made of tiny segments of wood pieced together like a mosaic, has limitations. The jigsaw-puzzle effect may clash with your decor, and over time individual pieces may loosen with contraction and expansion and "click" when you walk on the floor. Laminated flooring can provide you with the linear look of planking, and the larger sections in a glue-down application will be less likely to work free. There are now at least eight companies selling laminated wood floors, besides Tarkett, maker of one of the systems used in "Float a Fancy Floor" (see the box at the end of this article).

"European-style laminated flooring got its start in the United States in, of all places, the Pacific Northwest," says John P. Stern, president of Kentucky Wood Floors. "That kind of flooring was available only regionally until several years ago, when a Swedish company introduced its product

**New finishes** and fabrication techniques allow you to use wood easily in innovative ways (above) and in areas that were once thought to be unsuitable (right).

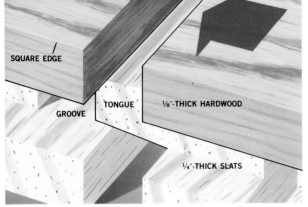

SQUARE EDGE

GROOVE  TONGUE  ⅛"-THICK HARDWOOD

¼"-THICK SLATS

**Hartco's Pattern Plus** is backed by cross-grained wood slats—with tongues and grooves machined into the edges—instead of plywood (see drawing in "Float a Fancy Floor").

nationwide. The flooring immediately gained acceptance, primarily because the product provided a prefinished no-wax, no-maintenance linear floor with square edges [as opposed to beveled edges] that also could go directly on a concrete subfloor."

All laminated flooring, except Hartco's Pattern Plus (see caption), is of a cross-laminated plywood construction, where the grain of alternating plies is placed at 90 degrees to each other. The beauty of a laminated product is dimensional stability: It can be used in applications to which solid wood flooring is not well suited, such as over existing floors and concrete slabs, or in areas like the kitchen, where spills and heavy traffic have traditionally posed problems for wood. Also, plywood can be finished in the manufacturing process to closer tolerances than solid wood, and you have less of a problem with warping and bowing.

The number of plies in laminated flooring ranges from three—in the Kährs (⅝ inch thick), Kentucky Wood Floors (⁹⁄₁₆ inch), and Robbins/Sykes (½ inch) products—to five—in the Anderson (⁹⁄₁₆ inch), Bruce (⅜ inch), and Mannington (⁹⁄₁₆ inch) flooring. The number of plies in BiWood flooring varies with the thickness of the material: four, six, seven, and eight plies in its ⁵⁄₁₆-, ⅜-, ½-, and ⅝-inch-thick flooring, respectively.

"Generally, the more plies you have, the stronger the product," says Robert C. Brown, president of Bi-Wood. "Our ⅝-inch Oak Plank, for example, has eight plies and so is really stronger than ¾-inch lumber [the thickness of conventional solid wood flooring] because of all that cross banding."

Although cross lamination does have its dimensional strength advantage, there is a disadvantage: "The more plies you have," Kentucky Wood Floors' Stern told me, "the thinner the top layer of hardwood is going to be." The top layer of BiWood's flooring is two millimeters, or just over ¹⁄₁₂ inch, while those of the Anderson, Bruce, and Mannington products are about ⅑ inch. Those of

Hartco, Kährs, and Kentucky are ⅛ inch thick, and Robbins/Sykes boasts a ⅙-inch finished oak face.

"I always maintain that the face thickness is really a moot point," says Mike Barrows, technical services manager for Mannington Wood Floors, which began manufacturing laminated wood floors in the United States about 2½ years ago. "The only time you'll be concerned about the thickness is if you're going to sand the face. With today's extra-hard no-wax factory-finished urethanes, you'll never have to sand as long as you maintain the finish properly and renew it before you wear through to the wood. Even so, the floor will withstand a couple of sandings—we figure our floors are good for at least fifty to sixty years."

As important as the face is for appearances, the plywood core is also important because that, after all, forms the bulk of the flooring. Some European-made flooring has a softwood core; other laminated flooring, including the material made in the United States, has a hardwood core. What's the difference?

"If the floor has a softwood core," says BiWood's Brown, "it can absorb moisture at a different rate than that of the hardwood face and buckle unless you've taken elaborate measures to prevent the presence of moisture. It's best to use a core that is about the same density as the face. The result is a balance in the construction of the flooring."

## Fabulous finish

A feature most of the prefinished laminated floors have in common is the no-wax finish. Whether it's called Ultra Violet Urethane, Swedish Finish, or UV-Cured Urethane, the coating is a super-tough factory-applied urethane that goes on in up to four coats, depending on the flooring, and is cured under ultraviolet light. "The UV induces linking of the polymers in the solution for an extra-hard surface, just as solvent evaporation in polyurethane does, but much more efficiently. The resulting finish is more

water and stain resistant than conventional finishes," says Barrows.

An exception to the UV-cured finish is Hartco's Pattern Plus. In a process called impregnated acrylic, a pigmented acrylic polymer solution is said to be forced all the way through the fibers of the ⅛-inch top layer of hardwood under high pressure to create a durable surface.

## Linear look

One identifying feature of many laminated wood floors that try to imitate the linear look of strip or plank flooring is a kind of segmented, patterned appearance. The face of a large section of manufactured flooring is actually composed of many small two-foot pieces in a repeating pattern. The result is, for every 8-inch-by-8-foot section you put down, it looks as if 12 to 16 individual pieces have been laid (see kitchen photo). New flooring from Anderson, Bruce, Mannington, Robbins/Sykes, and BiWood avoids this by using individual planks between three and seven inches wide by up to four feet long so that the installation more closely resembles the random-length appearance of solid wood planking.

What about price? "Generally, laminated flooring will cost a bit more than solid planking because of the manufacturing involved," says Barrows. "But because installation is easier and can be done by most homeowners themselves, the laminated route may be cheaper in the long run."

"Hardwood flooring is going more in the laminated direction," says Bob Brown. "That is mainly because of its ease of installation, the strength of the laminated product and its affordability, and the durability of the no-wax finishes. The situation is similar to what happened with furniture many years ago, when laminated materials first started to be used. People questioned lamination, but nearly all the furniture manufactured today is laminated to some extent. It makes practical sense"—
*by Timothy O. Bakke.*

# float a fancy floor

Bob Tallini looked up from the parquet pattern he'd just placed together on my floor. "Notice that we took wood directly from a standard package and made a custom pattern out of it," he said. "Because this floor is not tongue and groove, you can create any design you want just by cutting standard lengths."

Tallini, regional sales manager for Rowi USA (importer of flooring materials produced in Holland), had come to start me off on installing a Rowi hardwood floor in my attic bedroom suite. We were putting the floor down over a waferboard subfloor.

I chose the dramatic Marie Antoinette pattern from a page full of parquet designs in the Rowi literature. For the lighter-toned squares (each made up of five pieces 13⅝ inches long) I chose Rubea. The dark accent strips (34 inches long) are a wood called Merbau.

To echo the lines of the room's cathedral ceiling, we decided to install the pattern at a 45-degree angle to the walls. A more conventional design would have speeded installation, but the results justified the extra work.

Like the Tarkett floor Home & Shop Editor Al Lees laid (see companion article), the Rowi floor is a hardwood surface that "floats" over a foam pad. The polyethylene foam functions as a sound barrier for both floors, and allows installation without nails. But the similarity between the two floors ends there.

The Rowi system has an extra installation layer: An underlayment of medium-density hardboard goes down at a 45-degree angle to the top layer of solid hardwood boards (see drawing). Both layers are backed by a bright-green pressure-sensitive adhesive that's slightly tacky.

The basic directions for laying the floor are simple. You level the subfloor (if necessary), lay the foam blanket, and put down the hardboard panels with the adhesive side up. Next, you lay the hardwood boards, piece by piece, with the adhesive side down. A few blows with a rubber mallet activate the adhesive, which sets up fully in 24 hours.

Sound simple? It is, especially if you lay a conventional straight-planking floor. If you choose a showy custom floor such as the one I installed, you need to plan the placement of the first completed pattern block, or centerpiece, carefully.

"Starting in the center of the room is not that critical if you're just laying plain random plank flooring," Tallini explained. "But when you lay a pattern, whether it's herringbone, parquet, or an original design, you want the pattern centered in the room. So we'll make the centerpiece before we even lay the foam blanket."

As he talked he slit open one of the plastic-wrapped packages along both sides and tugged out several hardboard panels. He flexed them over his knee to separate the slightly tacky surfaces.

"We need enough underlayment to tie the pattern together," he explained, as he set two of the hardboard panels side by side.

"No matter what the design, we lay the hardboard in a parquet pattern," he said. "Two of these twelve-by-twenty-five-inch panels form a square, so we'll put the next two down at right angles to them." He added that you set out the underlayment only as needed, to avoid stepping on the adhesive as you work.

Tallini next slanted a piece of the dark hardwood across the underlayment. "This crosspiece ties the underlayment together," Tallini said as he pressed the dark wood in place and laid down a light board. With the rubber mallet, he hammered the seams where the boards met.

"You don't need to hammer these Rowi planks all over the board," he explained. "Just hammer along one length where the seams join. This snugs the two boards tight."

While Tallini pounded boards with the mallet, I laid the foam underlayment, measured the center points between opposite walls, and snapped two chalk lines.

Then Tallini and I picked up the completed centerpiece block and moved it into position in front of the platform bed. "Line up the four points of the pattern with the chalk lines," Tallini instructed. We maneuvered the square till it looked like a marquetry diamond inlaid on a green cross (see photo).

"All you have to do is repeat that pattern down the center of the room," Tallini said, "and then you fill in at

the edges. Don't forget to leave a ¾-inch expansion gap at the walls and any built-ins."

My L-shaped room, with its stairwell and built-ins, required what seemed like countless angled cuts. Tallini suggested the job would go faster if I got a carpenter's bevel square. To cut the boards, Tallini scored them deeply with a utility knife and snapped them. But he also had another tool that speeded the task—a Crane cutter, used by professionals to cut vinyl tile. The tool works like a super-tough paper cutter, and can be rented from flooring stores.

Once Tallini had left, it took my husband and me a number of days to finish the job—with the edge fitting consuming the most time. We then lightly hand-sanded the whole floor with 100-grit sandpaper, and applied a single coat of clear polyurethane. The Rowi floor already has three coats, but the final coat seals the joints.

The last step was to cover the gaps at walls and built-ins with one-inch pine molding. We nailed it to the wall —not the floor—then laminated leftover hardwood strips to it with contact cement.

The finished Rowi floor looks spectacular, and it's quiet and soft underfoot. Despite my husband's groans, I'm thinking of installing another one. This time, though, I plan a nice, simple random plank design—*by Susan Renner-Smith. Photos by John B. Carnett.*

DRAWINGS BY VICTORIA VEBELL

WINDOW

STAIRWELL

17'6"

7'

4'9"

3'

A  HARDWOOD PIECES
B  ADHESIVE UNDERLAYMENT
C  FOAM PAD
D  SUBFLOOR

BUILT-IN CABINET

PLATFORM BED

53"

13'

A

B

C

D

**L-shaped floor plan** created trim problems for diamond pattern centered on platform bed. Every piece that butted walls, stairwell, or built-ins had to be trimmed at 45-degrees. Layered system is sketched at right. Gap all underlayment planks using ⅛-inch hardwood piece set on edge as spacer.

**1. Resting a knee** on the foam-pad roll, the author stacks up three ⅛-inch thick hardwood pieces to mark clearance that's needed for the swing-out cabinet doors, which will later be removed for trimming. 2. Sealing butt joints of foam pad with waterproof tape is especially important if floor is being laid over concrete: The foam pad serves as a vapor barrier. 3. Now you can align the points of the centerpiece pattern with center lines snapped on the foam. A 5-foot straightedge will help while pattern is being moved as a unit. 4. Tallini gives the author advice on hammering. Always work from the wood, both to protect adhesive on adjacent underlayment and to facilitate tight butting strips. Don't hammer down strips, such as the dark one in the right foreground, until all adjacent pieces are placed: Leaving the pattern strips loose makes it much easier to fit in the field pieces. 5. The planks you use for underlayment should always be notched around fixed units, such as platform bed. Leave a ¾-inch gap at edges.

# floor finery

The inherent beauty of hardwood flooring and luxurious wall-to-wall carpeting provide such good decorating foundations that many people are content with a single color or pattern over an entire floor—often an entire house. But by overlooking opportunities to combine colors, patterns, textures and borders with "run-of-the-mill" flooring, you miss the chance to add something special. With imagination and an understanding of typical installations, you can build a richness of detail, starting from the ground up.

## Work in wood

The natural beauty and warmth of wood have made it a favorite flooring material for centuries. The development of new wood flooring, especially preassembled parquet units, prefinished products and "drop-in" borders, have made creating a fancy wood floor less pains-taking—and less expensive.

A patterned border not only adds distinction, it also helps define space within a room. A border can also serve as a unifying element or create a transition between spaces. Stock border designs are available in combinations of oak, walnut, teak, ma-

**A special border,** such as this one made of oak, walnut and mahogany, can be set into parquet or wood-strip flooring to add distinctive detail.

PHOTO AND FLOOR BY KENTUCKY WOOD FLOORS

*Reprinted by permission of Homeowner magazine.*

PHOTO BY RICK DAVIS; FLOOR BY BANGKOK INDUSTRIES

**Wood borders,** like this one made of walnut, birch and karpawood, are a highly effective way to define a specific area of space within a large room.

hogany, karpawood, purple heart, birch and other exotic woods. Ready-made borders are also available with marble, metal and ceramic tile inlays. Some companies will cut and assemble custom-designs. Generally, ready-made borders are ⁵⁄₁₆ inch thick and are preassembled on a paper or plywood backing. They cost from $15 to $30 per lineal foot.

To install a ready-made border or one made from raw flooring strips in an existing floor, you'll need to cut channels using a router fitted with a *straight-cutter* bit.

Start by snapping chalk lines to define the border's location. Mount the bit in the router and measure from a cutting edge to the outside edge of the router base. Use this measurement to set straight wooden guides parallel to the chalk lines on the floor so that the cutter can't travel outside the defined area, as shown in the illustration on page 00. Then set the cutter depth according to the thickness of the border, and cut the channels. Square out the rounded corners left by the cutter with a sharp wood chisel, and set the border units into the channels with a recommended adhesive.

Borders are usually unfinished, and it may be difficult to match a new polyurethane finish to the existing floor. In many cases, the entire floor will need sanding and refinishing. However, it is possible to match an existing oil finish. Sand the flooring adjacent to the new border, and feather in the oil finish.

For new floors, first install the *field* —the flooring that falls inside the area defined by the border. Let the last strips of the field overlap into the border area, and trim them back in place. Then install the border, then the *skirting*—the flooring outside the border—*by John Birchard.*

## Creative carpets

Wall-to-wall carpeting is a luxurious floorcovering, and if a color or pattern works throughout an entire room, fine. But you're not locked into using just one color or style on a floor. It's possible to mix colors, patterns and even textures in wall-to-wall carpeting.

A border in a contrasting color can define space within a room and can make a small room seem larger. Bold diagonal stripes set into a sedate car-

ART BY JOHN GIST

**To inset a border** in a wood floor, first snap chalk lines to define the border area. Tack wooden strips to the floor to guide the router, which you'll use to cut channels. Set with an adhesive.

pet can counteract the "tunnel effect" of a narrow hallway. Or it's possible to inset an "area rug" into a field of wall-to-wall carpeting.

There are two ways to combine carpets in a single installation: The first is to have standard-width carpet cus-

A simple two-color carpet inset is used as a border around the table and chairs in this formal dining room.

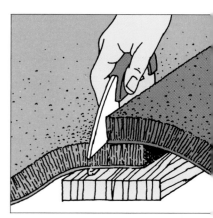

To create neat carpet seams, overlap the edges and cut as shown using the top piece of carpet as a guide.

Center the seaming tape under the edges, and heat it with an iron. Press down and butt the edges.

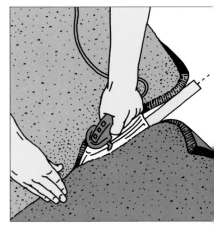

tom-tufted, or woven, to the exact measurements of a room. This method adds about 15 percent to the cost of the carpet. If you're interested in a custom design, add another 5 to 25 percent. The extras can add up, but, in some cases, custom tufting can save money because it eliminates seaming and waste. Wool is usually the fiber of choice for custom tufting because manufacturers can dye small quantities of yarn economically. Synthetic fibers must be dyed in large quantities to keep costs down.

The second method for combining carpets involves cutting and heat-taping the seams, as shown at the right. This is the best method for installing nylon carpet, which is less expensive than wool and is available in so many colors that dyeing isn't usually necessary.

It's a good idea to have seamed carpets with inset borders installed by a professional. Wall-to-wall carpeting must be stretched during installation, and while this isn't a particularly complicated procedure, the location of the border seams is critical, making installation tricky. If you do attempt it yourself, practice on scrap carpeting first since it's difficult to hide mistakes on a finished installation—by *Ola Pfeifer*.

The custom inset and contrasting border band help tie the color scheme of this room together. The design was assembled by seaming the carpeting.

# pre-assembled tongue-and-groove planks

I had to try it to believe it. Patterned hardwood floors—the luxurious kind we've all admired in the stately homes of Europe—are now available to do-it-yourselfers on a budget. You have your choice not only of a wide range of woods and patterns, but of varied installation systems.

You'll have less creative flexibility with the Swedish system I chose than with the Dutch installation described in the preceding article. Tarkett's basket-weave pattern is preassembled on plywood planks 6⅝ inches wide and over eight feet long. Each plank has an identical pattern; you create the basket-weave effect by offsetting the planks so the cross-banded squares align in every other course. Because there's a great deal of variation in the oak grain and coloration, the effect is dazzling.

The site of my installation was the Lockbox showcase home I built in the mid-1970s for a series of *Popular Science* articles. Because this is a pole house, its bottom floor is suspended from three to eight feet above a steep slope. The underside is insulated and weather-closed, but still exposed to winter blasts. So I was intrigued by the bit of extra insulation the Tarkett floor would provide.

The original floor I'd laid was cushioned sheet vinyl, cemented directly to the glue-nailed plywood subfloor. Because the room measures 16 feet square, I'd had to seam the vinyl. (Most do-it-yourself sheet flooring comes in 6- and 12-foot-wide rolls, so in a 16-foot room a seam is in-evitable.) Over the years, the seam had lifted in places. Before laying the new floor, I cemented the cupped edges back down by wetting a knife blade with epoxy adhesive and inserting it first under one edge, then the other; I covered the glued areas with waxed paper and weighted down the seam while the adhesive set.

## Vapor barrier?

The vinyl sheet forms an ideal vapor barrier for my new floor, so I could skip the six-mil PVC layer that Tarkett suggests you lay if your hardwood floor is to be applied over concrete or anywhere else you could expect moisture to rise. Unlike the Rowi pad, which is a four-pound-density closed-cell foam, Tarkett's pad is a two-pound-density open-cell foam that does not function as a vapor barrier.

There are other differences between the systems: The assembled thickness of a Rowi floor is between 5/16 and 3/8 inch, while Tarkett's will be nearly 5/8 inch thick. Both hardwood wear layers are about ⅛ inch thick, so it would be possible in future to sand and refinish either floor. However this is a tedious job with any patterned floor because of the varied grain direction. (It's poor practice to sand across the grain of any hardwood.)

The Rowi installation calls for an unusually wide expansion gap—¾ inch—at all walls and where the floor butts fixed objects. Most other systems—including Tarkett's—call for only a half inch. The wider gap would have

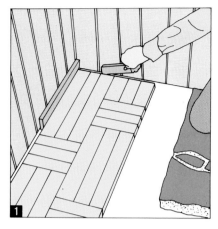

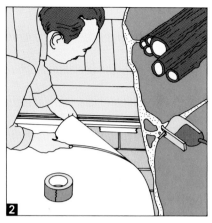

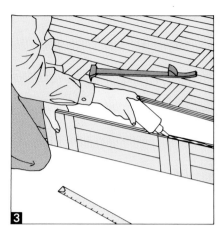

DRAWINGS BY VICTORIA VEBELL

**1. Half-inch expansion gaps** must be maintained at all edges as planks are driven together, so spacer blocks are inserted along walls. Note raised fieldstone hearth at right: The end of each flooring plank had to be trimmed to its irregular shape. 2. As you cover each width of foam pad, butt the next strip against the projecting edge, keeping the seam tight with strips of duct tape. 3. Run 8-inch beads of glue, spaced a foot apart, in the groove of each plank. 4. Fit the groove of a scrap piece over the plank's tongue, hook the TarkTool over the scrap, and hammer the anvil until the joint closes. 5. Fit around the base of the circular stair was accomplished by notching two planks at a joint line.

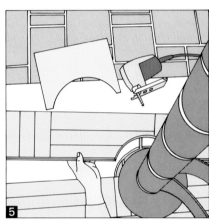

created a problem in my room because of all the edges I couldn't cap with moldings: along the window walls, around the hearth.

### Start the pattern

I began in the most visible corner, where the two window walls meet, and started my pattern with a full cross-banded square by trimming the left end of a plank with a back saw. The first course of planks was laid with their grooved edge ½ inch from the base of the window frame. The gap was minimized by running a strip of black electrical tape along the edge of the foam pad to keep it in place. The black tape is used to hide the color of the original floor, because this gap must remain open. (Several of the window units are patio sliders, and any attached molding would impede their movement.)

The roll of Volara foam pad that Tarkett supplies is five feet wide. You roll out one strip of it at a time, then cover it with flooring, leaving enough pad exposed beyond the last course of planks so that you can butt and tape the next pad strip to it. (If you covered your entire floor area with the foam, you'd track debris all over it as you worked; and you'd risk tearing it, because the pad is fragile.) Don't lap these foam strips. You can use four- or five-inch tabs of two-inch duct tape, spaced two feet apart to keep edges neatly butted.

To hold the ½-inch gap while you're hammering the groove of the next course of planks onto the tongue of the first course, you must place ½-inch spacer blocks at intervals of three or four feet along the starting wall—in my

case, against the window frames. As you add courses, drop an occasional spacer block along the side walls as well. Severe hammering is required to seat the long planks snugly, and without these holding blocks you can shift the entire hardwood membrane. You hammer until each joint line closes tight, then wipe up any squeezed-out glue with a damp cloth.

Always remember that this is—literally—a floating floor. At no point will it be anchored to the subfloor. Even at edges where ¾-inch molding strips are feasible, you nail the molding to the wall, never to the flooring. The entire membrane of your finished floor "floats" on the foam pad, gently expanding and contracting as weather and heating conditions alter.

At the far side of the room, where the flooring butts a built-in counter bar faced with Spanish tile right down to the original vinyl floor, I didn't want to crop the geometrical tile pattern by hiding the bottom edge with the ⅝-inch thickness of the new flooring. So I decided to cap this edge with a matching prefinished oak reducer strip available from the supplier of the flooring. Because this reducer tapers to its outer edge (see sketch), it obscures none of the pattern when viewed from above. A deep rabbet at its thicker edge caps the edge of the flooring and provides the ½-inch expansion gap along this edge of the floor.

This final course of flooring had to be trimmed lengthwise to fit. I set the reducer strip in place and scribed a line along its base inside the rabbet, then scribed a second line ½ inch out from the first. The flooring planks were then cut to fill the space between the last full course and second line. Because few rooms are precisely square, your trim cuts will probably give this final course a slight taper. For the trim work I found Porter-Cable's compact circular saw—called Saw Boss—ideal. The six-inch blade is positioned on the left-hand side for greater visibility.

I continued the reducer strip treatment the full room width, here, because at the end of the counter the strip serves as a threshold to a kitchen floor beyond. Also the effect was neater if this strip continued past this entry and along the wall behind the spiral stair (see photo).

## Comparing the systems

How does the Tarkett installation compare with Rowi's? Even though you're working with bigger sections of flooring at a time—the patterned planks—the Tarkett system will probably take you longer. The planks are ½-inch plywood, so they must be sawn. This becomes especially tricky when fitting around an irregular object, such as my fieldstone hearth. You must first make a precise paper template and transfer this pattern to the back of the butting plank. (Because a saber saw cuts on the *up* stroke, always cut from the back to avoid splintering the good face. You'll find that the finished face of Tarkett planks won't splinter readily. The hardwood is pressure-bonded to the core layer, and the acrylic polyurethane finish is rugged.)

My spiral stair also required fitting of the planks that butted its base and the end post of the railing; both of these were anchored to the original floor. Accurate cardboard templates were the key. Their patterns were transferred to the back of the panels that needed trimming.

Unlike the homeowner in the preceding article, I had no visiting pro to get me started. I've laid many floors, but never one of prefinished hardwood. Tarkett's instruction sheet clearly shows how you lay the beads of glue in both the long edge groove and short end groove of the plank you're installing. You fully glue the end joints, but apply only eight-inch-long beads spaced 12 inches apart in the side grooves. I differ with the instruction sheet, however, when it lists the TarkTool as "optional." Don't even *try* to pound an eight-foot plank securely home without this tool, which consists of a steel bar with a flange at one end to hook over the edge of the scrap block you've fitted onto the protruding tongue you don't want to damage. At the bar's other end is welded a sturdy anvil for striking with your hammer. When using the TarkTool, always spread a scrap of toweling under it so that its movement won't scratch the surface of the plank you're driving in place.

To keep the flange from bouncing out of contact with the scrap block as you hammer, you'll need to keep your foot lightly on it. It's hard to keep the edge of the flange from cutting through the foam; but because this foam isn't a vapor barrier, these little slits don't matter.

## Future repairs

If trimming and installing the thinner pieces for a Rowi installation go easier and faster, does the Dutch system offer any other advantage? Perhaps.

A bad mar on a Tarkett plank presents a repair problem. Because each plank is locked in place by tongue-and-grooved edges and ends, it is difficult to remove and replace. Rowi claims you will be able to easily pry out a damaged piece of its hardwood and replace it with a good one. (You will destroy the original adhesive interface, of course, so you would have to apply contact cement.)

So pick your system. One thing's assured—either way, you end up with a spectacular floor that's warm and cushioned underfoot. And it's a floor you can install yourself, at your own pace—*by Al Lees. Photos by David Stubbs.*

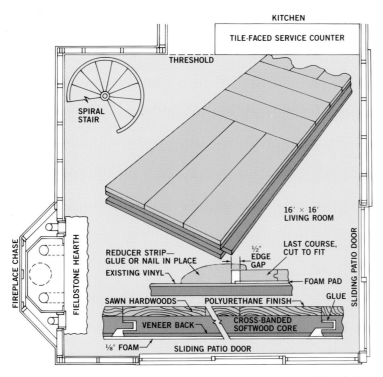

**Tarkett system** is superimposed on floor plan of Lockbox living room. Each tongue-and-groove plank is a three-layer lamination. Planks are glued into one large membrane floating on a foam pad. The only thing that's nailed down is the reducer.

# two routes to radiant floors

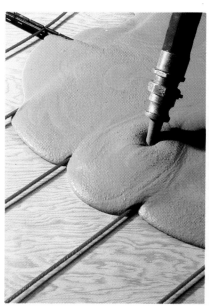

**A layer of gypsum cement,** called Gyp-Crete 2000, is poured over electric cable laid out on a plywood subfloor to form an electric radiant heating system.

**Warm-water pipes** embedded in the Gyp-Crete form hydronic radiant floors. Either system can be covered with various materials—carpet, tile, wood, or vinyl.

O n a frosty winter morning the thought of your snuggly warm toes traipsing across an ice-cold floor makes you gather your blanket up to your nose. With radiant floor heat you won't have that excuse to stay in bed.

Radiant floor heating systems generally heat your house by hot water running through pipes in a concrete floor slab, heating the slab and thus the house. Infloor Heating Systems, a division of Gyp-Crete Corp., now offers two systems: One uses plastic pipes to carry hot water; the other uses electric heating cables. Both can be laid over existing concrete slabs or wood flooring. Then they're topped with a special gypsum cement. An Infloor floor surface radiates an even, comfortable warmth. "We design our systems to keep floor temperatures below eighty-five degrees [F]," a stan-dard temperature limit for comfort, says John Fantauzzi, technical services manager of Infloor. "Beyond that, and your feet get too warm."

The Infloor hot-water system can tie into any heat source—boilers, heat pumps, solar collectors, water heaters—that can deliver water from 140 to 180 degrees F. At its heart is the Zone Control, a mixing valve and pump that maintain the desired floor temperature.

To install the hydronic system, po-lybutylene tubes are stapled to the plywood subfloor or laid over insula-tion board on a concrete slab, and a 1¼ inch layer of lightweight non-structural gypsum cement, called Gyp-Crete 2000, is poured over them. "Portland cement is around 150 pounds per cubic foot," says Phil Turner, new product development di-rector of Gyp-Crete Corp. "Our gyp-sum cement is approximately 110 to 115 pounds per cubic foot."

For electric-resistance radiant floors, spacer strips establish the floor pattern and maintain a constant dis-tance between the runs of cable. An Infloor thermostat controls the tem-perature; a sensor embedded in the gypsum keeps the cable from over-heating.

"Homeowners can save money on their heating bills," Fantauzzi con-cludes, "because the even distribution of heat reduces heat loss." Proponents also point out that radiant heat warms people directly, so you may feel comfortable at lower thermostat settings.

But the very best benefit of all: No more cold toes! Infloor Heating Systems, 920 Hamel Rd., Box 253, Hamel, MN 55340—

*by Cheryl M. Fiorillo.*

# repairing rotten wood

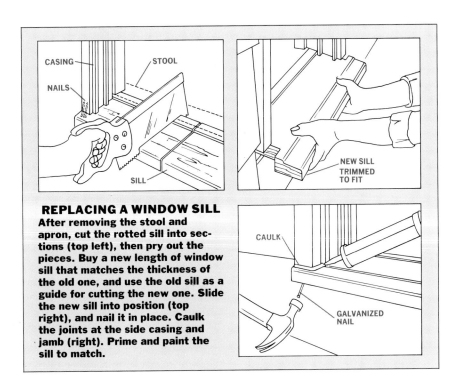

**REPLACING A WINDOW SILL**
After removing the stool and apron, cut the rotted sill into sections (top left), then pry out the pieces. Buy a new length of window sill that matches the thickness of the old one, and use the old sill as a guide for cutting the new one. Slide the new sill into position (top right), and nail it in place. Caulk the joints at the side casing and jamb (right). Prime and paint the sill to match.

*Reprinted by permission of Homeowner magazine.*

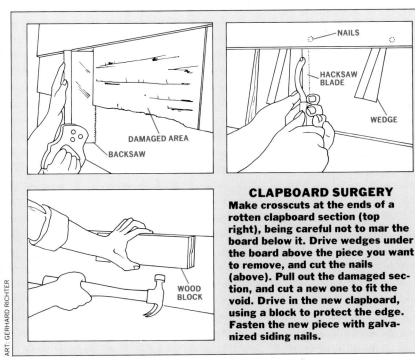

**CLAPBOARD SURGERY**
Make crosscuts at the ends of a rotten clapboard section (top right), being careful not to mar the board below it. Drive wedges under the board above the piece you want to remove, and cut the nails (above). Pull out the damaged section, and cut a new one to fit the void. Drive in the new clapboard, using a block to protect the edge. Fasten the new piece with galvanized siding nails.

Paints and stains usually protect wood from the ravages of moisture. But rain, snow and ice are persistent, and if water finds a chink in the protective coating, it can settle in and support the organisms that cause rot. Rotten wood is not only unsightly, it's also weak, which could lead to a dangerous situation if the wood in question is load-bearing. Now's a good time to inspect your wood siding, windows, posts, decking and any other wooden parts of your home that are routinely exposed to moisture.

The warning signs of wood rot are peeling paint, fungus stains, a spongy feeling, and a dead, hollow sound when you tap it with a hammer. If you suspect rot, check the extent of the damage by probing with an awl or ice pick. In most cases, the damage will be limited to a small section of wood, which you can repair without replacing the entire piece.

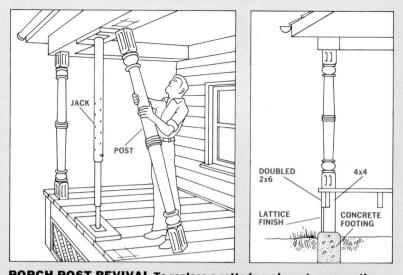

JACK

POST

DOUBLED 2x6

4x4

LATTICE FINISH

CONCRETE FOOTING

**PORCH POST REVIVAL** To replace a rotted porch post, prop up the beam that carries the roof with a jack post (top right), then swap the decayed post with a new one. Make sure that the new post is centered correctly over the post and footing that support the porch-floor frame (details, top right). Also, make sure the footing is sound.

## Surface treatments

Rot sometimes occurs only on the surface of a piece of wood. You can repair this by scraping or sanding down to sound wood, then refinishing it. If the damage goes a little deeper, dig out the decayed portion and fill the pocket with putty or another wood-patching compound rated for outdoor use.

Epoxy-based products are designed to soak into the wood and then harden. Some manufacturers recommend drilling holes in the wood to allow the epoxy to soak into the interior. Besides epoxy, there are other two-part fillers that can be shaped and carved after they've cured. These are good for rot-damaged moldings and other shaped pieces that would be hard to match.

## Major surgery

Surface remedies are usually fine for wood that's not too far gone, especially if it's used in a non-structural way—for moldings, fascia boards, cap rails and the like. But restoring damaged surfaces with filler won't renew the strength of the wood, so if rot is extensive, you'll have to reinforce or replace the entire piece. And if you find rot in joists, posts, stair stringers and other parts where strength is critical, a little surgery may be in order. Here are some approaches to repairing typical cases of wood rot.

*Window sills*. When rot occurs in a window sill, it's usually caused by one of three things: Poor upkeep of the paint finish, a missing or damaged drip cap on the window casing header, or imperfect caulking of the casing joints. Before repairing a sill, try to find the source of the moisture seepage and correct it.

If a window sill isn't too badly rotted, you can repair it with a surface treatment. But since sills are designed to deflect water from the window frame and keep it from getting into structural parts of the wall below the window, they should be absolutely watertight. Unchecked rot in a sill can easily spread to other parts of the window and its structural frame, so in most cases it's safer to replace rather than restore a rotted sill.

To take out a damaged sill, first pry out the stool (the interior window sill) and the apron (the molding below it). Then cut down and through the damaged sill (see the illustrations at the top of page 127). Avoid cutting into the framing. Cut the sill into a few sections, and try pulling them out one at a time. If the sections are hard to get out by hand, use a thin pry bar to separate them from the framing. There may be nails at the corners of the existing sill that are driven up into the side casings from underneath. If prying doesn't work, use a hammer and chisel to split the sill along the grain. This should be a last resort because the old sill can serve

as a template for cutting the new sill to size. As the illustrations show, window sills have recesses cut at the ends to allow them to slip between the jambs. The extensions along the outer sill edge, called "horns," wrap around the exterior wall and form tight joints with the ends of the side casing. Once the old sill is out, measure carefully and purchase a new sill from a lumberyard or millwork supply shop. Cut the new piece for an exact fit.

Lay a bead of fresh caulk on the wood surface that the new sill will rest on, then slide the new sill into place. Drive galvanized finish nails (usually 10d) through the top of the sill and into the framing member below. Also drive nails from underneath the sill horns up into the casing. Set all the nail heads and fill the holes with waterproof putty. Replace the stool and apron. Caulk the bottom of the finish pieces. Then sand, prime and paint to match the rest of the window.

*Clapboard*. Wherever the ends of two clapboards butt, and where clapboards join a vertical trim piece, there's a possible point of entry for moisture. In most cases of clapboard rot, it's only necessary to replace the decayed section.

Gently pry up the board above the rotted one. Using a backsaw or crosscut handsaw, cut out the damaged section (see the illustrations at the bottom of page 127). Wedge a plastic shield beneath the damaged board to

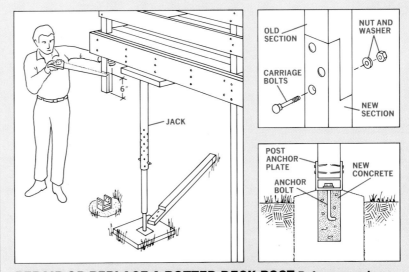

**REPAIR OR REPLACE A ROTTED DECK POST** Before removing a decayed deck post, install a temporary support. If you find rotten wood inside the concrete footing, dig it out, pour new concrete in the void, and set an anchor bolt and plate (lower right). You can either replace the entire post, or splice in a new section as shown (top right).

avoid marring the face of the board beneath it.

Once you've made the crosscuts, you'll have to cut the nails along the butt edge of the siding board above the section you want to remove. Drive wedges up under that edge, and insert a hacksaw blade in a holder in the gap. Cut through the nails and remove them. Pull the damaged section sharply downward.

Before replacing the clapboard, check the condition of the building paper covering the sheathing. If it's rotted or torn, replace it. Cut a new piece of clapboard to fit, and slide it underneath the overlapping board. Use a wood block to protect the edge of the new board as you drive it into position. Secure the board with galvanized siding nails driven through the butt edge. Then caulk, prime and paint the new section.

*Support posts.* Look for signs of damage where posts contact the ground and at joints where the post meets another framing member. Before cutting or removing a post, set up a temporary brace to carry the load that the post supports. If the deck is close to the ground, you can stack lumber underneath it for temporary support. Otherwise, use a jack post to support the load. They're inexpensive to buy and also available through rental outlets.

Once the temporary support is in place, remove the damaged post. If the post wasn't supported by a con-

crete footing, pour one now. If the damaged post was set in concrete, pry out the rotted wood with a wood chisel. Fill the void with new concrete and place an anchor bolt in the wet mix (see the illustration at the bottom of the page).

When the concrete cures, put in a post anchor plate. Then set the new post into the plate and secure it with nails driven through the plate's flanges. The anchor plate supports the post and keeps it off the ground, which helps prevent rot.

If only part of a post is damaged, you can splice in a new section without removing the entire post. Cut out the damaged section. On the replacement piece, cut an L-shaped notch half the thickness of the post and about six inches long (see the illustration on this page). Make a matching cut on the section of post that remains in place. Before joining the two sections, soak the parts of the joint in wood preservative. Secure the splice with ⅜-inch carriage bolts.

*Horizontal Supports.* Check where joists supporting a deck or floor join a ledger board or band joist—these joints are the likely places for rot to begin. Severely damaged joists should be replaced.

In most cases, all you need to do is take the old joist out and put a new one in. While it's not necessary to provide temporary support when only one joist is being removed, you should remove heavy objects from the deck-

ing and keep people off it until the job is done. Attach the new joist with joist hangers.

You can also support a weak joist by "sistering-in" a new joist alongside the damaged one: Hold the new joist flush against the existing member and attach it to the ledger or end joists with metal joist hangers or angle plates. Nail the two joists together about every 12 inches, staggering the nails at the top and bottom of the boards. Only use the joist-sistering method if you can arrest rot in the existing joist—otherwise, the rot will spread.

## Preventing rot

Good construction practice is the best way to prevent rot. Use decay-resistant lumber—pressure-treated wood, cedar or redwood—for all exterior work. Even with pressure-treated lumber, it's wise to soak all cut ends in wood preservative before nailing them in place. Most good carpenters prime wood or apply preservatives and water repellents to all new wood surfaces as they go.

Always construct joints so they can't trap water. Whenever possible, put in a metal flashing or drip edge to deflect water from joints and seams. Where joints can't be flashed, they should be caulked. Moisture has a tough time penetrating wood that is already sealed against it—
*by Tim Snider.*

# tile repair

Just as one bad apple can spoil a whole barrel, one bad or broken tile can make an otherwise perfect tile installation look perfectly awful.

Ceramic tiles have a well-deserved reputation for durability; but like any material, they are not impervious to damage. Individual tiles can chip, spall, crack and break loose from their base or substrate. When this happens, it's usually up to the homeowner to either live with the problem or repair it, because finding a tile setter to replace just one tile can be a difficult—and expensive—proposition.

However, replacing a single tile, or a small area of damaged tiles, is a job that do-it-yourselfers can accomplish in only a few minutes using the typical hand tools most homeowners have. The adhesive needed for the task is sold by the quart at hardware and tile-supply stores, and that amount is often more than enough for a small repair job.

Because tile styles change, like fashions, finding the right size, type and color replacement tile can be tricky, unless you have extras left over from the original job. Since many tiles are made in standard sizes and patterns, it is usually possible to find a match when necessary. Even the fancy "Valencia" pattern shown in this repair is available from a number of tile manufacturers. But before you begin a repair, first check your local tile stores to see if you can find a pattern that matches your own.

Removing a damaged tile and replacing it with another of the same size and shape is a fairly uncomplicated operation, as the photos illustrate. The steps involved are generally the same for replacing tiles of marble, plastic and other materials. Just be sure the adhesive you buy is compatible with the tiles used. If you shop for your materials at a tile distributor or a home center that has a good selection of tiling products, a salesperson should be able to provide the correct items for your needs.

Here are a few valuable tips to keep in mind that will make the job go smoothly:

**Use a cold chisel** to break apart and remove tile without disturbing surrounding tiles. The fragments are sharp: Wear eye protection, gloves and knee guards, or kneel on a piece of carpet or a mat while working.

*Reprinted by permission of Home Mechanix magazine.*

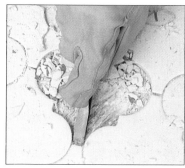

**Use chisel** to carefully clean substrate below tile, removing built-up adhesive and old grout around adjacent tiles. Surface must be flat. New tile should not sit higher than its neighbors when glued down.

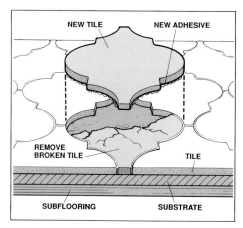

NEW TILE    NEW ADHESIVE

REMOVE BROKEN TILE    TILE

SUBFLOORING    SUBSTRATE

ART BY DON MANNES
PHOTOS BY SUZANNE DECHILLO

**Shop vacuum** picks up even minute, almost-invisible tile fragments in and around work area. Keeping bath floor free of shards is especially important for barefoot use.

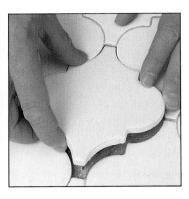

**Use your best judgment** when applying adhesive to bottom of new tile: 'butter' tile (as shown below) with enough to grip substrate, but not enough to cause adhesive to squeeze up between tiles.

**Set tile in place** and let adhesive dry, following manufacturer's recommendation (be sure to protect tile from traffic). When adhesive is dry, mix an adequate amount of grout to fill the tile joints.

**Test-fit replacement tile** (right) before you glue it down. Check that it doesn't rock or sit higher than the surrounding tiles.

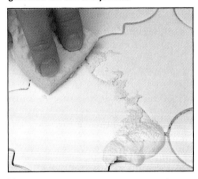

**Use sponge** to squeeze grout into place, making sure to completely fill joint cavity around replacement tile. Thin grout to creamy consistency to avoid air pockets in narrow joints.

**You can use** adhesive to fill any chipped-out areas or depressions in substrate caused by chiseling or removal of old tile. However, be careful not to get adhesive on the edges of the surrounding tiles. When you work with adhesive, it's always a good idea to keep a can of solvent handy (see label for manufacturer's recommendation).

**Keep a water bucket** handy and rinse sponge often as you wipe up excess grout. Do not allow the grout to become hard on the face of the tiles.

● Wear protective gear for your hands and face. When you start hammering on tile, the chips fly in all directions—a real hazard to unprotected eyes. And because tile shards can be as sharp as shattered glass, be careful around the work area. If you are working on a floor repair, have something soft to kneel or sit on, and check occasionally to see if any tile shards have found their way under your position.

● Use a hammer and cold chisel to break out the damaged tile, but keep the amount of hammering you do to a minimum. Too much pounding can crack other tiles, loosen grout in nearby joints and even fracture a mortar substrate, which could allow moisture to penetrate the tile barrier into the wall or subfloor. Also use caution to avoid damaging the area under the tile. Substrates may be poured concrete, masonry backer board (Durock, Wonderboard, etc.), plywood, Masonite or other material.

● After you break up and remove the damaged tile, thoroughly clean out the hole to remove all old adhesive and grout. The surface should be level and free of bumps or gouges that would interfere with the fit of the replacement tile.

● Always test-fit a new tile before gluing it down. A floor tile that doesn't have a flat installation base will rock back and forth, and crack when weight is placed on it; a wall tile with a cavity behind it is an invitation to moisture problems—*by Michael Morris.*

# airing it

PHOTOS BY SUZANNE DECHILLO

Whether you use the space directly under your home's roof or not, your attic plays an important role in keeping your house comfortable year-round.

In the summer, an overheated attic acts like a giant radiator atop a home, taxing occupants and air conditioning below. During winter, heat and moisture emanate upward from the living quarters, resulting in condensation under the roof and even within the walls where it can render insulation ineffective. In addition, high humidity levels can cause mildew and paint failure.

Often, the solution is to increase attic ventilation. It will reduce heat buildup, carry off trapped moisture and discourage mildew growth. The general rule for venting is 1/300th of the ceiling area. For example, a home with 1,200 square feet of ceiling area should have a minimum of 4 square feet of ventilator area.

Powered attic ventilator installs easily in existing roofs, has automatic fan to exhaust hot or humid air. Intake vents in gable walls or soffit (roof over-hang) provide positive airflow.

## installing a powered attic ventilator

*Reprinted by permission of Home Mechanix magazine.*

Mount ventilator high, below ridge. Measure from ridge to unit center, locate fan between rafters from inside the attic.

Bore locator hole to center unit between rafters. Nautilus has two-way template for shingle and roof sheathing cutouts.

Mark and remove shingles within larger circle, then reposition template to mark smaller circle for cutting roof sheathing.

Because units are sized to fit between rafters, sabre or keyhole saws easily cut opening through roof sheathing.

Use pry bar or hand-saw blade to lift shingles, remove roofing nails within lines corresponding to unit flange size.

Wiring for unit's thermostat is two-wire connection, with ground. Use humidistat for automatic moisture control.

This relatively new type of non-powered roof ventilator is installed in a continuous strip at the house ridge, the highest point on the roof. It is easily retrofitted to existing roofs of virtually any material or slope, and is widely used in new construction. Ridge vents are especially useful above cathedral ceilings because they create an upper outlet for airflow between rafters along the entire length of a roof. For this applicataion, continuous soffit vents should also be installed at the lower end of the rafters to allow free air flow between ceiling and roof. Ridge vents generally provide 18 square inches of ventilation area per lineal foot (to convert square inches to square feet, divide by 144). Most types of roof and wall ventila-

**WORTH WRITING TO**
**Air Vent Inc.**, 4801 N. Prospect Rd., Dept. HM1088, Peoria Heights, IL 61614 (ridge and soffit vents); **Arvin Industries**, 500 S. 15 St., Dept. HM1088, Phoenix, AZ 85034 (wind turbine); **Home Ventilation Institute**, 30 W. University Dr., Dept. HM1088, Arlington Heights, IL 60004 (Home Ventilating Guide, Publication 12, a free booklet); **Nautilus**, Box 159, Dept. HM1088, Hartford, WI 53027 (powered attic ventilator).

# ridge vent installation

PHOTOS BY THE AUTHOR

**For existing roofs,** ridge shingles are removed to install vent. Snap chalk lines for cutting 2-inch-wide slot along ridge.

**Use razor knife** to cut away shingles. Cut tabs from new shingles to cover exposed roof below ridge shingles.

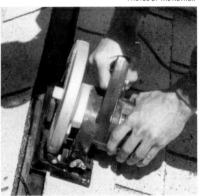

**Set saw blade depth** to penetrate roof sheathing without cutting rafters or ridge board. Cut to 4 inches from roof ends.

**Plug seals vent** at gable end. Note new shingle tabs installed up to ridge opening and ridge shingle at end of run.

**Special connector plug** is used to join vent sections. Use hacksaw to cut aluminum sections (generally 8 and 10 feet).

**Nail through prepunched holes** to fasten vent to roof. Use only ringed aluminum nails, available in colors to match vent.

**Cover strap** is nailed over connector at joint between sections. Nails secure to roof sheathing but don't create rain leaks.

**To install continuous soffit vent,** snap chalk lines and cut slot to product width. Check that soffit interior is open into attic.

**Use nails** to secure vent strip. Ridge vent requires 9 square inches of vent area per lineal foot at bottom of roof slope.

tors can be found wherever roofing or building products are sold.

Wind-turbine ventilators work like powered attic ventilators—although with less air-handling capacity. Their advantage: They don't need electrical power and, in their own way, they work very efficiently. The slightest air movement sets the turbine spinning, and the faster it spins on its low-friction jeweled bearing, the more hot, humid air it evacuates from the attic. Homes with adequate gable and soffit vents may need only one turbine, while large homes or houses with complex roofs may require several. Turbines should be installed high up—so the turbine clears the ridge—to catch breezes from all directions. If two units are installed on one roof, place each one a fourth of the distance from the gable ends, allowing the turbines to share ventilation of the center section.

Most older homes can benefit from increased attic ventilation to help supplement vents that may clog with built-up paint, webs and nests, etc. The simple vent shown below is inexpensive and installs quickly—several may be added at points around the attic perimeter for optimum effect. Also inspect eaves from the inside to keep vents clear of insulation, storage items and debris—
*by Michael Morris.*

## letting wind do the work

**Separate base from turbine** and position on roof (wear gloves to protect hands). Use snips or knife to trim shingles.

**With base in position,** mark shingles around inside of base circumference. Use razor knife to remove shingles in circle.

## adding soffit vents

**Tap soffit** to find hollow area between framing members, and mark opening. Cut hole slightly smaller than vent size.

**As with powered ventilator,** be sure to position roof opening between rafters to avoid having to cut structural members.

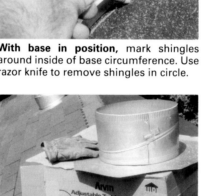

**Cut hole in roof sheathing** same size as shingle opening. If installing more than one turbine, space them equally on roof.

**Use power or hand saw** (bore access hole first) to make cuts. Check soffit interior to be sure air can circulate freely into attic.

**Fasten base to roof** with 1½-inch No. 10 pan-head galvanized screws. Use roofing cement to seal screwheads and base.

**Loosen base clamp screw** and rotate sections until collar is level. Install turbine, secure it with sheet-metal screws.

**Nail or screw vent** over hole. Insect screen may be added above vent but it will reduce air passage slightly.

# refrigerator tune-ups

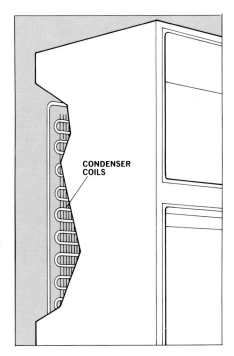

CONDENSER COILS

### Finding the coils
**Refrigerator coils** need routine vacuuming. If coils are mounted on the back of the unit (right), move the refrigerator out to get at them. To clean bottom-mounted coils (below), remove the grille at the base of the refrigerator. Be careful not to bend the coils as you clean them. To clean the circulator fan on bottom-coil units, remove the access panel behind the refrigerator.

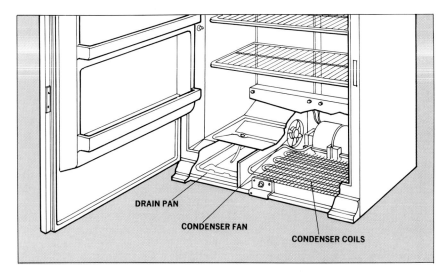

DRAIN PAN

CONDENSER FAN

CONDENSER COILS

### Door gasket details
**To remove a** faulty gasket (right), pull it back to reach the hex-head screws holding it in place. Use silicone caulking to fix isolated cracks.

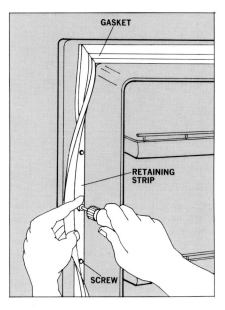

GASKET

RETAINING STRIP

SCREW

Of all home appliances, refrigerators may be the most taken for granted. You have to defrost the older ones every once in a while, but outside of an occasional clean-out, most people are content to let the fridge chug along dependably and unnoticed. But even the most modern iceboxes need tuning up from time to time. It doesn't take much time or effort, but if you give your refrigerator the attention it needs, it'll do a better job for less money and have a longer life.

*Reprinted by permission of Homeowner magazine.*

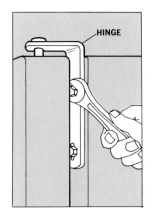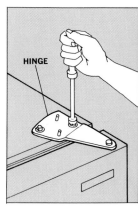

## Adjusting the hinges
**Refrigerator door** hinges have slots that allow you to adjust alignment. Two hinge styles are shown above.

### Keep it clean

To operate efficiently, a refrigerator needs an unimpeded thermal path so heat can be expelled from the interior. If the internal heat-exchange surfaces are coated with ice, or if the external coils are covered with dust and grime, the refrigerator has to work that much harder to keep its cool.

If your refrigerator is a manual-defrost model, make sure you defrost it whenever the ice gets thick in the freezer. On an automatic defrost type, check the ice build-up to be sure the defrost control is set properly. To minimize ice build-up on any refrigerator, don't keep the door open unnecessarily, especially during hot, humid weather.

The external heat-exchange coils should be cleaned every three months. In most cases, these coils are mounted on the back of the refrigerator, although some models have them mounted beneath or on top of the unit. With a refrigerator that has coils at the back, you'll have to move it to get at them. Plan the job for a time when the refrigerator is relatively empty so it'll be easier to move. If the unit has built-in wheels, follow the manufacturer's instructions for moving the unit. If there are no wheels, check your local hardware store for an inexpensive dolly designed for refrigerators. These dollies have wide rollers that won't mar or tear soft resilient flooring.

Once you can get to the coils, use a vacuum cleaner to remove built-up dust and dirt. On newer "reduced clearance" models, the coils are mounted under the unit. You'll have to remove the grille below the refrigerator door to reach them. Space is limited down there and access for a vacuum hose is awkward, so be care-ful not to bend or damage the coils.

Bottom-coil refrigerators have an electric fan that circulates air past the coils. It needs cleaning about once a year. The access panel is at the back, so you'll have to move the refrigerator to get to it. Remove the access panel, and clean the fan gently with a vacuum cleaner. Most fans are permanently lubricated, so you don't have to worry about that.

Auto-defrost and frost-free units have a defrost drip pan that should be scrubbed out periodically. It's a prime source of unpleasant odors in an otherwise-spotless refrigerator.

Follow the manufacturer's instructions for general clean-up of the refrigerator's interior and exterior. A solution of two tablespoons of baking soda in a quart of warm water will handle most cleaning jobs. A mild solution of dishwashing liquid and water also does the trick. Never use flammable or abrasive cleaners.

### How cold?

Ideally, a refrigerator will maintain an average internal temperature of 40 degrees Fahernheit. It might be a bit warmer in the butter compartment and a bit cooler in the meat bin. The target freezer temperature is 0 to 5 degrees Fahrenheit. These temperatures represent the ideal balance point of reasonable operating costs and adequate food protection.

Refrigerators have a built-in thermostat that's supposed to maintain these temperatures, but these automatic controls aren't adequate to handle the wide swings in room temperature that can occur throughout the year. That's why refrigerators also have manual temperature controls.

You can make sure the temperatures are right with inexpensive re-frigerator and freezer thermometers. Twice a year—once in late spring and again in late fall—check the temperatures and set the controls accordingly. Allow several hours between adjustments to give the internal temperature a chance to stabilize.

### Gasket case

The door gaskets are the only other parts of a refrigerator that need routine attention. If your gasket leaks, cold air escapes and is replaced by warm air. Happily, gasket leaks are rare, now that magnetic gaskets are the standard door seal. One indication of leaky door gaskets is when ice accumulates on a door's inner surface. To check whether gaskets are sealing properly, open the door, place a dollar bill against the front edge of the refrigerator cabinet and close the door. If you can pull the bill out with the door closed, the seal is imperfect.

One cause of leaks is built-up dirt on either the gasket or its mating surface. A simple clean-up with a mild detergent will cure the problem. A mis-hung door, too, can cause large-scale leaking. Leveling the refrigerator and, if necessary, readjusting the door-mounting hardware will correct the problem.

If you inspect the gasket and find an isolated crack or split, try to repair it with a silicone caulk. Work from the inside of the gasket and use the silicone sparingly. If there's extensive cracking, you'll have to replace the gasket. It's an inexpensive and simple job that can be done with just a screwdriver.

A refrigerator doesn't require much attention. Giving it the care it needs can pay off handsomely in higher efficiency, lower operating costs and a longer life—*by Lee Green.*

# appliance tune-ups

*Reprinted by permission of Homeowner magazine.*

Making the time to give your household appliances some TLC is a good idea for a few reasons: With a little attention, you can keep them running at their peak for as long as you own them. It follows, too, that machines tuned to run efficiently usually last longer than those left to strain along at less-than-perfect pitch. And regular maintenance can help you spot small problems before they turn into big emergencies. So for whiter washes, cleaner dishes, lower utility bills and some peace of mind, look into our guide for the things you can do to keep major appliances humming happily along.

## clothes washer

### Check the shaft seal

**Unscrew** or pull off the cap on top of the agitator, then lift it out. This exposes a shaft within a shaft, with a rubber seal between them. Check the rubber for deterioration and for a gap between the inner shaft and seal. If the seal is bad, replace it. Many gear-case problems start when the detergent solution bypasses the seal and flushes lubricant from the bearings or gets into the gears. So check the seal about once a year.

### Lubricate the pump

**Find the pump** by following the large hoses that come from the bottom of the tub. They attach to the pump housing. Look around the pulley shaft for a cavity containing a felt wick. About once a year, saturate it with turbine oil or SAE20 nondetergent motor oil.

### Tighten the belts

**Slightly loosen** one or both of the bolts that hold the motor bracket to the chassis, and tap the motor mount back to tighten the belt. Under moderate pressure, the belts should deflect no more than ½-inch at the center. Proper belt tension helps the machine wash better and spin-dry more effectively.

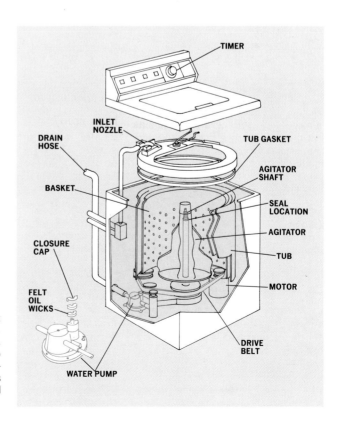

TIMER

INLET NOZZLE

DRAIN HOSE

TUB GASKET

AGITATOR SHAFT

BASKET

SEAL LOCATION

AGITATOR

CLOSURE CAP

TUB

MOTOR

FELT OIL WICKS

DRIVE BELT

WATER PUMP

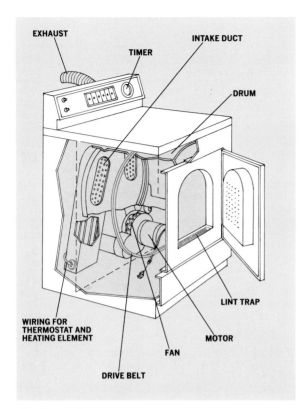

## clothes dryer

### Clean out the lint
Lint can block airflow and insulate electrical contact points, causing spotty switching, damage to parts and sometimes even fires. Twice a year, inspect the cabinet and vent pipe, and vacuum lint away.

### Check electrical connections
Once a year, after unplugging the machine, check where the wires attach to the heating element, and tighten the connections. If they're corroded or burned, take them apart and polish the contacts with an automotive point file. Cut back wires to a shiny point if necessary.

### Lubricate pulleys and rollers
Most dryers have a self-tensioning idler pulley, so belts don't need adjusting. But the idler pulley itself and the main bearing at the back of the drum (or on some models, the drum rollers) can benefit from a few yearly drops of SAE20 nondetergent oil applied at hub.

### Check the thermostat
Many gas dryers have a sensing tube inside the exhaust outlet; the sensors are metal discs about the size of a quarter. Once a year, remove any built-up lint.

### Check the outlet
Examine the exhaust outlet often, and check the operation of the exhaust-hood flapper door. When it sticks open, the hood makes an inviting nest to let energy-wasting air enter house.

## water heater

### Flush the tank
How often water heaters need flushing depends on the mineral and sediment content of the water, but it should be done at least once a year. If allowed to accumulate, deposits can corrode tank and cause noisy operation. Attach a garden hose to the drain valve, let water run until it's clear.

### Check the safety-valve
The safety-valve is located at or near the top of the tank. It's designed to relieve excess pressure that can build up in the tank. It should connect to a separate drain line. Three or four times a year, place a small pan underneath the drain line, raise the valve handle and allow it to flush. This keeps it in shape for emergencies. When the handle is released, the water flow should stop completely. If it doesn't, replace valve.

### Check electrical connections
Turn off the power and tighten all electrical connections once a year. If they're burnt or corroded, disassemble and clean them: If a wire looks discolored, clip it back to a shiny point.

### Check the setting
Unless you've got a dishwasher, turn the thermostat down to 120 degrees F for comfortable water temperatures and energy savings.

### Check gas burners
On gas water heaters, periodically clean the main burner and pilot with a brush. If flame isn't bright blue, adjust the air supply.

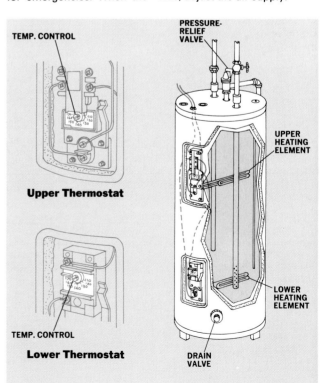

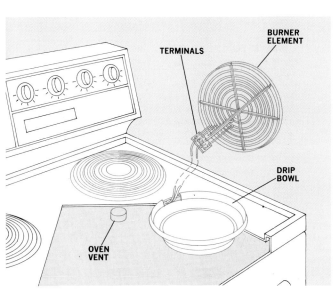

## electric range

### Check electrical connections

**Unplug the range,** and check all connections to burner elements. Tighten screw terminals. If they're discolored, clean them until they're shiny with a point file.

### Adjust the oven door

**A twisted door** can cause an oven to cook unevenly and use more energy. To straighten one, loosen the screws that hold the inner panel to the outer panel, gently twist the door back into shape, and then retighten the screws.

### Check the oven vent

**It's usually located** under the right rear burner. Once a year, check for blockage, which impedes air currents in the oven. Some self-cleaning ovens have a catalytic screen in the vent; don't remove this screen.

### Level the surface units

**Check** that the surface units are secure and level. If they're not, adjust the mounting tabs.

## garbage disposer

### Use it regularly

**That's the best way** to keep a disposer in good shape. Grinding bones helps clear away buildups. To discourage odors, pour in a foaming cleanser every few months.

### Clear jams immediately

**Turn off** the power and follow the instructions in your owner's manual. Some disposers come with a hex wrench that can be inserted in the bottom. Unlock jams by turning the rotor in both directions. Or, insert a broomstick and try to dislodge the jam by turning the disc, first in one direction then the other. Then use tongs to remove the object.

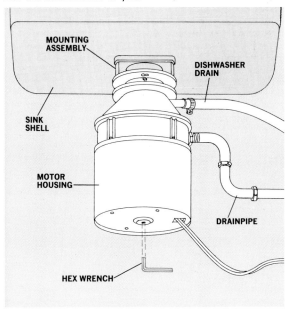

## gas range

### Adjust the flame

**Use the air shutter** on each burner to adjust the flame so that each burns efficiently, with a soft blue outer cone and a brighter inner cone. If you see yellow tips, add air; if the flame "pulls away" from the ports, reduce it. Air shutters come in three basic types, but all have a retaining screw that loosens to adjust the shutter. Readjust whenever necessary.

### Clean igniters

**Clean** the contacts with a point file once a year.

### Adjust the oven vent and doors

**Follow** the procedure listed for electric ranges.

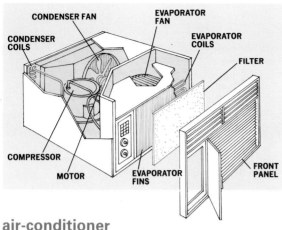

## air-conditioner

### Clean the filters
**Clean or replace filters** every 30 days during the operating season. Dirty ones restrict airflow and interfere with effective heat transfer.

### Wash the coils
**At the start** of each season, clean dirt from the coil fins with a spray cleaner, then rinse thoroughly. Clean machines cool much better.

### Straighten the fins
**Once a year,** use a fin comb, available through parts suppliers, to straighten bent fins and improve heat transfer.

### Clean the fans and chassis
**During** the preseason checkup, slide the chassis out and clean the fan and the drain trough.

### Oil the fan motor
**Look** for small plastic caps at each end of the fan-motor housing. Each season, apply a few drops of turbine oil or SAE20 nondetergent motor oil to each of the caps.

### Clean the drain
**To keep it clear,** pour bleach solution into the drain trough, flush with water.

## refrigerator/freezer

### Clean the condenser coils
**Vacuum the coils** every three months. If they're underneath the refrigerator, unplug it, remove the front grille, and use a crevice attachment to vacuum. Be careful around electrical connections and tubing.

### Clear the drain
**Clean the mouth** of the drain, and occasionally pour a tablespoon of chlorine bleach, followed by some water, into it. This kills algae and mold, and keeps blockages from forming.

### Sanitize surfaces
**At least once a month,** clean out leftovers and out-of-date foods. Wipe down the inside with a baking-soda solution. Clean the door gaskets frequently to keep them pliable, so they'll maintain a seal.

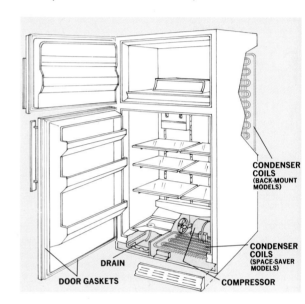

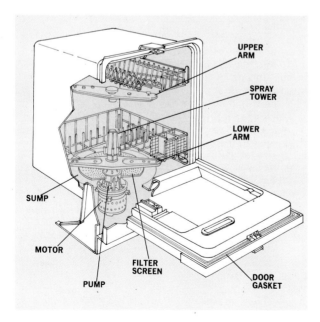

## dishwasher

### Check the water temperature
**Fill the dishwasher,** then turn it off. Test the water with a thermometer. It should be at least 130 degrees F. If it's not, repeat the test after letting the kitchen faucet run until the water gets hot. If the water still isn't hot enough, raise the water heater setting.

### Check the filter screens
**The dishwasher tub** has a depressed sump area that contains the deepest water and the pump intake. If your tub has a filter screen there, remove and clean it every three months or so.

### Check the door seals
**Examine seals** and gaskets closely, particularly the ones at the lower edge of the door. Clean away deposits of grease or residue. Heavy grease deposits are a sign of low water temperature.

# waterline leak? patch it with glue

When you're closing a house (whether for a winter vacation or after winter weekends at your country place), it's always best to drain all waterlines—even if you set the thermostat to keep the indoor temperature above freezing while you're gone. Severe cold snaps can freeze standing water and burst pipes.

But even following this advice, it's easy—if the hour is late and you're eager to be off—to drain imperfectly.

This happened last January at my weekend house. On my next trip up I restored the supply only to hear the sound of water thundering against the floorboards—and none at the sink.

Then I remembered I had previously used Copper-Bond Epoxy Adhesive to glue up lead-free water lines, so I dug out the yoked-plunger dispenser from a shop drawer and ducked under my floor to locate the damaged pipe. My lines are heat-traced and wrapped with strip insulation, so I uncoiled the soggy wrap and detached the heat cable. Because the rupture was at a spot near a plastic drain line, I was grateful not to have to torch any solder joints. In-

stead, I hacksawed out a six-inch section, then cut a replacement nipple of the same length from identical copper tubing.

The only copper connectors I could find had a center ridge inside that kept them from slipping more than halfway onto the tubing. That was OK for the sleeve on the left, which I could epoxy onto the cut line in advance and let set; but the sleeve at the right had to slip all the way onto the replacement section while I aligned it with the run, as in the photo. For this I had to insert a rattail file through the sleeve and abrade the ridge flush with the inside diameter.

Then I mixed a large second batch of epoxy and liberally applied it to both sides of the exposed joint before slipping the sleeve to the right, centering it on the joint. (The wrap of electrical tape helps position it.) Actually, it's a good idea to coat the inside of the sleeve as well, to ensure a leak-proof seal and to provide lubrication.

The patch has been in service now for over a year. Copper-Bond Epoxy is made by Marsh Laboratories, 2437 Waverly Ave., Pittsburgh, PA 15218 —by Al Lees.

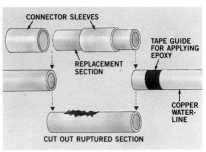

**Use copper connectors** to attach the new section of tubing to the waterline pipe.

# doctor radiator

Your front-wheel-drive General Motors car with a transverse-mounted engine has been running hotter than normal. The car has begun to lose its cool in bumper-to-bumper city traffic, overheating on a few occasions.

After a quick check, you can't find any coolant leaks, so you decide the root of the trouble has to be a clogged radiator. Although you've never removed a radiator, you are confident you can handle the job. But as you are about to find out, there is a right way and a wrong way to do it.

In the following pages I will guide you through diagnosing cooling systems and the delicate job of removing a radiator and installing a new one. Along the way I will point out several common errors made by beginners.

The primary rule when it comes to radiator repair is to diagnose the cooling system before doing any repair work. Just as a good physician will determine a patient's disease before operating, you must become a radiator doctor to figure out what is at fault before lifting a wrench.

When a radiator is operating properly, it extracts the engine's waste heat from the coolant and transfers it to the outside air. To do that, coolant must flow freely through the radiator tubes. Air must also flow freely over and around the radiator's individual tubes. At highway speeds fresh air is directed to the radiator, but when the going gets slow, the radiator fan must force cool air through the radiator.

Everyone knows that when the core's surface becomes covered with dirt and debris, or the radiator's internal tubes become clogged with corrosion, heat quickly builds up, resulting in the familiar clouds of billowing steam vapor that accompany overheating. But in my experience as a professional mechanic, I've found that clogged radiator tubes are often blamed for poor cooling-system performance, whether they are at fault or not. Based on that often erroneous assumption, would-be mechanics remove the radiator without knowing the true cause of the problem. That is what you are about to do.

You start out by opening the petcock at the base of the radiator, draining the coolant into a pan. After putting the pan aside, you disconnect the upper and lower radiator hose clamps. The upper hose slides off with no problem, but the lower hose is stuck fast to its connector. You think you might be able to pry it free with your largest screwdriver, but you only succeed in mangling the soft brass connection pipe.

nection pipe. On your last swipe the screwdriver slips, scoring the core's surface and leaving a deep groove. You aren't too concerned, though, because the radiator has to be repaired anyway and a few extra leaks won't make a big difference.

When hoses are difficult to remove, the best way to get them free is to cut several slices in the hose, near the connector. In this way the hose can be

**Getting to know your radiator** inside and out is essential to diagnosing a cooling-system problem. Diagnosis is the first step to doing the correct repair job.

peeled away without damaging the connector. In any event you should replace old hoses and clamps.

*Your next area of attack is the transmission-coolant lines. Using only an open-ended wrench you try to loosen the fittings, but the upper fitting holds tight. As you force it, the fitting's brass nut becomes rounded. So you clamp vise-grip pliers onto the nut. The fitting still holds firm, but the soldered connection between the tube and the radiator shears off.*

Whenever you disconnect a fitting from a radiator, use a tube nut wrench that wraps around the fragile nut to protect the fitting. It is also a good idea to use a backup wrench whenever possible. As for tough-to-remove fittings: Do not force them; try using a small tubing cutter to cut away a straight section of the pipe. Later, you can install a compression fitting to reconnect the tubing. At this point it's a good idea to plug the transmission lines to prevent transmission fluid from draining out. And always check the transmission-fluid level after the radiator is reinstalled.

*Once you disconnect all the hoses and tubes, start to unbolt the radiator. Remove the fan shroud if it might get in the way later.*

Radiators are generally attached with four or six bolts on either side. If they haven't rusted, they are simple enough to remove. However, it is easy to miss some of the square rubber cushions on which the radiator sits. Sometimes they stick to the bottom of the radiator or to the rail on which the radiator rests, or they may be lost in transit. Make sure the cushions, which protect the radiator from shocks and vibrations, are present before you reinstall the radiator. On this transverse-engine General Motors car there is an extra hazard—a motor mount that extends from the car's frame to the front of the engine. You should carefully loosen such a mount and keep it away from the radiator's surface.

*Once the radiator is completely disconnected, it's time to pull it out. Standing in front of the car with your hands on the radiator's sides, you manage to angle the radiator safely out of the engine bay. You avoid contact with any sharp edges, like the fan blade, exhaust manifold, or the loosened motor mount. Now you are ready to take the radiator to the repair shop.*

The soft radiator core is vulnerable, and once it has been removed, it should be sandwiched between two pieces of corrugated cardboard. If you are in doubt about there ac-

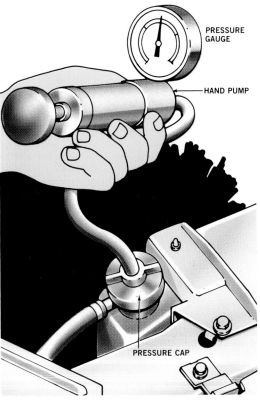

**1. Pressure-test** the cooling system by pumping it up to operating pressure while the engine is cold. Leaks can be safely traced without running the risk of being sprayed by hot antifreeze.

tually being a problem with the radiator, ask the radiator repairer to tell you about any leaks, clogs, or defects that were found. Explain that you are trying to solve an overheating problem.

If the radiator flow is restricted, the radiator repairer may suggest removing the tanks to check each tube individually or just replacing the entire core. Often cars with radiators damaged in a front-end collision have core areas that were soldered off. While this technique saves money on the repair bill, it cuts down on the cooling capacity and efficiency of the radiator, making it, in effect, a smaller radiator.

*As it turns out, the radiator shop's owner tells you your radiator is free of defects, except those you inflicted during removal. With the core surface so badly cut, the damage done to the transmission-fluid cooler, and the badly mangled hose connection, the cheapest way to get your car back on the road is with a new radiator. The only real defects in the original radiator were those caused by your inexperience.*

*After buying and installing a new*

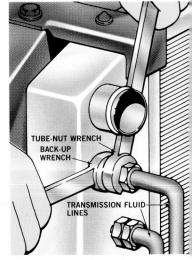

**2. When opening** the transmission-line fittings, always use a tube nut wrench, and a back-up wrench when space allows. It is easy to damage the fitting's nuts with an open-end wrench.

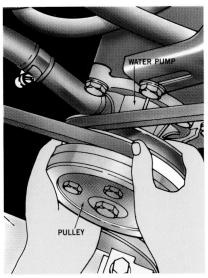

**3. Check the water pump** by pulling on it and trying to rock the pulley back and forth. If there's too much play, the bearing may be worn out and the water pump should be replaced.

radiator, your car still has the same overheating problem, so you go to a mechanic for help. He starts out with a cooling-system pressure test, which shows there are no leaks. Next he does a combustion-leak test to make sure there are no internal leaks that might allow exhaust gas to bubble into the cooling system. He draws air from the radiator through a blue test liquid. Any trace of combustion gas would make the liquid turn yellow. Your engine passes the test.

Everything else, including the thermostat, core plugs, and pressure cap, checks out fine, yet the car still runs hot and begins to overheat in city traffic. The mechanic decides to see if he can duplicate the conditions by running the car in drive with the wheels blocked to simulate city driving. This puts stress and load on the engine and cooling system similar to what you would encounter in a typical traffic jam. After about 15 minutes the engine gets hot, with occasional bursts of bubbles in the coolant recovery tank. At that point the engine's electric cooling fan should be turning to pull cool air over the hot radiator tubes; it is not. On some cars with electric fans, turning on the air conditioner automatically engages the fan, but most of them use a temperature sensor to start the fan.

It doesn't take long to figure out that the engine coolant sensor, which triggers the fan circuit, is defective. Using jumper cables to ground the sensor wire turns on the fan, and the temperature gauge begins to drop slowly. Once the engine cools down, a new coolant sensor is installed. Your car now keeps its cool wherever you drive it.

Solving the overheating problem was more complicated than necessary because you didn't diagnose the problem; and the solution came at a high price. Getting your car's coolant system under control ended up costing $220. The price of the coolant sensor was only about $20, but you also had to pay $200 for the new radiator, which you didn't need in the first place. In any auto repair, diagnosing the problem before you undertake a repair is the key to success—by Bob Cerullo. Drawings by Russell von Sauers.

**4. On newer cars** a coolant sensor (next to the distributor on this car) operates the radiator's electric cooling fan. If it is defective, the car will quickly overheat in start-and-stop driving of city traffic.

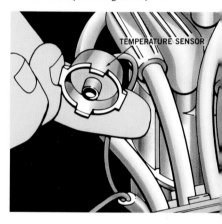

**5. When all the hoses** and tubes have been removed, the radiator must be carefully angled out to avoid sharp objects still in the engine bay (shown with arrows): motor mount, exhaust manifold, and transmission-fluid lines.

## Your car's cooling system: What's wrong, and where

Before attempting any repair work, it is best to know where you stand and what needs fixing. A step-by-step plan of attack for diagnosing your car's problem will be time well spent, avoiding costly unneeded work.

It is easier to find a coolant leak under pressure, so the first step is to pump up the cooling system. While this can be done by letting the engine heat up and the coolant pressurize, it is safer and easier to use a pressure tester. (When you find a leak, it is better to be sprayed by cold coolant than to be scalded by hot antifreeze.) The pressure tester consists of a hand pump that fits over the radiator cap and a pressure gauge. Do the same pressure test after you complete the job.

All modern automotive cooling systems are designed to operate under pressure to raise the coolant's boiling point and efficiency of heat transfer. Not only will a leak cause the system to loose coolant, it will cause the coolant to boil at a lower temperature, making a boil-over easier.

Coolant can escape through a number of places; the most common are a leaking hose and clamp. If the pressure test reveals no leaks, check the engine core plugs. Core plug leaks are generally difficult to spot, and you will need to get under the car and search carefully and check each plug. The best clue to a leaking core plug is a greenish drip of coolant you might find clinging to the starter or motor mounts. While under the car, check the water-pump weep hole where possible (found on the bottom of the water-pump casting) for drips or coolant residue.

When you're stumped, look for more exotic leaks, such as the heater core. Drips of coolant may show up on the floor mat on the driver's side or may come from the air-conditioner evaporator housing. One sure sign of a heater core leak is the sweet smell of coolant accompanied by a fogging of the windshield when the defroster is used. Examine the coolant-recovery tank and its plumbing for leaks.

The thermostat can be quickly checked by putting it into a pan of water on the kitchen stove. As the water heats up to boiling, the thermostat should pop open. It should then close as the water cools. This simulates the thermostat's action as the engine coolant heats up to operating temperature. If it opens too soon or remains open, performance, efficiency, and emissions will suffer.

The real trouble begins when the thermostat doesn't open. Coolant will be trapped in the water jacket and will not transfer heat away from the engine. A loud banging sound usually precedes the geyser of billowing vapor that accompanies overheating.

Next, look at and grasp the water pump's pulley, trying to rock it back and forth. It should move freely. If it feels loose, the bearings may be worn out.

Remember too that air must flow across the radiator tubes. If the airflow to the front of the radiator is restricted by debris on the radiator's face or a problem with the cooling fan, cooling will be seriously reduced. Older cars will have either a direct-drive fan powered by a belt, or one that is activated by a heat-sensitive clutch: Check the belt tension for slippage. On newer cars there is a temperature-sensor control and an electrical fan; both should be checked.

Even after you think you've found the source of your cooling-system failure, continue along with the diagnostic checks. Multiple causes could be at the root of your car's overheating.—B. C.

# car care quiz

## problems

### 1. Black smoke

The 1986 Ford was a delight to its owner. It started in any weather, its electronically controlled V8 engine had plenty of power, and it averaged 20 mpg. But trouble surfaced when the engine began to run a little roughly. Convinced that a bad tank of gas was the culprit, the owner ignored this initial symptom.

Soon, however, he noticed black smoke belching from the tailpipe at all speeds. Then the car began to stall in traffic. To keep it running at a light, he had to race the engine slightly while applying the brakes. What's more, fuel mileage dropped to about 11 mpg. A review of the car's maintenance record showed that the engine had not been tuned for more than 14,000 miles. So the owner set aside time to do a routine tuneup.

As he expected, the spark plugs were fouled with carbon. The air, fuel, and emission-system filters also showed signs of severe service. He installed new spark plugs and a new distributor cap, rotor, PCV valve, engine-breather filter, air-cleaner filter element, and fuel filter. He also did a compression test. All cylinder pressures were within the allowable range.

After checking ignition timing and finding it on spec, he took the car for a road test. At first the engine ran well, but within a few minutes the tailpipe began to emit black smoke again. Back to square one.

Black smoke is a telltale sign that the air-fuel mixture is too rich. Could the electronic feedback carburetor be faulty?

To find that out, he drove the car to a local repair shop for an exhaust-emission test. Sure enough, as soon as the test probe was inserted into the tailpipe, the test machine registered abnormally high emissions of hydrocarbons and carbon monoxide. There was no question that the engine was running too rich.

The mechanic testing the car began his trouble-shooting with a check for possible fault codes stored in the electronic control assembly (ECA), the computer that controls the engine.

He attached an analog voltmeter to the self-test connector in the engine compartment. After observing the movement of the voltmeter's needle, he confirmed that the ECA was sending out a code indicating that the engine was running rich. When questioned, the mechanic listed the most likely causes of a rich air-fuel mixture. At the top of the list were a dirty feedback carburetor or a malfunctioning evaporative emission control system. After paying the diagnostic fee, the owner headed home to do his own trouble-shooting.

It seemed logical that the carburetor could be at fault: A partially closed choke valve will restrict airflow and cause a rich mixture. But when he removed the air-cleaner assembly with the engine hot, he found that the choke valve was completely open. And the choke valve and its connecting linkage moved freely, without binding or sticking.

A maladjusted carburetor was ruled out because the idle-mixture screws were blocked off with metal caps. So the owner moved on to the next area of testing: the fuel evaporation control system. To check whether this system was working properly, he started the engine and allowed it to reach operating temperature. Then with the engine at high speed, the owner pulled off the vacuum hose to the carburetor-bowl vent tube. When he placed his finger over the hose opening, he felt a strong suction.

To test whether the canister was purging, he removed its purge hose. At idle no vacuum was present; but when the throttle was accelerated, a strong vacuum was present at the hose end.

As a final test of the system, the canister was removed from the vehicle to check whether it was saturated with fuel. From its light weight, it was evident that the canister was not filled with gasoline. It appeared that the rich-fuel-mixture problem had to be caused by a dirty feedback carburetor.

After finding out that a new carburetor cost more than $800, and that

rebuilt units cost about $250, the owner decided to spend $35 for a carburetor kit and attempt an overhaul job. That way if the carburetor still didn't work, all that was lost was $35 and some time—and a new carburetor could still be installed.

Following the step-by-step procedure in the shop manual, the owner took the carburetor apart, then cleaned and assembled it with new parts. During the overhaul procedure all adjustments were set to the factory specifications. But when the car was retested on the highway, the tailpipe still blew out black smoke. What was causing the black smoke and power loss?

### 2. Lazy heater

A car equipped with an automatic heating and air-conditioning system has developed a strange problem. When the car is first started cold, the heater-blower motor will not switch on until the car has been driven for about 20 minutes. Then, like magic, the blower begins to work normally. The owner is puzzled because the system uses only one blower—and it works just fine when the air conditioning is used. The blower is only temperamental when the system is in the heater mode.

But in the middle of the winter driving around for 20 minutes without heat is no fun. Moving the blower-speed selector switch through its full range from economy to high speed doesn't have any effect on the blower. And rotating the temperature control from cold to hot also fails to energize the recalcitrant motor. To add to the mystery, the blower motor will run if the selector is positioned in the defrost mode. This is the case regardless of the temperature inside or outside the car.

This mysterious blower condition didn't develop overnight. It began a few months earlier during the autumn when the blower motor hesitated a few minutes after the engine was started before it would come on. The motor seemed to be waiting for the engine to warm up a bit before it would circulate air. But then the time

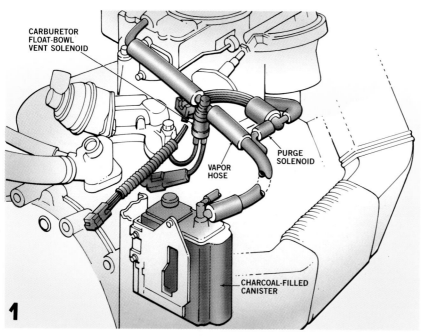

**When engine is shut off,** evaporative control system's vent solenoid opens, directing gasoline vapors to canister. When engine is running, vent solenoid closes and purge solenoid opens, sending vapor to the intake manifold.

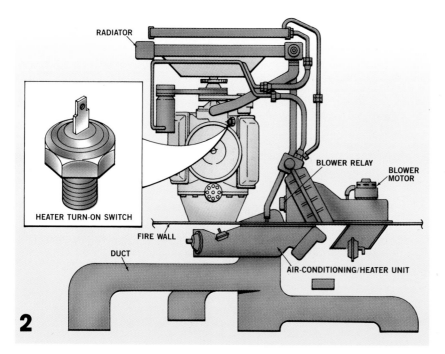

**The climate control** system's blower is activated by an instrument-panel switch when air-conditioning or defrost modes are selected. For heat, a temperature-activated switch on the engine's cylinder head turns on the blower.

before the blower started in the morning grew longer and longer, eventually reaching 20 minutes.

It seems logical that the stubborn blower is reacting to a tired cooling-system thermostat. Maybe the thermostat is opening too soon and failing to allow the coolant to reach the proper temperature. If the blower turn-on action is dependent on engine temperature—as it appears to be—it's possible that low coolant temperature is causing the delayed reaction. The owner installs a new thermostat, but it doesn't solve the problem.

He decides to investigate further. Perhaps a loose connection in the blower-motor electrical circuit is the culprit. Following the schematic in the shop manual, he carefully inspects each wire for possible looseness, corrosion, or frayed insulation.

The electrical disconnect terminal at the blower motor is clean and tight; so is its grounding connection. Wires to the blower relay also pass the visual test. The motor circuit is protected by an in-line fusible link. Its connections also prove tight, and a 12-volt test lamp illuminates when touched to either side of the link.

Maybe the brushes in the motor are worn or one of the wires leading to them is only making intermittent contact? He rules this out one cold morning when he disconnects the wire to the blower and runs a jumper wire from the battery's positive terminal to the motor's feed terminal. The motor comes to life each time a connection is made to the battery.

The engine is equipped with a fluid-coupling radiator fan, a type that's designed to freewheel when the engine coolant is at normal temperature. If the under-hood temperature rises beyond the normal range, the fluid coupling locks the fan hub to the drive pulley, and the fan pulls cooling air through the radiator. Perhaps the coupling has seized, causing the engine to run too cold? This theory is ruled out when the owner is able to spin the blades by hand when the engine is shut off and cold.

Poring over the shop manual, he identifies the blower-motor circuit components and their functions: The battery supplies electrical power to energize the blower motor; the fusible link protects the circuit from overload; the relay controls the blower feed; and two switches control the blower relay. During the summer when the air conditioning is used, an in-car temperature switch grounds the relay when the interior temperature reaches 73 degrees Fahrenheit, closing its contacts and energizing the blower motor. This gives almost immediate air circulation when the weather is hot.

The manual explains that the heater turn-on switch provides delayed blower operation in cold weather. It also controls the blower relay. The switch is screwed into the right-side engine cylinder head, where it contacts metal but not engine coolant. The switch closes and grounds the blower relay when cylinder-head temperature climbs above 120 degrees Fahrenheit. This delayed action prevents the blower relay from energizing the blower when the engine is cold and cold air would be blown into the passenger compartment.

What's causing the delayed blower motor operation?

## 3. Chronic battery drain

The battery in your Dodge van does not hold a charge. A recharge seems to give fresh life to the battery, but within a week it fails again, and you're unable to start the engine. Before the battery goes dead each time, you notice something unusual. At idle speed the directional signals flash slowly.

An old receipt indicates that the battery was purchased about three years ago, so you decide to replace it with a new one. About a week later, the old symptoms reappear: slow directional-signal action followed by slow engine cranking at start-up. Now you're confused. The instrument-panel indicator light does not show a charging-system problem. It goes out as soon as the engine fire up, and it stays off while you're driving.

Determined to get to the root of the problem, you check the condition of the alternator drive belt. With the engine turned off, the belt looks OK: It's not glazed, worn, or cracked. To check for looseness, you manually try to spin the alternator cooling fan. It won't budge an inch. The belt isn't slipping.

Looking for possible electrical short circuits, you remove the negative cable of the battery and connect a 12-volt test lamp between the cable and the battery terminal. The ignition key is turned off and the car doors are closed. By keeping the doors shut, you know the interior dome light won't switch on and cause a misleading battery-drain reading. The test lamp doesn't light. You think this test rules out the possibility of a battery drain or short.

You continue by inspecting the charging circuit wires for corrosion or a loose connection. All connectors are tight and clean, including the connections at the alternator, voltage regulator, and engine-compartment fire wall. Convinced that the alternator is at fault, you install a rebuilt unit. To your dismay, the battery goes dead again a few days later. Nothing has changed.

Realizing that you have exhausted your knowledge of the charging circuit, you take the van to the local repair shop for a complete electrical-system diagnosis. The mechanic rechecks the components you've

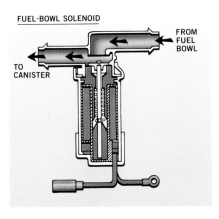

FUEL-BOWL SOLENOID

FROM FUEL BOWL

TO CANISTER

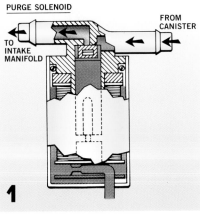

PURGE SOLENOID

FROM CANISTER

TO INTAKE MANIFOLD

**1**

**The fuel-bowl solenoid** (top) vents the carburetor to vapor canister when engine is off. Venting is blocked when the ignition is turned on. The canister purge solenoid (above) remains closed until the engine is warm and running at cruising speed, when it directs fuel vapors to the intake manifold. Vapors burn in engine.

already looked at and recharges the battery. Then he connects a voltmeter, an ammeter, and a carbon-pile rheostat to the battery to prepare for an alternator current output test. When he performs the test, the reading indicates the alternator's output is below specification.

The mechanic explains that further testing is required to find out whether the wires in the charging circuit are electrically sound. With the ignition key turned off, he connects a 12-volt test lamp to a good ground and touches the lamp probe to the "BAT" terminal of the alternator. The test lamp illuminates.

Following the steps in a repair manual, the mechanic continues by testing the wires going from the alternator to the voltage regulator. He also tests the wire going to the ignition switch from the regulator. All wires pass the electrical continuity test.

Finally, the mechanic repeats the

alternator-output test. But during this second test, he removes one of the alternator field wires and connects a jumper wire between the open alternator field terminal and ground. As soon as this connection is made, the meter shows that the alternator is delivering its maximum rated current output.

By this time, you're thoroughly confused. What's causing the battery to be undercharged?

# solutions

**1.** Remember when the owner felt a strong suction at the carburetor float-bowl vent hose with the engine at idle speed? There shouldn't be vacuum at this opening when the engine is idling. Therefore, a faulty carburetor-bowl vent solenoid or its electrical circuit was causing the rich fuel mixture.

The repair manual explains that the evaporative emission control system's purpose is to limit emissions of unburned hydrocarbons by venting vapors from the fuel tank and the carburetor float bowl to a special charcoal-filled canister. The canister is located in the engine compartment and stores fuel vapors for eventual burning by the engine. Studying the system diagram reveals the components that could cause the rich-fuel-mixture condition.

Two electric solenoids are used to control the evaporative system: a float-bowl vent solenoid and a purge solenoid. The bowl solenoid is a normally open valve when not energized. It is installed in the hose that goes from the carburetor float bowl to the carbon canister. When the engine is off, the solenoid is open and vapors from the float bowl are delivered by a hose to the canister for storage.

As soon as the ignition key is turned on to start the engine, the solenoid is energized and closes the bowl vent hose to the canister. If the solenoid fails to block off the bowl from the canister when the engine starts, fuel vapors that are in the carburetor float bowl will be drawn into the intake manifold, which causes the engine to run rich. Such was the case in this instance. Because the solenoid did not close, the owner felt vacuum at the hose end when the engine was running.

Repair manuals contain the procedure for checking a float-bowl vent solenoid. They describe the tests to make on the solenoid feed and ground circuits. If the electrical circuit ,

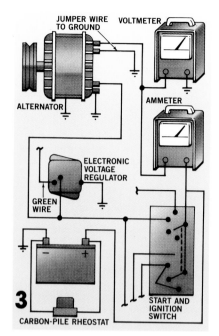

**A voltmeter,** ammeter, and a carbon-pile rheostat are used to check alternator's current output. Continuity testing pinpoints any wiring faults that may exist.

checks out OK, the solenoid itself must be replaced.

The purge solenoid is located in the hose that goes from the canister to the intake manifold. It is a normally closed valve that blocks vacuum to the canister when the engine is off, below its normal operating temperature, or running at low speeds.

When the ECA energizes the purge solenoid, the solenoid will open and allow intake manifold vacuum to purge or pull fuel vapors from the canister. The ECA energizes the purge solenoid when the engine is at operating temperature or running at

cruising speeds. The purge solenoid was functioning correctly in this instance.

**2.** The blower-motor turn-on switch located in the engine's right-side cylinder head is faulty. It does not close at the correct temperature and ground the relay to energize the blower motor. Instead of closing at 120 degrees Fahrenheit, it's closing at a much higher engine temperature, which delays the blower operation.

The clue to solving the problem was the lengthening time delay before blower turn-on caused by the failing switch. The fact that the blower worked when the driver selected the defrost position meant that the blower and its power-feed circuit were in good shape.

A quick test to isolate a faulty temperature-sensing blower turn-on switch is to disconnect and ground its wire when the engine is cold. Then turn on the heater. If the blower responds, it's an indication that the heater turn-on switch is faulty. Remember also to check the wire to the switch when trouble-shooting a similar problem. The wire is exposed to heat and dirt under the hood and may have suffered abrasions or breaks.

**3.** The voltage regulator is defective and must be replaced. One clue to a pending charging problem is a slow signal flasher or dim lights at idle speed. When the alternator and regulator are supplying the proper current, the signals and lights will function normally.

On most late-model Chrysler products the voltage regulator is mounted in the engine compartment. To find out whether the regulator is the cause of a low- or no-charge condition,

it is often necessary to bypass or isolate the regulator from the charging circuit during testing. Briefly, the test goes like this: With a voltmeter and ammeter connected in the circuit and the engine running at about 2,000 rpm, one of the two alternator field wires (the green one) is removed from the back of the alternator. Then one end of a jumper wire is connected to the open field terminal, and the other end of the jumper wire grounded.

If the alternator begins to deliver its full output, as it did in this case, the voltage regulator needs to be replaced. If, however, the alternator fails to reach its full output, then it's the alternator itself that needs replacement.

When you set out to perform this test, it is important to remember that the alternator's "BAT" terminal is always hot. If this terminal is accidentally shorted by a screwdriver or wrench while you are working on it, it's almost a sure bet that the alternator diodes will be destroyed. Bad diodes result in low- or no-current output and the expense of a replacement alternator. So it's always wise to disconnect the battery's negative cable before going to work under the hood.

Why didn't the warning indicator light up when the engine was running and alert the driver that the battery charging rate was low? These simple on-off lights are only designed to show whether or not charging current is present. They don't tell you how much current there is. If you want more information, you should install a needle-type gauge—*by Steve Mercaldo. Drawings by Russell von Sauers.*

# taking care of your car

DRAWINGS BY RUSSELL VON SAUERS

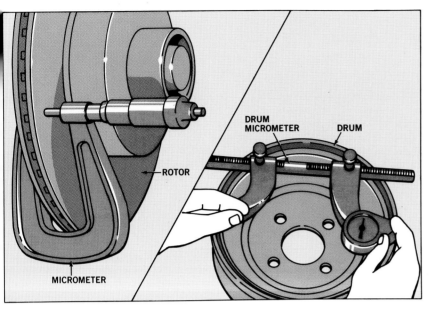

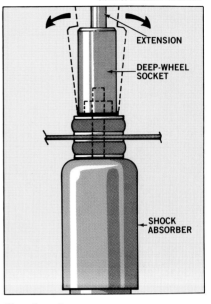

## Breaking away from the worn-parts routine

Brake drums or rotors that have worn beyond their normal life can cause dangerous brake fade, seriously decreasing your car's stopping power. The pedal will remain high and feel firm, but the friction surface will lose its gripping force due to excessive heat. The shoe or pad will not apply sufficient pressure on the drum or rotor. Use an outside micrometer caliper to measure the thickness of the suspected rotor; use an inside micrometer to measure the inner diameter on the drum. Immediately replace any drum or rotor that is out of manufacturer's specification.

## Shock solver

When replacing shock absorbers the toughest job is usually removing the old shock. Try this technique: Using a ½-inch-drive deep well socket with an extension, rock the stud back and forth until it breaks. The stud and nut flex on the rubber bushing, leaving the frame undamaged.

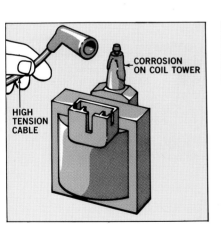

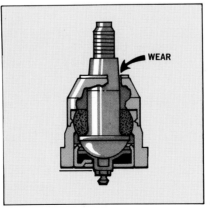

## Coil corrosion

Hard starting during wet weather? Corrosion at the high tension tower of the ignition coil could be robbing spark from the plugs. Carefully inspect beneath the ignition wire's rubber boot for corrosion and damage. Clean corrosion from the tower—but if the tower shows signs of major corrosion or is cracked, replace it.

## Ball-joint game

Before replacing a ball joint, inspect the tapered hole for size and roundness. If it has worn, the ball-joint stud can move, rock, and possibly break when stressed. The best test is to insert the new ball joint into the hole and try to wiggle it side to side. Any movement indicates that the control arm requires replacement.

## Spinning wheels

When tires spin wildly on ice or snow, it can not only get you stuck, but can also destroy your tires. The centrifugal force created by the wheel rapidly turning can tear a tire apart from the inside out. If stuck, try gently rocking the car back and forth, use traction pads or chains, or else put in a call for a tow truck.

# taking care of your car

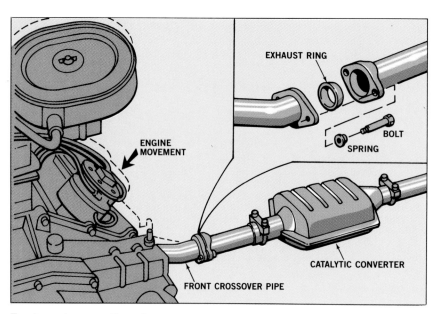

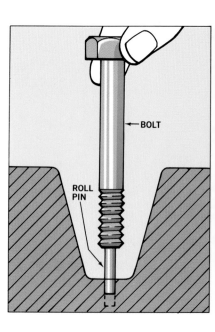

### Engineering exotic exhaust rings

When cars with transverse-mounted engines accelerate, their exhaust parts are subjected to tremendous stress. Today's exhaust rings are made of exotic and expensive materials to compensate for as much as a four-degree movement between the exhaust manifold and pipe and still maintain a gas-tight seal. Stainless-steel mesh and expanded graphite provide the needed flexibility and durability under operating conditions. It is important to install the correct parts and always use the spring-loaded bolt between the crossover pipe and front intermediate pipe.

### Roll-pin starter

If you're having trouble starting a roll pin in a tight place, try using this easy-to-make tool. Take a ⅜-by-3-inch cap bolt and drill a hole the size of the pin into the threaded end. Slip the roll pin straight into the hole, and press the tool and pin into place; carefully pull the bolt out.

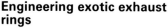
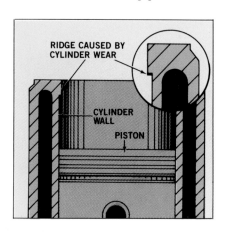

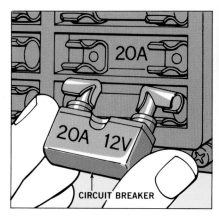

### Piston pitfall

Before removing an engine piston, check for a ridge at the top of the bore. If you can feel a raised lip, use a ridge reamer to smooth the inner surface of the bore. Failure to do this may result in piston damage when it is removed. Do the job correctly the first time by carefully following the reamer marker's instructions.

### Oxygen-sensor killer

When reassembling an engine that contains an oxygen sensor use only "sensor safe"-labeled silicone sealant. The wrong RTV (room temperature vulcanizing) sealant can contaminate and destroy the engine's vital oxygen sensor, causing an inefficient air-fuel mixture in the combustion chamber. Poor fuel economy will result.

### Fussy fuse

If the same fuse keeps blowing but you can't find an electrical short anywhere, try this temporary fix. Replace the fuse with a plug-in circuit breaker. The breaker will open when the circuit overloads to protect the car's electrical system, but will close when it cools. Replace the fuse with a circuit breaker of the same rating.

# taking care of your car

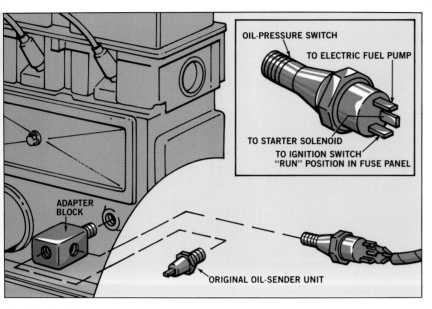

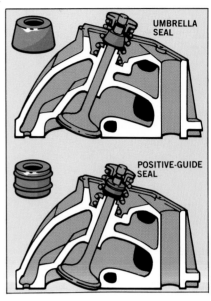

## A safer fuel pump

Whenever a mechanical fuel pump is replaced with an electric pump, there is an extra step you can take during the installation job that will prevent engine damage due to low oil level and also will guard against a possible fire in the event of a collision: Install an oil-pressure shut-off switch in the feed wire to the electric fuel pump.

If the engine runs low on oil, the switch will turn off the pump, saving the engine from the ravages of insufficient lubrication. The switch will also turn off the pump if the engine stalls because of carburetor flooding or during an accident.

## Replacing valve seals

When changing valve-stem oil seals, be sure you use the same type as the original seals. Umbrella and positive-guide seals are the two common types. Using the wrong type of seal may starve the valve stem and guide areas of oil or allow too great a flow of oil, causing high oil consumption.

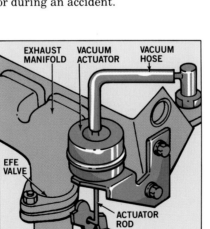

## Stiff steering

A power rack-and-pinion steering unit that's about ready for a rebuild can feel as follows: When the vehicle is started cold, the steering wheel will be tough to move for the first several turns, then it will become normal. Hardened oil seals in the steering gear are the cause of the stiffness; replacing the seals is the cure.

## Slow warm-up

Does your engine hesitate when cold? Does it have a vacuum-controlled exhaust manifold heat riser? If so, see whether the actuator rod on the early fuel evaporation (EFE) valve moves when the engine is started. If not, disconnect the vacuum hose and feel for suction. If vacuum is good, suspect a leaky actuator diaphragm.

## Caliper repair tip

Doing a front-disc-brake job? Break open the bleeder screws with a piece of hose attached before pushing the pistons back into the calipers. This allows you to push out the old brake fluid, which contains moisture and dirt that can cause corrosion and result in a seized caliper. This can save replacing the calipers later.

# secrets of the superglues

PHOTO BY JOHN B. CARNETT

Have you recently tried one of the super-fast cyanoacrylate glues only to be disappointed by a weak bond or even no bond at all? If so, you are not alone. When those tiny tubes of revolutionary adhesive came out several years back, I tried them dozens of times on all kinds of materials and finally gave up in disgust. Sometimes they worked perfectly, but more often they failed miserably. And everyone I've ever talked to has had the same experience.

It doesn't have to be that way. About two years ago I stumbled onto a brand of cyanoacrylate that really works. This stuff comes in three different viscosities, and the maker, Satellite City, Inc., also offers a spray-on catalyst, or cure accelerator. With this superglue I started getting consistently good results. I talked to experts, learned more about these glues, and began getting even better results. Recently I've found other brands of high-quality cyanoacrylates. I've also learned the reasons behind those early problems.

## Super discovery

Serendipity played a starring role in the discovery of superglue. During World War II, its inventor, Dr. Harry Coover (now president of Loctite Corp.'s new business development group), was a young chemist working at the Kodak Research Laboratories in Rochester, New York, looking for an optically clear plastic for gun sights. "I was working with some ac-

**Cyanoacrylates,** in one- and two-ounce bottles, come in various viscosities. Shown (zigzag from upper left) is Sig Manufacturing's thin type; Pacer Technology & Resources's Zip Kicker (an accelerator that speeds the cure); Slow Jet, an extra-thick formula from Carl Goldberg Models; Pacer's Flex Zap, a thick formula that's more flexible than most when cured; PIC's Stic medium-viscosity formula; and Satellite City's thin formula, Hot Stuff. Set times range from two seconds to two minutes.

rylate monomers that showed promise," he relates. "But everything they touched stuck to everything else. It was a severe pain."

1951 found Coover supervising a group of chemists at the research laboratories of Tennessee Eastman Co. Their mission: To find a tougher, more heat-resistant acrylate polymer for jet canopies. One of the group, Dr. Fred Joyner, spread a film of ethyl cyanoacrylate between a couple of prisms of a refractometer to check its refractive index. He made the measurement, but couldn't pry the prisms apart. "He came to me to report that he had ruined a seven hundred dollar instrument," Coover recalls. "It was then I suddenly realized that we had a unique adhesive." Years of work remained before cyanoacrylate became a viable product. Eastman 910, an industrial adhesive, was introduced in 1958.

Cyanoacrylates are reactive monomers that polymerize (chemically link) when pressed into a thin film—and only then. Under normal conditions "all surfaces have at least a monomolecular layer of water on them," Coover explains. "It's actually the water, or any weak base, that is the catalyst causing the polymerization."

The original cyanoacrylates were water-thin and good for gluing nonporous surfaces only: Metal, glass, rubber, some plastics. Later, thickeners and other agents were added by some companies to adapt the adhesive for wood, leather, ceramics, and such.

All cyanoacrylates bond flesh well, as nearly every user knows. This generally causes no problem, for acetone (lacquer thinner or nail-polish remover) will dissolve the glue and free your flesh. But beware of tots bearing superglue. A medical journal recently described the case of a man who had to have a plug of cyanoacrylate surgically removed from his ear. It seems his three-year-old son squirted in a glob of glue while daddy slept.

## Trouble with superglue

The problems most people have with cyanoacrylates are tame by comparison: merely poor or failed bonds. Why does this happen?

There can be many reasons. Sometimes the trouble starts in the plant. Bob and Bill Hunter, a father and son who head Satellite City, Inc., voiced the same opinion: "Inferior drugstore cyanoacrylates often are of poor quality to begin with."

"Most are imported from Japan or Taiwan, where some producers don't spend enough time in refining," Bob Hunter explains.

"If the cyanoacrylate isn't properly prepared, it will have a short shelf life," Coover elaborates. So the makers of the low-quality stuff add excessive stabilizers to keep it from curing in the tube. "The result is poor performance," Coover goes on, and he explains why: "The stabilizers are acidic materials. If the concentration is too high, it will overcome the catalytic effect of the minute amount of moisture on the substrate and nothing will happen. A lot of the imported materials perform well," he adds, "but those sold at the low end of the market have given cyanoacrylates a bad name."

"Somebody buys the inferior stuff to do a specific job, bonding things that are important," Bill Hunter laments. "The glue fails, and he gets the impression that CA [cyanoacrylate adhesive] is just for fun."

But good CAs—used properly—are not just for fun. They are used every day by hundreds of different industries. Museums soak brittle bones and fossils with the glue; it helps bind them together and give them strength. Burt Rutan used Satellite City adhesives extensively in the construction of his *Voyager,* the lightweight airplane that flew around the world.

CAs can have a tensile strength of 4,000 to 5,000 psi, or roughly four times that of white oak. Says Bill Hunter: "For all practical purposes it's overkill."

## Glues to choose

Some of the products you buy in the tiny tubes at the hardware or drugstore are fine for the quick repair jobs they're made to do. (Coover claims that his company's Duro Quick Gel is "technically the best one out there. It has an additive that makes it, in my judgment, foolproof.")

But the tiny tubes are not convenient for me: I use CAs too profligately. And they are not economical:

**Color-matched wood filler** is easy to make right on your work (above left). Just dribble one of the thicker cyanoacrylates into a crack, hole, or gouge, then sand to pack a slurry of glue and wood dust into the blemish. Mist with kicker, and the repair is cured and ready to finish.

Superglues are super handy for lathe work (above). You can glue small workpieces to a faceplate or, as shown, tack the plate in position on large work to keep it from shifting while you screw it down. The author also used cyanoacrylate to laminate the turning blank that became this Egyptian-style vase—a five-minute job.

Cyanoacrylate plus fiberglass cloth becomes fiberglass-reinforced plastic in less than a minute (left). Here a wood-aluminum joint is being reinforced. The glass was tacked down with a mist coat of 3M 77 rubber-base spray adhesive. A thin cyanoacrylate was then soaked into the cloth and misted lightly with kicker. Strength is exceptional.

I buy cyanoacrylate in one-ounce bottles for around $10. At my local drugstore, a tube containing 0.07 ounce costs $2.50. That works out to nearly $36 per ounce!

After working with Satellite City glues for over a year, I started running into other makers, all marketing CAs for the hobby trade, and like Satellite City, all offering various viscosities—in one- and two-ounce bottles—plus spray-on cure accelerators. Among these makers are Pacer Technology & Resources, Sig Manufacturing Co., PIC, and Carl Goldberg Models. Now (too late to be included in our photos) I've learned that 3M has joined the ranks. There may be others.

I tried some of these products around the shop, and for my purposes, they seemed to work as well as Satellite City products. Others have found significant differences though. When *Scale Radio-Control Modeler Magazine* tested the tensile strength of two cyanoacrylates for a piece it ran in its January-February 1987 issue, Satellite City's Hot Stuff came out on top, "... almost two times stronger on average than the brand with which it was compared," according to the article. In that test fiberglass circuit board was glued to itself. Fiberglass was chosen because it's a difficult test material: smooth, non-porous, and strong enough not to fail before the glue itself.

Nevertheless, when I spoke with the magazine's publisher, Norm Goyer, he pointed out that for most jobs around the home all the products named above serve him well too. Generally, the material being glued will fail before the bond does.

The moral of all this? For simple gluing jobs—involving wood, most plastics, rubber, etc.—any good CA should work. If you have a particularly difficult job—gluing metals or composite materials, for example—it may pay to choose your glue more carefully. Check to see if it conforms to Military Spec MIL-A-46050-C, or ask the maker for test data on the actual materials you plan to glue.

## Use it right, too

Getting good results is more than a matter of buying a quality glue, however. You also need the right formula for the job you're doing, and you have to use it correctly. Rule one is this: Don't expect the water-thin cyanoacrylates to do every job. (Most drugstore brands, unless the tube says otherwise, will be this type.)

"With CAs," notes Tom Nightingale of Pacer Technology & Resources, "the gap-filling capacity is directly related to viscosity." You use the watery versions on parts that are smooth, tight-fitting, and relatively nonporous. These glues set fast; so when gluing a joint you must assemble the parts dry, then apply the adhesive around the edges of the seam. It wicks deep into the joint by capillary action and cures in seconds.

Because these CAs are so thin, they will not wick into loose joints, and they won't bridge gaps. They're not much good on porous materials either. They get soaked up before they can wick throughout the bond area.

That's where the higher-viscosity formulas come in. Makers offer medium viscosities (like syrup) and thick glues (like a mixed epoxy). These are thick enough to bridge small gaps and to resist being sucked out of the joint. You apply them to the surfaces first, then assemble the joint. Consquently they have slower cure rates The thickest usually take about a minute to cure.

But if you are using them on sloppy joints with wide gaps to fill, cure time may extend to minutes or even hours. This is one case where the spray-on cure accelerators are indispensable. Just mist a light coat on one of the mating surfaces. It will dry almosst instantly, but remain active for several minutes. Apply your glue to the other part, then assemble the joint. The accelerator will normally kick the glue over in seconds.

In addition to different viscosities, Pacer makes special formulas such as Poly-Zap for bonding difficult plastics like polycarbonate and polyamide nylon, and Plasti-Zap which contains ingredients to overcome the mold-release agents often found on the surfaces of plastic model parts.

If you have specialized needs—and need large quantities—you might want to investigate the industrial lines of cyanoacrylates. Says Nightingale: "We have over one hundred different formulations and materials in the CA family."

For use around the shop and home, however, the three basic viscosities I've mentioned should be adequate. In fact, I find I don't have much use for the medium-viscosity materials. I either want the fast set and excellent wicking of the thin formulas, or I want the gap-filling ability and the longer assembly times of the thick formulas.

## Sticky but tricky

Cyanoacrylates are odd beasts. So sometimes, despite your best efforts,

you may still have problems with them. Common causes are:

● Poor fit. Even though thick formulas can fill small gaps, the better the fit, the better the bond. Always check mating surfaces before bonding. Smooth them up and remove any burrs or rough spots. Kickers help, but it's best to aim for a good fit in the first place.

● Too much glue. Never use more than necessary. According to Bill Hunter, "Optimum results are obtained with the minimum quantity of adhesive required to fill the joint. In general, one free-falling drop spreads over one square inch." It takes some experience to know how much glue is enough, so it's a good idea to experiment on scraps of your material—making joints, then tearing them apart to check coverage.

● Premature curing. Do not spread your glue before you assemble the parts. This encourages it to start curing. Instead, lay down a serpentine bead, then assemble the parts, letting pressure squeeze the bead out into a thin film.

● Premature stressing. Although CAs cure in a matter of seconds, this initial cure is only about 20 percent of full strength, which is only reached after 8 to 24 hours. Give the bond ample time to cure before subjecting it to much stress.

● Surface contamination. CAs are more tolerant of this than most glues, but they still work best on clean surfaces. Waxes, oils, and *excess* moisture can act as barriers between glue and substrate, and this can lower bond strength.

● Acidic surfaces. Since alkalinity triggers the cure, it's not surprising that acidity inhibits it. To solve this problem, you can use a kicker on one of the mating surfaces. These are essentially organic amines that "supply a heavy dose of alkalinity," as Bill Hunter puts it.

● Low shelf life. The Hunters recommend storing unopened bottles of CA in a freezer. Frozen, the adhesive should last at least two years. Once the bottle is opened, however, shelf life drops to about six months. Moisture in the air gets in, starts the curing process, and the glue gets progressively thicker until it is too gummy to use. They do not recommend refrigerating or freezing bottles that have been opened.

● Cold. Users who store CA in the fridge or freezer may take it out and use it cold. They apply it as usual, and the joint simply falls apart. What happened? "The polymerization is not

terribly sensitive to temperature," explains Coover, "but when the glue is cold it gets thicker, and it may not get squeezed into a thin enough film to expose it adequately to the surface moisture it needs to catalyze."

## Pet projects

Although CAs will do just about any job other glues can handle, most often I find myself using them in unusual ways.

I use them almost daily in the home and shop for dozens of little odd jobs. The most common is tacking. A drop or two will tack a workpiece, a hinge, or a curtain-rod bracket in place so it can't skid out of position while I nail or screw it down. If work tends to slide around on my drill-press table, I tack it down.

To whip the end of a rope I soak it with glue and mist it with kicker. If I need to drive a screw in a tight or awkward spot, I tack the screw to the tip of my screwdriver so I can work one-handed. The photos and captions show more applications.

Bill Hunter has used CA as a wood finish on both his kitchen table and the walnut instrument panel of his Sunbeam Tiger. His technique? Dribble Hot Stuff (Satellite City's thin formula) on the wood, spread it around with a business card, then mist lightly with kicker. Sand lightly with fine paper on a block. Then repeat, applying two or three coats. You can get a matte finish by rubbing with steel wool, or use polishing compound to achieve a high gloss. A complete multi-coat job takes less than half a day.

Using CA with kicker opens up a realm of possibilities. You can lay a thick bead of the viscous stuff and spray kicker over it to create a neat fillet along a seam. By alternately applying glue and kicker you can build up acrylic plastic to any shape you like. A fishing fanatic, I use this technique to build plastic-bodied flies.

The only way you'll ever realize the full potential of CAs is to buy some and have them on hand. I'd suggest a bottle of the thin stuff, a bottle of one of the thickest formulations, and a spray bottle of kicker.

You aren't likely to run into one- or two-ounce bottles of CA in the local drugstore. I've seen these products in hobby shops (model makers love it), but I usually turn to mail-order catalogs aimed at model makers and woodworkers. If you have special needs, or have trouble locating an adhesive, contact the manufacturers directly—*by A. J. Hand.*

# glue guns
# go cordless

When I first reported on glue guns for *Popular Science,* I had to snip off their power cords to arrange them attractively for photography. Such picture-taking peccadilloes aren't required with this latest batch: They're cordless. Hassle-free photography aside, you may find that many of the places you want to use a glue gun are more accessible when you're unhampered by a cord.

As I write, there are six cordless glue guns available, but the way they are proliferating there may be more by the time you read this. New hot-melt adhesives are also sprouting like mushrooms. Not long ago there was one all-purpose glue stick and one kind of caulk available to consumers. Now there are lots of different formulas for different functions. More on that later.

Five of the six cordless glue guns—from Black & Decker, Emhart, Loc-

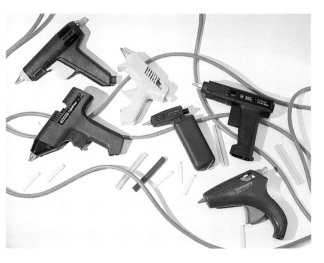

**MANUFACTURERS OF CORDLESS GLUE GUNS**
**Black and Decker,** Box 798, Hunt Valley, MD 21030-0748; **Emhart Home Products Div.** (Thermogrip), Box 13716, Reading, PA 19612; **Loctite Corp.,** 4450 Cranwood Ct., Cleveland, OH 44128; **Parker Group,** 10 Bearfoot Rd., Northboro, MA 01532; **Stanley Tools,** 600 Myrtle Street., New Britain, CT 06050; **Ungar,** Box 6005, Compton, CA 90224-6005.

**On display** (from the left) are some new cordless glue guns: the Parker, Stanley, Loctite, Black & Decker, and Thermogrip.

tite, Parker, and Stanley—have much in common:
- They are batteryless.
- They run cordless for 12 to 15 minutes.
- They heat up in 1½ to 5 minutes.
- They have a dual-connect feature allowing both corded or cordless use.
- They reheat in one to three minutes.
- They accept standard ½-inch glue sticks.
- They are trigger-fed.
- Prices range from $15 to $30.

But be forewarned: These five guns can't stray far from a power source for long. Without batteries, the guns rely instead on an insulated heating chamber to keep the glue at its optimum working temperature. While manufacturers are reluctant to discuss design details, Emhart says its Thermogrip gun's heating chamber is larger than in an AC-powered gun and made of materials that absorb and retain heat.

The batteryless glue guns won't emit a steady bead of hot-melt glue or caulk for their 12- to 15-minute cordless work time, but I found that they remain hot enough during that period to do average, intermittent jobs. You then have to plug them in for two to three minutes to get them back up to temperature. I found that the length of time they function also varies with the brand and type of glue stick or caulk used.

The guns are similar in style, but differ slightly when it comes to their charging stands. Parker's glue gun doesn't have a stand—only a retractable wire bail to keep the gun erect, nozzle pointing down. Thermogrip's and Loctite's both have basic charg-

ing stands. Stanley's bench-mountable work station provides a drip tray as well as storage for extra glue sticks and three additional nozzles. Black & Decker has the most elaborate setup. Its glue gun is sold with or without a Glue Gun Center, which includes storage space for glue sticks and a drip tray. In addition, this base has hot-melt application instructions printed on the side.

The maverick of the untethered breed is Ungar's rechargeable glue gun ($40). It is much smaller than the other five. Nevertheless, it can deliver hot-melt adhesive for approximately 30 minutes—about twice as long as the others. The reason: It's powered by rechargeable nickel-cadmium batteries housed in the handgrip.

The batteries take 14 hours to recharge. After switching on, it takes about 90 seconds for the gun to heat up. The Ungar does have its drawbacks. The gun accepts only ⁵⁄₁₆-inch glue sticks—the standard size is ½ inch—because company designers foresaw their cordless gun gluing in hard-to-reach spots requiring smaller amounts of adhesive. Unlike the other five guns, the Ungar is thumb-fed. Ungar vice president of sales and marketing Richard Shivers reports that continuous thumb feeding should deliver enough hot melt for any task. Like the Parker, the Ungar has no base from which to recharge. It doesn't even have a bail. It does however have a wire loop for convenient hanging. And Ungar offers only one general-purpose-type glue stick to fit this gun.

Along with the new glue guns have come glue innovations, and different formulas are identified by colors.

Thermogrip has introduced three hot-melt adhesives. Besides its Amber All-Purpose, Clear Craft & Hobby, and White Sealer Caulk sticks, the company now features Weatherstrip (a removable nonpermanent clear sealer for windows and doors), Slow Set (formulated for wood and other porous materials, it takes 90 seconds to set), and Color/Craft (available in red, brown, and green).

But the fount of hot-melt innovation is Black & Decker. The company has introduced color-coded glue sticks to make choosing the right glue for a specific project easy. Ten—count 'em ten—formulations, no less. There are five types: All purpose, wood/repair, fabric/leather, plastic/caulk, and ceramic, each in fast- and slow-dry varieties. Color stripes run the length of the sticks, indicating what material they will bond. Orange, for example, identifies the fabric/leather formulation. One color stripe equals fast dry (30 to 60 seconds), two mean slow (90 to 120 seconds). The B&D glue sticks are available in packs of six, boxes of 25 (four-inch), or a four-pack of 10-inch sticks.

I found that being able to control setup time on both big and small jobs and being able to select the best glue for various jobs cut out a lot of guesswork and saved time in the shop.

But what about all those partially used glue sticks as you switch from one formulation to another? For $10 B&D offers a GlueSaver mold set —a small stand with four silicone mold sleeves. Just squirt the molds full of hot glue; when cooled, they peel back to yield new and near-perfect reshaped glue sticks—
*by Phil McCafferty.*
*Photos by John B. Carnett.*

# gel stains

You've just finished stripping and lovingly restoring your grandfather's favorite side table, with its intricate carvings and turned legs. Now you're ready to stain it. But you remember that the watery stain splashes when you stir it and can spray off the end of your brush, puddle in the carvings, drip and run on the turned legs, and, even if you're extra careful, form lap marks between adjacent areas finished at slightly different times. You dread having to face the mess.

You don't have to.

With modern stains called gel or wiping stains, you wipe the color onto the wood with a cloth and avoid all the problems listed above and more. The stains—Behlen's Master Gel, Fabulon's Gel-Eze, Flecto's Varathane X-3D, Formby's Wiping Stain, Minwax's WoodSheen, and Wood-Kote's Gelled Wood Stain—are oil-based formulations that are easier to work with and more forgiving than conventional stains. They also allow you to do things that are difficult if not impossible to do with conventional stains, such as lightening the color or color-matching existing stains as you apply the gel stain.

What exactly are these stains? How

**MANUFACTURERS OF GEL STAINS**
**H. Behlen & Bros.,** Rte. 30 N., Amsterdam, NY 12010; **Fabulon Products,** Box 1505, Buffalo, NY 14240; **The Flecto Co.,** 1000 45th St., Oakland, CA 94608; **Minwax Co.,** 102 Chestnut Ridge Plaza, Montvale, NJ 07645; **Thompson & Formby,** Box 677, Olive Branch, MS 38654; **Wood-Kote,** Box 17192, Portland, OR 97217.

did they originate? How do they differ from conventional stains? How do they perform and what can you expect of them? I visited a leading wood-finish manufacturer's labs and spoke with other experts in the field to find the answers to these questions and more.

Thickened wood-finishing stains are not new. There have been other such products over the years, but according to a spokesman from Thompson & Formby, with the exception of Wiping Stain and Wood-Kote's stain, which were introduced in the late 1960s and have since been reformulated, those products did not perform well and have gone the way of the dodo. This past year, however, seems to have been the year of the gel stain, with the introduction of three new products: Behlen's Master Gel, Minwax's WoodSheen, and Fabulon's Gel-Eze.

The Master Gel and Gel-Eze lines contain separate stains and tung-oil-like top coats, both in thickened form. (Formby's, Flecto's, and Wood-Kote's are stains only.) WoodSheen, says Dorey Lum, Minwax group leader of research and development, is different. "It is a one-step wood-finishing product. Tung oil is mixed in with the stain so it colors and coats the wood at the same time [basically the same principle as the company's conventional-technology Polyshades]," says Lum. With that exception, however, all the products are similar: They are thick rather than watery, and they are applied by wiping onto wood with a cloth or fine (0000) steel wool. I traveled to the research center of Pratt & Lambert (parent company of Fabulon) in Buffalo, New York, to find out more about gel stains.

## Where it all starts

The enameled concrete floor shines under fluoresent lights as I look around me at lab tables, stacks of small birch panels used for color testing, and shelves upon shelves of plastic bottles with hand-lettered labels —resins, colorant dispersions, extenders like calcium carbonate, surfactants like lecithin, solvents, pigments: The stuff of wood-finish research.

Research and Development Group Leader Michael DePietro, a suave bearded gentleman with flecks of salt in his pepper-dark hair and whiskers, explains gel stains to me: "These stains basically contain the same ingredients that conventional stains do, but they have more pigment and vehicle, and therefore a higher solid content. And they contain a polyamide-modified thixotropic alkyd and other thixotropic agents that are mixed into the solution by a high-speed dispersion.

"Thixotropy can be described as false body. Through hydrogen bonding, the molecules in the solution form a soft gel structure. When you shake the solution, you break down the structure. The solution becomes fluid and easy to work with. When it sits, it settles back into a thick consistency. And when you apply shear forces to it, as when you rub it with a cloth, it spreads easily. A similar thixotropic technology is standard in water-based products like latex paint and enamel, and it is easy to 'build a puff' with them. It's much harder with oil-based solutions like these stains."

Paul Schlagter, a slightly rotund jolly technician with over 30 years' tenure at Pratt & Lambert, reaches under one of the lab tables to pull out a cardboard box full of containers of various sizes and descriptions. "Actually, developing the formula wasn't all that difficult," he says as he hoists the box. "That took only a few months' work. It was designing the packaging that was difficult. That held up product development for about a year."

## Squeezing stain

"We thought we wanted a pressurized aerosol dispenser, similar to shaving cream, mousse, or whipped cream, but that gave us all kinds of problems," explains Schlagter. "Once, when I was testing one of the containers, I turned it upside down and pressed the nozzle. Nothing happened. I called my assistant, and as I did I held the can up at an angle. I guess I pressed the nozzle a little, because a wad of coagulated stain shot out of the can with a whoosh! It just missed his head and splattered on the wall. Well, we killed that idea in a hurry."

What Fabulon and other manufacturers settled on was a squeeze bottle made of polyethylene terephthalate (PET) or polyvinyl chloride (PVC) plastic. DePietro says the PET was chosen because, unlike some other kinds of plastic, it doesn't allow oxygen crossover, which would quickly break down the stain. (X-30 and Gelled Wood Stain come in cans; the others, in squeeze bottles.)

Gel stains don't necessarily do a better job than conventional stains. In fact, says Minwax's Lum, "for large jobs such as staining big flat

**Unlike watery** conventional stains, thickened gel stains like this one from Minwax will not run uncontrollably.

panels, conventional stains can be applied twice as fast." It is for the small job—staining a chair or small table with difficult-to-stain vertical and turned surfaces—that gel stains are intended. I found them easy to use with a cloth application, and because there is no settling, especially convenient as I didn't have to stir them every few minutes. The Wood Stain is creamier than the others, all of which are a bit more runny. Because wood doesn't absorb higher-solid-content stain as readily as it does conventional stain, color is easier to control, and you don't get any lapping. Color coverage and quality for all the products are excellent.

Gel stains certainly won't displace conventional wood-finishing stains, especially for those who do high-volume work. But if you just stain small pieces and you want to keep the mess to a minimum, they are hard to beat —*by Timothy O. Bakke. Photo by John B. Carnett.*

# cheaper biscuits

Back in March 1985 when I first reported on biscuit-joining machines for *Popular Science,* two things about them impressed me:

• They were the slickest, fastest, and simplest joint-making tools I had ever seen. (Their business end is a small circular saw blade made for plunge-cutting arc-shaped slots. You squeeze some water-based glue into the slots, then insert mating compressed-beech splines. Soon the glue causes the biscuits to swell. Result: A tight, almost foolproof joint.)

• The pint-size cutters were also the most overpriced tools I had ever seen. My favorite—the Lamello Top —sold for a whopping $580. The cheapest I tested—the Elu—sold for around $330, even at discount.

That's why I was glad when two new biscuit joiners—Freud's import, the JS100, and Porter-Cable's model 555—hit the market recently. Although both carry a list price of around $270, I have seen them for about $180 in discount-tool catalogs. That's low enough to catch the eyes of serious do-it-yourselfers. So I got these two new tools for a hands-on appraisal.

When I unpacked the tools and looked them over, the Freud seemed the winner. Its fence system is far superior to that of the Porter-Cable. It has two clear scales, one calibrated in metric, the other in English units. As you slide the fence up or down to set it, a track system keeps it parallel to the blade. To change it from right-angle to miter work, you loosen two knobs, slide off the fence, flip it over, then slide it back on. Easy.

In contrast, the Porter-Cable has a crude, hard-to-see scale with no calibrations. The fence can easily slip out of line with the blade as you adjust it. And to switch from right-angle to miter work, you have to remove two thumb screws and washers, turn over the fence, then reinsert the screws. Advantage, Freud.

## Put to the test

When I plugged in the machines and put them to work, however, the advantage swung the other way. The Porter-Cable (P-C) is quieter, smoother, and delivers more power to the blade. Though both machines have five-ampere motors, the P-C makes faster cuts. Unless you feed the Freud slowly and carefully into your stock, it will bog down and "walk" to the left (enlarging your slot and throwing the joint out of alignment). It may even stall.

Once its tedious fence is set, the P-C cuts with greater speed. It is also easier to use on miter joints, locking onto your stock to ensure perfect blade alignment. With the Freud, if you don't guide the tool carefully, you can rock it out of line while making miter joints.

Other points: The P-C instruction booklet is better than Freud's. If you don't know how to use a biscuit tool, the instructions that come with the Freud won't help much.

I also like the P-C's trigger switch better than the Freud's slide switch (which is located inconveniently at the side of the housing). In the Freud machine's favor, I like its grip system better. It is in line with the cutter and seems to give better control than the P-C's pistol grip does.

How do these bargain biscuit machines compare with their high-priced predecessors? The Lamello Top is still the tool of choice for a professional woodworker. It will hog out a slot in a second flat, while the P-C might take three and the Freud five or six seconds. The pro looking for a bargain might favor either the Lamello Junior or the Elu. I've recently seen the Junior selling for $299.

That's still too high for the average do-it-yourselfer. If you have $180 to spend, the Freud and the Porter-Cable are both worth considering— *by A. J. Hand.*

**Biscuit-joining tools** cut arc-shaped slots that take football-shaped wooden splines. The "biscuits" come in three sizes (they are shown at center of the photograph) and will reinforce glue joints in hardwoods, softwoods, plywood, and particleboard.

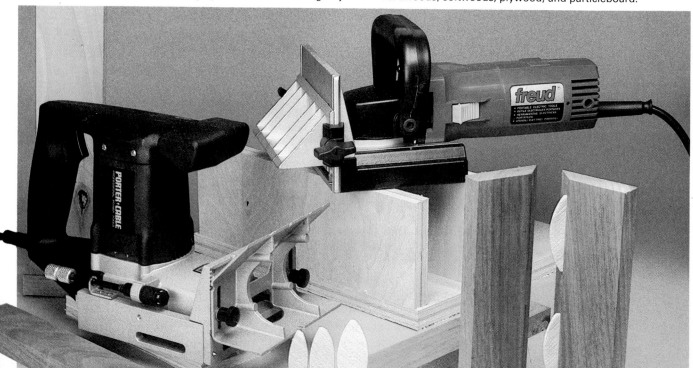

# anti-crush cushions

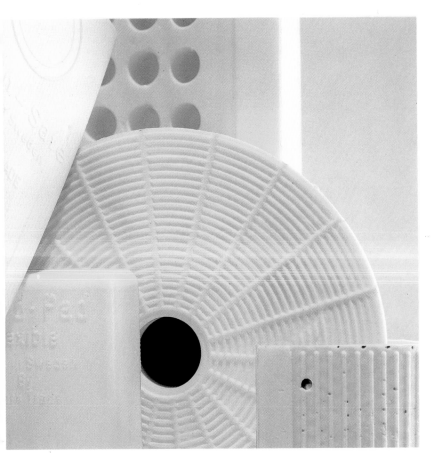

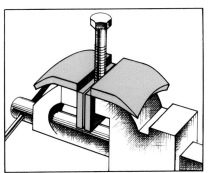

**Vise Pad** (above) prevents damage to delicate screw threading by spreading the applied force over a large area.

During the course of many mechanical tasks, chances are you'll need cushions to protect your workpieces. Now there are specially designed cushioning pads, cast from a tough but pliable plastic, made by Mark Trade Innovations in Stenungsund, Sweden. Mark Trade engineers call the plastic "microcellular polyurethane," a proprietary polymer compound that can deform under pressure up to 85 percent of its volume and still distribute the applied weight evenly over a pad's contact surface.

"The material conforms to any contact surface according to the contour of that surface," says C. W. Lage Jonsson, president of Super Cushion Inc., Mark Trade's United States im-

porter. "It has total molecular memory: Once the pressure is released, it comes back to its original shape," he explains.

Jonsson points out that several other physical properties of the plastic make it well suited for cushioning jobs: It absorbs up to $6\frac{1}{2}$ tons of pressure per square inch, is highly resistant to tearing, and can withstand extreme temperatures (−30 to 120 degrees Centigrade).

The Mark Trade pads come in five shapes and are available from Super Cushion Inc. (Box 302, Ramsey, NJ 07446). Vise Pad ($\frac{1}{4}$ by 4 by 11 inches; $19.95) allows a safe but strong grip of oddly shaped or delicate objects such as the threaded bolt in the drawing above. When using a

car jack or pneumatic lift, Jack Pad (2 by 6 by 7 inches; $23.95) prevents slips that can damage vehicle undercarriages. Marine Pad ($\frac{1}{4}$ by 3 by 15 inches; $23.95 a pair) is designed to be placed between a boat's stern and its outboard-motor screw holds to reduce vibration and wear. Sand Pad (2 by 2 by 6 inches; $8.95) has slots to hold sandpaper or cloths, to make sanding, scrubbing, and polishing uneven surfaces easier. Multi Pad (2 by 5 by 15 inches; $26.95) can be used for a variety of things, such as protecting a car body when towing a trailer or as a fender for a boat's hull. Super Cushion plans to introduce more, possibly larger, shapes for industrial applications—
*by Eduardo R. C. Capulong.*

# air power

Imagine you're at the local home-improvement store, wheeling a shopping cart through aisles of tools. Into the cart go an impact wrench, sabre saw, sander, pneumatic stapler, grinder, and chisel-hammer (or impact chisel). Now imagine the total on the cash register: $300, $500, or more? Not if you're buying the newest breed of hard-working air-powered tools. The total price for the same selection of air-powered tools will be closer to $170.

Since *Popular Science* last looked at air tools, prices have dropped and more tools are available for under $35. The same trend is true for air compressors. Prices are geared more for the home user, and the tools are available in sizes varying from totable ½ horsepower (hp) to heavy-duty 5 hp. And now there are accessories that make the air tools easier to use.

They solve tool-compressor incompatibility and other problems that in the past have steered the do-it-yourselfer away from air tools.

Air tools can do most of the things electric tools can, and they do some jobs much better, such as painting and anything involving a series of impacts—like a power lug wrench. For other jobs—greasing, caulking, power washing and inflating—air tools are the only choice other than muscle or lung power. Air tools are usually lighter than a similar electric tool, they don't overheat, don't lug down, and are generally less expensive to fix when something goes wrong. That's because they run cold and have relatively few parts. They also spare you the hazard of electric shock.

Air tools come in two varieties: air pressure and air power. The first type

includes dusters, washers and paint guns, which do their jobs with escaping pressurized air. Some air-powered tools, such as the scaler, stapler, and chisel hammer, are run by a piston reciprocating in a cylinder. Other air-powered tools, including grinders, drills and shears, are powered by a tiny rotary air motor that, depending on how it is designed, can develop awesome speed and power. A mini-die grinder (used for wood-lettering and etching surfaces), for example, has an air motor that winds up to about 57,000 rpm, yet the whole tool is not much bigger than a fat pencil.

Many of the air tools now available are engineered and priced as consumer versions of industrial-type tools. An example is the versatile air-impact chisel-hammer, which will rip open a rusty muffler connection, cut a panel, punch a hole, or remove a rivet

**The air-tool squadron has arrived**: Central Pneumatic (CP) punch-flange tool from Harbor Freight Salvage Co. (HF) 1. is used for flanging and punching holes in sheet metal. The body saw 2. from HF cuts through sheet metal like butter. CP air file 3. shaves time. HF's die grinder 4. grinds and cleans tight welds. HF offers a CP adjustable-torque reversible screwdriver 5. and an inexpensive ⅜-inch drill 6. HF's Chicago Forge shear 7. cuts up to 18-gauge sheet metal. CP ratchet wrench 8. can be used with standard sockets. CP nibbler 9. is perfect for contouring up to 16-gauge sheet metal.

**WHERE TO GET THEM:**

Air tools and compressors are available in many DIY, auto-supply, and builder's stores, but these firms sell a large variety of equipment by mail: **Dynamic Power,** 1401 Business Center Dr., Conyers GA 30207; **Eastwood Co.,** Box 296, Malvern PA 19355; **Harbor Freight Salvage Co.,** 3491 Mission Oaks Blvd., Camarillo CA 93011; **Kitts Industrial Tools,** 22384 Grand River Ave., Detroit MI 48219; **Northern Handyman's Headquarters,** Box 1499, Burnsville MN 55337-0499; **Sears, Roebuck & Co.,** Sears Tower, Chicago IL 60684; **Trend-Lines,** 375 Beacham St., Chelsea MA 02150; **U.S. General,** 100 Commercial St., Plainview NY 11803; **Wholesale Tool Co.,** Box 68, Warren MI 48090

Some manufacturers of air tools and compressors: **Black & Decker Corp.,** 10 N. Park Dr., Hunt Valley MD 20130; **Campbell Hausfeld Co.,** 100 Production Dr., Harrison OH 45030; **DeVilbiss Co.,** Box 913, Toledo OH 43692; **Ingersoll-Rand Co.** (ChargeAir Pro brand), Box 241154, Charlotte NC 28224; **Sanborn Mfg.,** 5909 Baker Rd., Suite 515, Minnetonka MN 55345; **Thomas Industries,** 1419 Illinois Ave., Sheboygan WI 53081-0029

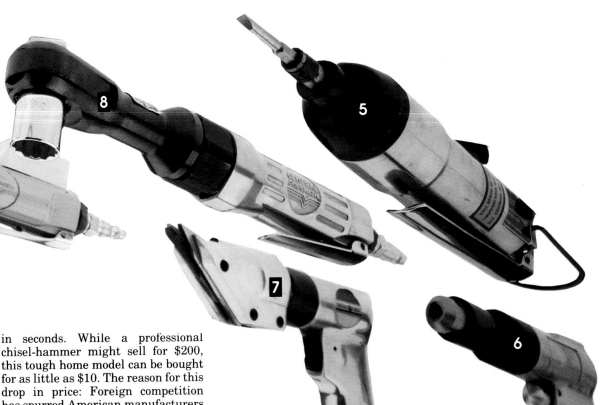

PHOTO BY MITCHELL & BENSON PHOTOGRAPHY, INC.

in seconds. While a professional chisel-hammer might sell for $200, this tough home model can be bought for as little as $10. The reason for this drop in price: Foreign competition has spurred American manufacturers to lower their prices and increase the volume of do-it-yourself air tools.

One factor that used to cause do-it-yourselfers to steer clear of air tools was the initial investment in an air compressor. Now compressor prices are down too. Those designed primarily for home use range from ½ to 5 hp and cost $100 to $600 for some versatile new models. In the past compressors with more than 1½ hp generally required 220 volts, and therefore a special circuit, for home use. But now innovations in motor technology have brought 2-hp engines to 110-volt compressors. This is good news for the home user because a two-horse compressor gives you enough extra power to get the best results from a wide range of air tools without having to spend too much money.

## Choosing a compressor

Now that there are so many home-size compressors on the market, it's hard to decide which one is right for your needs. The table accompanying this article is a good guide. Some tools require large volumes of air, measured in cubic feet per minute (cfm), while other tools, like the chisel-hammer, require lots of air pressure, measured in pounds per square inch (psi). But then there are tools like grease guns and air brushes that require relatively low psi and cfm. Almost all air tools will list required air volume and pressure in their specs. Although many tools will run with a less powerful compressor than shown in the

**1. Combination filter-oiler** from Robert Bosch mounts on a compressor's air tank and filters out water, oil, and foreign material, and also regulates and mist-lubricates the air. Portable air tank (right), shown with inflator unit provides air for smaller jobs.

**2. Plug them in anywhere:** These new 2-hp tank-mounted compressors run on 110V rather than the usual 220V. The Ingersoll-Rand unit at the right is a belt driven one, while the Campbell Hausfeld compressor operates on direct drive.

**3. Central Pneumatic's new variable-speed sabre saw** is cool running but hard working. Here it's paired with a handy retracting hose reel from Harbor Freight Salvage that keeps the hose safely away from the saw's blade and neatly coiled when not in use.

table, they are not likely to perform as they should.

The specifications for home-size compressors give the units' rated cfm capacity at 40 and 90 psi because as air pressure increases, volume of air delivery decreases. The specs also list maximum operating pressure, which increases with compressor horsepower. The maximum pressure on most ½- to 1½-hp compressors is 100 psi; 125 psi on 2- to 5-hp models.

Besides horsepower and air delivery, there are other differences among compressors. For one, you can choose between an oiled or an oil-less unit. An oil-less model is most convenient if you are going to be using a paint sprayer. Dirty oil from the crankcase mixed in with the paint you're applying can be disastrous. Oil-less compressors are generally

low-horsepower models only. In some a motor drives a flexible diaphragm that compresses incoming air. Others use pistons made from no-stick materials to compress the air. Piston-type oiled compressors are the only choice for compressors over 1 hp.

Compressors up to 2 hp also come with either direct or belt drives. Direct-drive units are more compact; they don't need shielding to keep hands and debris away from the belt; and they may be less expensive.

The final choice you have to make is whether to buy a compressor with a tank or without. Compressors with tanks can store air, so the unit only runs when tank pressure drops below the outgoing air-pressure setting. Tank sizes vary (generally they hold 12 or 20 gallons), depending on how much reserve you want. Tankless

compressors (only available in units of 1 hp and below) run all the time, so that any air not used is bled off.

## Cleaned and oiled (a little)

Compressed air can be dirty, wet, and oily. That's because air coming into the unit may be dusty; when air is compressed, water condenses out; and outgoing air picks up oil from the compressor pistons. Most compressors do not come equipped with filters on the output line, and this can be bad news for a paint job. Solution: Add a filter to the system, either in the air line or at the compressor.

In some cases, though, more oil is desired. Air tools with reciprocating pistons and rotary air motors need tiny amounts of clean oil for internal lubrication. One way to handle this is to put a drop of oil in the tool's air inlet each day. A more certain way is to use an air mist lubricator at the tool or at the compressor air line.

A new accessory for solving filtering and oiling problems is an innovative combination filter, regulator, and lubricator from Robert Bosch Corp. (North Suburban, IL). The one-piece unit combines three functions in about the same space a conventional filter takes. And as a plus, it also reduces the pressure drop caused by three separate units.

Possibly the biggest reason for homeowners' wariness of air tools is that you cannot automatically expect to couple any tool with any compressor. But this incompatibility problem can be easily overcome if each tool is fitted with a quick-separating snap

coupler that will automatically shut off the air as it is uncoupled from the compressor.

Other accessories that are easing the way for air tools include a retracting hose reel and Ingersoll-Rand Co.'s new AirBench. The AirBench is a combination portable workbench and storage chest specifically designed for air-power equipment. It has three air outlets, a gauge, regulator, and hose, and storage for a compact compressor and auxiliary air tank.

I'm often asked what my favorites are. I recommend one of the new 110-volt two-horse compressors. If you have the money (I saw them priced at under $500), the space, and 220 volt service, one of the light-duty 5 hp compressors would be ideal. If you're

inclined to take your air on the road, a tankless 1-hp rig and a totable storage tank are good choices.

As far as tools go, a high-quality paint gun is a must, as is a tiny airbrush for touch-ups, shading, and the like. I seldom find use for anything bigger than a ⅜-inch-drive impact wrench. For metalwork I wouldn't be without my filer, nibbler, and shear. I guess I've worn out a couple of chisel-hammers because they get used so much. And I'll never drive another staple or lay a bead of caulk by hand as long as I have air. Finally, I use sand blasters frequently for more than just cleaning and rust removal: They're fantastic for etching glass, making wood signs, and more—*by Phil McCafferty*.

## Air-tool and accessory application chart

| Tool/Accessory | ½ Hp No tank | ½ Hp Tank | ¾ Hp No tank | ¾ Hp Tank | 1 Hp, No tank | 1 Hp, Tank mounted | 1½ Hp, Tank mounted | 2 Hp, Tank mounted | 3 Hp, Tank mounted | 5 Hp, Light duty | 5 Hp, Single stage |
|---|---|---|---|---|---|---|---|---|---|---|---|
| ¼–⅜-in. ratchet-impact wrench | | | | ○ | ○ | ○ | ● | ● | ● | ● | ● |
| ½-in. impact wrench | | | | ○ | ○ | ○ | ○ | ● | ● | ● | ● |
| 1-in. impact wrench | | | | | | | | | | ○ | ● |
| All-purpose spray gun | ● | ● | ● | ● | ● | ● | ● | ● | ● | ● | ● |
| Professional spray gun | | | | | | | | ● | ● | ● | ● |
| Heavy-duty spray gun | | | | ○ | ● | ● | ● | ● | ● | ● | ● |
| Spray cleaner | | | | | | ○ | ○ | ● | ● | ● | ● |
| 6-in. dual-action sander | | | | | | | ○ | ● | ● | ● | ● |
| 4-in. orbital pad sander | | | | | | ○ | ● | ● | ● | ● | ● |
| 7-in.-dia. sander polisher | | | | | | | | ● | ● | ● | ● |
| Paint tank (small) | ● | ● | ● | ● | ● | ● | ● | ● | ● | ● | ● |
| Stapler (small) | ○ | ● | ● | ● | ● | ● | ● | ● | ● | ● | ● |
| Nailer (small) | ○ | ● | ● | ● | ● | ● | ● | ● | ● | ● | ● |
| Heavy-duty nailer or stapler | | | | | | | | | | ● | ● |
| Chisel-hammer | | | | ○ | ○ | ○ | ● | ● | ● | ● | ● |
| ⅜-in. drill | | | | | ○ | ○ | ● | ● | ● | ● | ● |
| Sandblaster | | | | | ○ | ○ | ○ | ● | ● | ● | ● |
| Duster | ● | ● | ● | ● | ○ | ● | ● | ● | ● | ● | ● |
| Heavy-duty blow gun | | | | | ○ | ○ | ● | ● | ● | ● | ● |
| Inflator | ● | ● | ● | ● | ● | ● | ● | ● | ● | ● | ● |
| Airbrush | ● | ● | ● | ● | ● | ● | ● | ● | ● | ● | ● |
| Drain cleaner | ● | ● | ● | ● | ● | ● | ● | ● | ● | ● | ● |
| Caulk and grease guns | ● | ● | ● | ● | ● | ● | ● | ● | ● | ● | ● |
| Sabre saw | | | | | | | | ● | ● | ● | ● |
| Die grinder | | | | | ○ | ● | ● | ● | ● | ● | ● |
| Nibbler | | | | | | | ○ | ● | ● | ● | ● |
| Shear | | | | | | | | ● | ● | ● | ● |
| Flanger punch | | | | | | | ○ | ● | ● | ● | ● |
| Needle scaler | | | | | | | | ○ | ● | ● | ● |
| Filer | | | | | | | ○ | ● | ● | ● | ● |
| 3-in. disc abrasive cutoff | | | | | | ● | ● | ● | ● | ● | ● |
| Undercoating gun | | | | | | | | ● | ● | ● | ● |
| 4-in.-dia. angle grinder | | | | | | | | | ○ | ● | ● |
| Hacksaw | | | | | | | ○ | ● | ● | ● | ● |
| In-line body sander | | | | | | | | ● | ● | ● | ● |
| Screwdriver | | | | | | | | ○ | ● | ● | ● |
| Air-hydraulic rivet gun | | | | | | | ○ | ● | ● | ● | ● |

●–Needed for heavy-duty use    ○–Suitable for light-duty use

DRAWING BY ELIOT BERGMAN

# 8 tricks with air tools

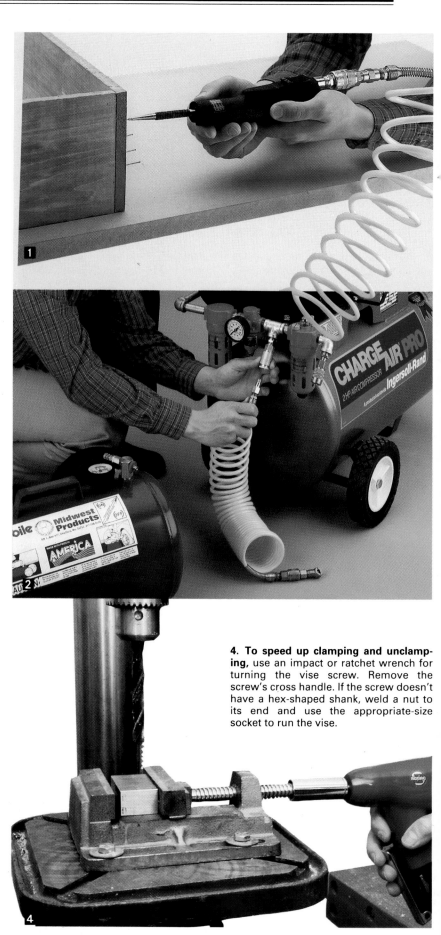

**1. An air filer** makes a great close-quarters brad driver. Just grind or turn down nail-set shanks to fit the filer chuck—a bit under ¼ inch as shown. The rig quickly and effortlessly drives in the fasteners.

**2. You can have** both clean dry air and clean oiled air available at your compressor if you modify a filter-regulator-oiler unit as shown—with a pipe T inserted between the regulator and oiler. Hooking up right out of the regulator gives dry air; hooking up to the oiler gives lubed air.

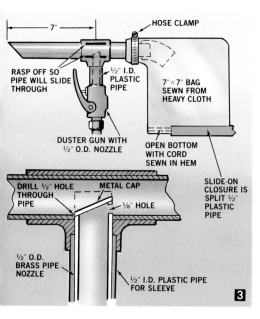

RASP OFF SO PIPE WILL SLIDE THROUGH

7"

HOSE CLAMP

½" I.D. PLASTIC PIPE

7" × 7" BAG SEWN FROM HEAVY CLOTH

DUSTER GUN WITH ½" O.D. NOZZLE

OPEN BOTTOM WITH CORD SEWN IN HEM

SLIDE-ON CLOSURE IS SPLIT ½" PLASTIC PIPE

DRILL ½" HOLE THROUGH PIPE

METAL CAP

⅛" HOLE

½" O.D. BRASS PIPE NOZZLE

½" I.D. PLASTIC PIPE FOR SLEEVE

**3. Make an air-powered vacuum** from a duster gun, pieces of plastic pipe, and a stitched-up cloth bag. It's handy for quick vacuum cleanups around the shop and car. Cut the gun's brass nozzle to about 1¾ inch with a ten-degree bevel. Solder a thin metal cap over bevel, as sketched above, and adjust the nozzle within the ½-inch plastic sleeve so bottom of the ⅛-inch hole clears inside of the big pipe by about 1⁄16 inch. Don't bond pipe joints till you make trial assembly for testing.

**4. To speed up clamping and unclamping,** use an impact or ratchet wrench for turning the vise screw. Remove the screw's cross handle. If the screw doesn't have a hex-shaped shank, weld a nut to its end and use the appropriate-size socket to run the vise.

**5. A die grinder** is for shaping and polishing metal, but its ¼-inch collet chuck lets you use rotary burrs, rasps, and the structured carbide burrs shown, turning it into a powerful woodcarving tool.

PHOTOS BY PHIL MCCAFFERTY

**6. Regrind appropriately shaped metal** cutting bits to wood-chisel cutting angles (check any hand-tool manual), and you've got a power woodcarver/chisel. Just throttle the impact tool so it hammers slowly, and guide the chisel shank when you start to make a cut.

**7. A straight-line sander** for auto-body use works on long boards as well. Tape a small cloth patch over the exhaust to prevent oil spatters on fine woodwork. The same holds true for the pad sander that is in the background.

**8. Make a simple blaster cabinet** for cleaning and etching small parts with a portable gun. It keeps abrasive from being blown around and collects it for reuse. Select a sturdy carton, and tape the frames and plastic in place with duct tape. You should still use gloves, a respirator, and goggles.

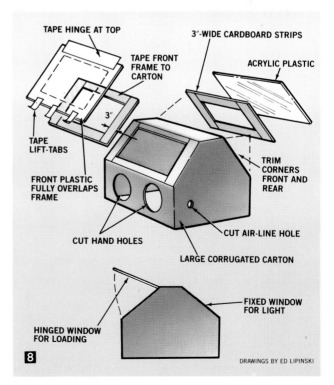

TAPE HINGE AT TOP

3"-WIDE CARDBOARD STRIPS

TAPE FRONT FRAME TO CARTON

ACRYLIC PLASTIC

3"

TAPE LIFT-TABS

TRIM CORNERS FRONT AND REAR

FRONT PLASTIC FULLY OVERLAPS FRAME

CUT AIR-LINE HOLE

CUT HAND HOLES

LARGE CORRUGATED CARTON

FIXED WINDOW FOR LIGHT

HINGED WINDOW FOR LOADING

DRAWINGS BY ED LIPINSKI

# instant workshop

This Australian-made tool table is for do-it-yourselfers who own portable power tools but lack the stationary—or even bench-top—tools required to do quality woodworking. "It's a machine that I began developing in 1975 because I couldn't cut straight with my power saw and I didn't feel comfortable using it hand held," says George Lewin, the inventor.

With the Triton Workcentre MK 3 plus the appropriate tool, you can mimic several workshop mainstays: Mount your portable circular saw below the work surface, and you have a table-saw equivalent. Mount it on rails above the work surface, and it performs radial-arm-saw functions.

With the optional router/jigsaw package, you can transform your router into an overhead router when you mount the tool above the table—or into a shaper when you mount the tool below. Your jigsaw, mounted beneath the table, performs band-saw-like functions.

According to Triton's inventor as well as several woodworking experts, it is a safe and precise piece of machinery. "There is no slipping," says Lewin. "You soon find that your limitations come from your tools, not the table," agrees Grant Pearce, an enthusiastic user, in the British magazine *Woodworker*.

The Triton adjusts to accept any circular saw, from 6½ to 10¼ inches, and takes most routers and jigsaws. It measures about 25 by 40 by 14 inches and folds down flat, so it's stowable in a basement or garage and is easy to tote to the car. A 28-page instruction manual and an optional three-hour videotape make assembly clear.

The Workcentre with saw carriage is about $199; the router/jigsaw table is $40. Triton Manufacturing & Design Co. Pty. Ltd. is located in Cheltenham, Australia. The U.S. distributor is Fred Meyer (Box 42121, Portland, OR 97242)—
*by Jennifer Hume.*

**With Triton's two table-top** configurations you can use your circular saw in the radial-saw mode for cross cuts (lead photo) then convert it to the table-saw mode for ripping (insert).

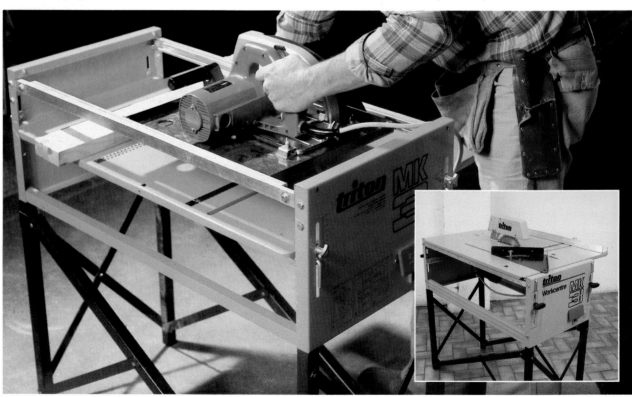

# master your monster (router)

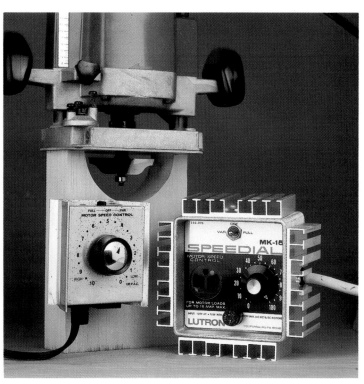

**The Lutron MK-15** (right) and MLCS RSC-15 variable-speed controls let you dial the ideal router speed for any bit in your arsenal, even a big panel raiser.

Remember the basic routing law: The bigger the bit, the slower the router should run. Until lately you had two choices: Obey the law and spend $500 for a variable-speed router, or break it and use a cheaper single-speed model. The penalty for law breaking? Possible burning, chipping, chatter—even broken bits.

Now two little silver boxes—the MLCS RSC-15 and Lutron MK-15—offer another solution: They're electronic speed controls. After a week's testing, I decided they're an indispensable accessory for a single-speed half-inch router. Just plug your router into one, make a test cut or two, and you can quickly find the ideal speed for any bit. And having the controls in a separate box is safer and more convenient if you use your router in a shaper table: Mount the box where it's easy to reach, and you needn't fumble under the table for the router switch.

How do they work? In both, an inner electronic device rapidly turns the circuit on and off, changing incoming voltage to maintain the desired speed.

Both also have nearly identical controls, a three-position switch with settings for full-speed on, variable-speed on, and off, plus a control dial with numbered settings. But the smaller, lighter MLCS has a clip so you can fasten it to your belt for hand-held routing. It also has the lower price: $40. The Lutron is more impressively built, with a heavy-duty aluminum heat sink, and lists for $160.

Is the Lutron worth the extra money? I don't know. Both operate about the same. The Lutron has smoother no-load performance at low speeds. But when you apply a load to the router, it runs smoothly with either control. I also tested for overheating by running a router on each at half-speed nonstop for 20 minutes. The MLCS warmed a bit; the Lutron remained stone cold. In a production situation it would probably outlast the MLCS, but for home-shop work the MLCS should be adequate.

Because these controls will work with all universal motors that don't exceed their 15-ampere rating, you can also use them with other portable power tools, including drills, grinders, buffers, sanders, and saws —*by A. J. Hand.*

**MANUFACTURER'S ADDRESSES**
Lutron Electronics, 205 Suter Rd., Coopersburg, PA 18036; MLCS, Box 4053, Rydal, PA 19046.

This sanding station ensures that sanded workpiece edges remain square to surface. Always apply work against the downward-rotating face of the drum. Plans for making this and other accessories are on following pages.

PHOTO BY RAY CURLETTI

# get more from your drill

*Reprinted by permission of Home Mechanix magazine.*

Accessories have so changed the way many people think of a portable drill that perhaps it's time to rename the tool. The name implies that the tool has only one function, namely, drilling holes.

Instead, the simple electric drill has evolved into—at its versatile best —a "variable-speed, reversible, hand-held motor for turning accessories." And these accessories, in turn, allow it to sand contoured surfaces, do buffing and wire brushing chores, mix paint, cut plugs or short dowels, pump water in emergency situations and perform like a small drill press.

On top of all this, magnetic screw-bit holders and specialty devices like the Dimpler pictured on page 171 make the difficult task of driving screws so easy that, if you never drill a hole, it would still be worth buying the tool just to drive and remove screws.

Be warned, however, that the list of available accessories may be larger than your bank account. For the sake of economy and to avoid cluttering your work area, the first rule is to buy accessories only as you need them. And before you buy, consider the following: how much does an accessory cost, what work will it do, how often will it be used and what are the alternatives? See page 173 for my personal evaluation of popular drill accessories.

## Tips on various accessories

● A problem with freehand drilling is the difficulty of holding the bit perpendicular to work surfaces. Although you can judge by eye or use a square—there are even levels that attach to a drill—you can't expect freehand operation to produce precise results.

A vertical drill guide accessory is

# accessorize your drill

PHOTOS BY THE AUTHOR

Start a hole saw (above) at very slow speed. Increase speed only to the point that the tool cuts consistently and without motor strain. (Photos show band and cup types.)

Impact mode on a hammer drill can be used with special cutters like gouges and straight chisels (left). Its reciprocal action occurs only when the cutter is pressed against work.

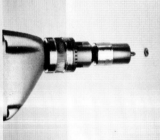

Dimpler (above), with optional magnet, converts a drill to a drill/driver. It installs drywall screws to precisely the right depth.

the next best thing to a drill press. A guide is not as precise as a stationary press but it has the advantage of portability. And, at $30 to $40, it is much cheaper. With most guides the chuck of the drill is removed from the shaft and attached to the guide, which in turn is attached to the drill shaft.

Manufacturers also offer a special stand which allows a portable drill to be used as a miniature drill press. Be sure to check if your drill and the stand are compatible. Bolt the stand to a solid surface or to a block that can be clamped in a vise.

● A glue joint reinforced with dowels is a good method for joining boards edge-to-edge. The holes for the dowels must be positioned accurately and be bored at precise right angles to the work's edge. A doweling jig accurately locates and bores perpendicular holes; and a stop that is secured to the bit ensures correct drilling depth. (Stops are often supplied with jigs but can be purchased separately). Various doweling jigs, adjustable for different stock thicknesses, are available.

● Hiding screws is done by driving them into counterbored holes and then filling the hole with a plug. Use a plug cutter accessory to form plugs. You can cut plugs, with or across the grain, from any available piece of

## SANDING STATION AND ACCESSORIES

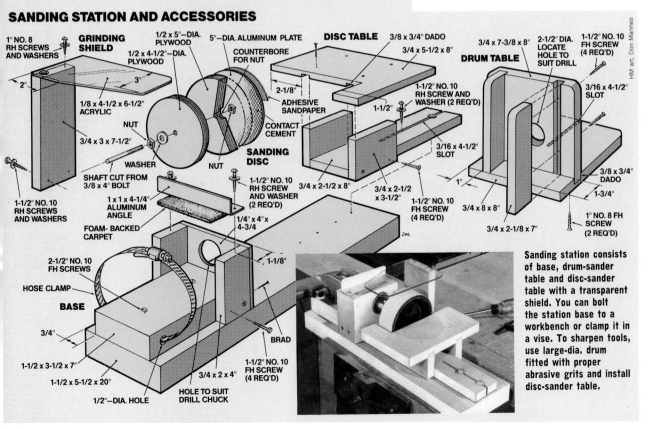

Sanding station consists of base, drum-sander table and disc-sander table with a transparent shield. You can bolt the station base to a workbench or clamp it in a vise. To sharpen tools, use large-dia. drum fitted with proper abrasive grits and install disc-sander table.

# accessories that you can buy

Vertical drill guide bores holes perpendicular to work surface. By extending the posts through base, guide centers holes in stock edges.

Drill-operated pump saves time and effort when you're faced with draining a fountain or clearing a clogged drain. It can move up to 200 gal. per hour depending on drill rpm. Outlet hose can be up to 100 ft. long, but intake hose is limited to 10 ft.

Boring dowel holes is best done with a doweling jig. One type, left, automatically centers the bit. Others, like the one shown at right, adjust to stock thicknesses. All allow boring of various hole diameters.

wood and from any wood species. Alternately, dowels can be cut off to be used as plugs, but dowels are usually only available in birch or maple, may not be handy when you need them and their diameters are not always consistent. Some plug cutters form straight cylinders while others are designed to round off the top end of the plug for its easy insertion in the hole.

● Special cutters called hole saws can bore larger holes than conventional bits. Some are cup-like devices with saw teeth on the rim, each saw producing a specific size hole. Others are adjustable for cutting a range of hole sizes. The cutting capacity of the latter ranges from 1 inch to 3 inch diameter, while individual hole saws are available up to 6 inch diameter.

● Chisel and gouge accessories, like those commonly used with compressed-air tools, can be used in a hammer drill to carve wood, clean out drilled mortises and remove plaster and tile. Set controls for hammer-action alone. And don't forget that a hammer drill can operate like a conventional drill.

Some accessories or jigs are simple to make, requiring just minutes; others, like the sanding station, need more time to construct but still make

# accessories that you can make

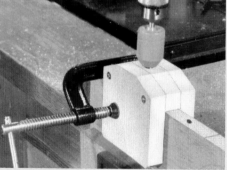

You can make a doweling jig for a particular stock thickness, in this case ¾ in. The jig can be clamped to the work or hand-held. Marks on workpiece indicate jig position.

**EDGE DRILLING GUIDE**

3/8"–DIA. HOLE
3/8–DIA. x 1-1/4" BUSHING
1-1/2"
3/4"
1/2"
1"
1-1/2" NO. 10 FH SCREW (4 REQ'D)
3/4 x 4 x 4" BLOCK (2 REQ'D)
3/4 x 1-1/4" x 4" BLOCK

**CENTERING DRILL GUIDE**

WASHER (2 REQ'D)
3/8"–DIA. BUSHING
WING NUT (2 REQ'D)
1"
3/8"–DIA. HOLE
1/2 x 1 x 16"
3/16 x 1-1/2" FH MACHINE SCREW (2 REQ'D)
1/2" x 1" x 3" (2 REQ'D)
1/2" RAD.

Shop-made centering guide (art, photo) allows accurate boring in exact center of boards up to 12 in. wide or in stock edges. If you want to mark (not drill) the center, use a pencil in bushing instead of drill bit.

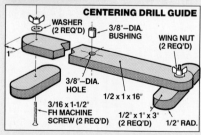

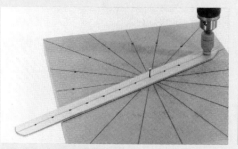

This easily made guide is used for drawing circles and for boring or marking a series of holes in various circumferences from 1-in. to 12 in. The point aligns it with radial lines marked on the work. The stop on the drill bit controls the depth of holes.

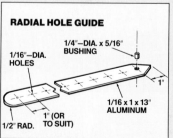

**RADIAL HOLE GUIDE**

1/4"–DIA. x 5/16" BUSHING
1/16"–DIA. HOLES
1"
1/16 x 1 x 13" ALUMINUM
1/2" RAD.
1" (OR TO SUIT)

# what do you really need?

The chart below rates some of the more popular drill accessories according to how valuable they've been to me over the years.

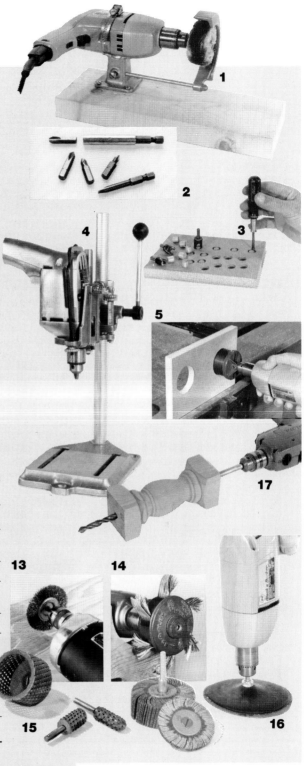

## I'D NEVER BE WITHOUT THESE...

| | | |
|---|---|---|
| **1** | **Horizontal stand** | Allows use of drill as stationary tool for buffing, polishing and sanding. |
| **2** | **Magnetic bit holder** | Frees one hand to hold workpiece, interchangeable bits. |
| **3** | **Plug cutters** | Make screw-hiding plugs from any wood species available. |
| **4** | **Drill press stand** | Makes drill a miniature drill press. |
| **5** | **Adjustable hole saw** | Makes hole sizes that can't be bored using conventional bits. |
| **6** | **Drill stops** | Maintain precise control of hole depth. |
| **7** | **Screw-hole bits** | Bore the countersink, pilot and shank holes for screws in a single step. |
| **8** | **Countersinks** | Necessary for flat-head screws in metal; also available for wood screws. |
| **9** | **Doweling jig** | Positions and guides drill bit to bore dowel holes in board edges to be joined. |
| **10** | **Drill guide** | Ensures that holes will be perpendicular to work surface. |
| **11** | **Water pump** | For emergency use to clear a clogged drain or flooded basement. |
| **12** | **Paint mixer** | Inexpensive aid for stirring paint. |

## THESE ARE NICE TO HAVE...

| | | |
|---|---|---|
| **13** | **Wire brush** | Hastens cleaning and buffing of metals. |
| **14** | **Flap-type sanders** | Reach into recesses on curved surfaces, wrought-iron furniture. |
| **15** | **Rotary rasps** | Reduce irregular surfaces. |
| **16** | **Flexible disc sander** | For preliminary work when smoothing rough surfaces, minor auto body repair. |
| **17** | **Extension drill or shaft** | Bores extra-deep holes. |
| **18** | **Buffing pad** | Used over flexible sanding disc for polishing work. |
| **19** | **Right-angle drive** | Good for working in tight spaces. |
| **20** | **Flexible shaft** | A favorite accessory of wood carvers, it allows drilling in tight spaces. |

## I DON'T RECOMMEND...

| | | |
|---|---|---|
| **21** | **Major tools (band saw, belt sander, small lathe) powered by drill motors** | Don't perform well, are underpowered and may result in damage to drill. |
| **22** | **Edge-shaping cutters (router-bits)** | Difficult to control; drill lacks adequate speed to cut well. |

fun weekend projects. Why make them? They often improve your accuracy or save you time when you need them. They extend the usefulness of a drill. And many accessories and jigs are not available commercially. Perhaps the best reason is because of the satisfaction you can get from just inventing and building the device—*by R. J. DeCristoforo.*

**WORTH WRITING TO**

Drill bits and accessories not found at home centers or hardware stores are available by mail.
**Brookstone Company,** 127 Vose Farm Rd., Dept. HM688, Peterborough, NH 03458; **Constantine's,** 2050 Eastcester Rd., Dept. HM688, Bronx, NY 10461; **Garrett Wade,** 161 Avenue of the Americas, Dept. HM688, New York, NY 10013; **Trend-lines,** 375 Beacham St., Dept. HM688, Chelsea, MA 02150; **Woodcraft,** 41 Atlantic Ave., Box 4000, Dept. HM688, Woburn, MA 01888; **The Woodworker's Store,** Dept. HM688, Rogers, MN 55374; **Woodworker's Supply of New Mexico,** 5604 Alameda Pl. N.E., Dept. HM688, Albuquerque, NM 87113.

# smart house

**Remote monitoring will be possible: Where's Charles the Snacker? The occupancy detector says someone's in the kitchen. The fridge door's sensor tells all.**

"**F**ire in den! Fire in den! Exit through bedroom door. Fire department alerted. Exit immediately!" The insistent voice, with its syntho twang, repeated the urgent message.

Instead of exiting through the bedroom door as instructed, we stood intrigued—in the den, no less—and discussed the electronics that made the message possible.

With me were Robert K. Aasen, senior principal engineer in Honeywell's corporate systems development division, and Keith Phillips, vice president for the marketing of a group called Smart House Limited Partnership. Location: Honeywell House, a home-automation laboratory built to look like a real house, but built *inside* the companay's sprawling research facility in Golden Valley, Minnesota.

To demonstrate the fire response, Aasen had taken a spray can of smoke and squirted a shot into a smoke detector in the den. That triggered a string of events—from the smoke sensor, microprocessors, a voice-enunciation chip, occupancy sensors, and a telephone linkage. It was the capstone to Aasen's demonstration of home-automation possibilities that are built into the test house.

To achieve the desired effects, though, Honeywell applied lots of technical expertise and spent some $400,000 on wiring and electronics. But imagine a house that could perform feats like this for an affordable price; a house that would have all the wiring in the walls to allow your appliances—gas and electric—to communicate with each other and with such outside services as utilities, cable and satellite television, and even the appliance repair shop.

Impossible?

More like inevitable.

My visit to Honeywell House was actually an adjunct to another mission: To pick the brains of a group of engineers, dubbed the Tiger Team, who spent last summer and fall at Honeywell's lab working out the initial technical details of a sweeping program intended to make the automated home the standard dwelling before we're far into the new century. The concept, called Smart House, was conceived by the National Association of Home Builders Research Foundation and eventually spun off as Smart House Development Venture (then changed to Smart House Limited Partnership).

Basically, Smart House is an integrated wiring scheme with a battalion of microprocessors running the show. Smart House advocates say it would bring improved safety, better security, advanced entertainment features, greater convenience, improved comfort, superior communications capability, and reduced energy costs. But others are traveling toward similar goals. And they may be catching different buses. More on that later.

## Smart idea

In November 1984 David MacFadyen, then executive vice president (now president) of the NAHB Research Foundation, and generally considered the father of Smart House, invited more than 100 manufacturing firms, trade associations, and government agencies to a seminar to discuss the concept, which would require redesigning the electric and electronic services of a house in a coordinated fashion.

The just-passed National Cooperative Research Act modified certain provisions of antitrust laws to allow re-

**Smart House controls need not be centralized. Small panels, much like a programmable thermostat, can be located wherever they're wanted.**

Moisture sensors, a set program, or some combination can determine when the lawn gets watered. If a water shortage necessitated rationing, the water utility could overrule the program and only allow watering according to its rules.

Control of doors can be based on voice-recognition circuitry. Thus members of the household can come and go with a spoken command. With a camera aimed at the door, occupants can screen visitors—and unlock the door from a remote location.

Smart heating, cooling, and ventilating systems will respond to factors besides room temperature. Humidity, indoor air quality, whether a room is empty or occupied—even the utility rate—can be factored in. Comfort will be improved and less energy used.

Smart appliances can communicate with each other. For example, the washer could flash a message on the TV screen: WASH CYCLE FINISHED; MOVE CLOTHES TO DRYER AT NEXT COMMERCIAL.

search and development consortiums, and Smart House Development Venture was the first to be formed under it. Eventually 44 manufacturers signed on, including such biggies as General Electric, Whirlpool, Honeywell, Apple Computer, Kohler, Carrier, Lennox, Square D, and many more with similar standing. In addition, service providers such as electric and gas utilities signed on as advisory council members.

Builders got their first look at Smart House wizardry at the NAHB's 1986 convention. Two vans, one for gas appliances and one for electric, were set up in the Dallas convention center to show what Smart House could do.

It was an impressive demonstration: An articulate young man walked to a wall switch and turned on the living-room light. Then he touched the screen of a television set. "I'm now assigning this light to the motion sensor

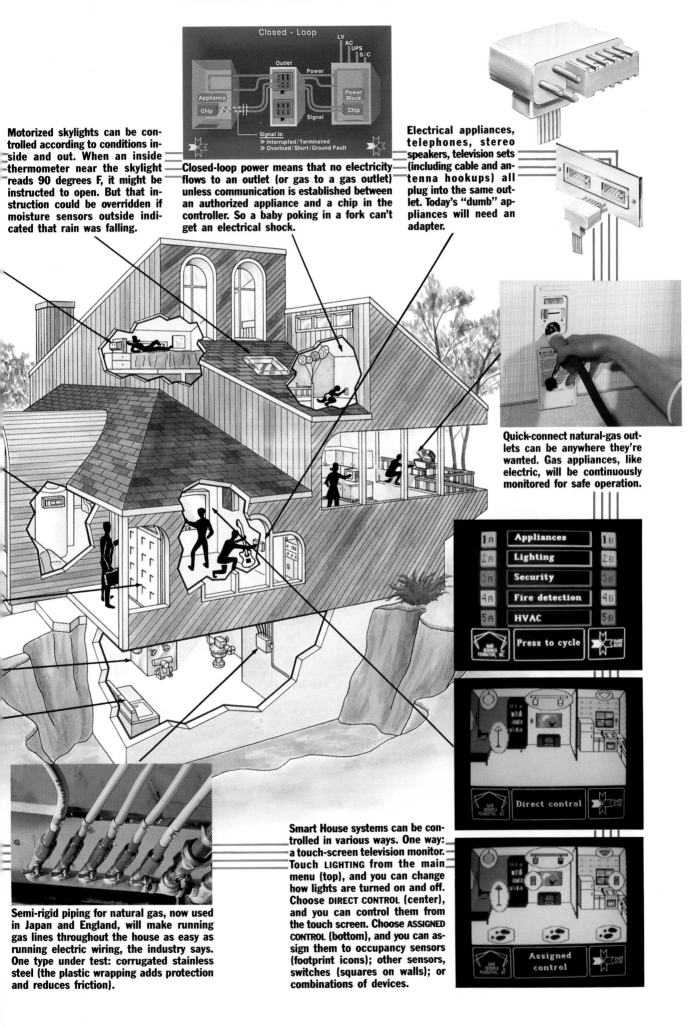

**Closed - Loop**

LV
AC
UPS
S/C

Outlet

Power

Appliance

Chip

Power
Block

Chip

Signal

Signal Is:
▷ Interrupted / Terminated
▷ Overload / Short / Ground Fault

Motorized skylights can be controlled according to conditions inside and out. When an inside thermometer near the skylight reads 90 degrees F, it might be instructed to open. But that instruction could be overridden if moisture sensors outside indicated that rain was falling.

Closed-loop power means that no electricity flows to an outlet (or gas to a gas outlet) unless communication is established between an authorized appliance and a chip in the controller. So a baby poking in a fork can't get an electrical shock.

Electrical appliances, telephones, stereo speakers, television sets (including cable and antenna hookups) all plug into the same outlet. Today's "dumb" appliances will need an adapter.

Quick-connect natural-gas outlets can be anywhere they're wanted. Gas appliances, like electric, will be continuously monitored for safe operation.

| 1A | Appliances | 1B |
| 2A | Lighting | 2B |
| 3A | Security | 3B |
| 4A | Fire detection | 4B |
| 5A | HVAC | 5B |

Press to cycle

Direct control

Assigned control

Semi-rigid piping for natural gas, now used in Japan and England, will make running gas lines throughout the house as easy as running electric wiring, the industry says. One type under test: corrugated stainless steel (the plastic wrapping adds protection and reduces friction).

Smart House systems can be controlled in various ways. One way: a touch-screen television monitor. Touch LIGHTING from the main menu (top), and you can change how lights are turned on and off. Choose DIRECT CONTROL (center), and you can control them from the touch screen. Choose ASSIGNED CONTROL (bottom), and you can assign them to occupancy sensors (footprint icons); other sensors, switches (squares on walls); or combinations of devices.

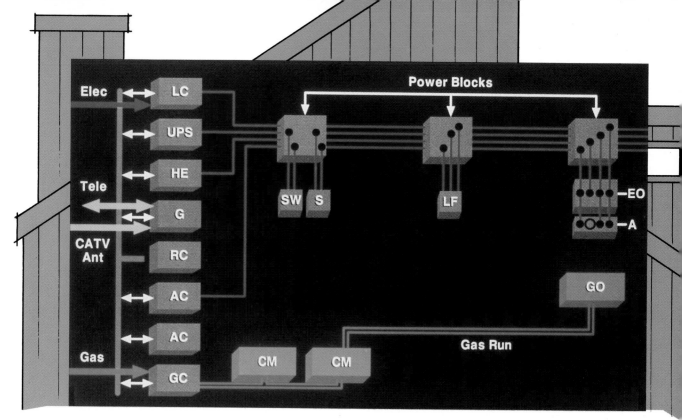

Power Blocks

Elec — LC

UPS

HE

Tele — G

CATV Ant — RC

AC

AC

Gas — GC

SW S

LF

EO

A

GO

CM CM

Gas Run

in the bedroom," he explained. He walked into the bedroom and the living-room light went off.

The Smart House vans could do much more. But they were made smart the way Honeywell made its lab house smart: By applying brains and bucks to force hundreds of off-the-shelf devices to work together—often against their will. The two vans came at a cost of about a half a million dollars.

### Smart House basics

In a real Smart House, the system integration would all be built in. Picture your present house wiring as a net-

**Smart Houses** will bring in outside services as shown above: LC (load center) is the point of entry for electric power, HE (head end) for cable TV and antenna, G (gateway) for telephone service. All are distributed via a common wiring cable. A low-voltage DC line on the cable carries the uninterruptable power supply (see text). At each point on the cable any or all conductors can be accessed. An outlet would tap all; a light, switch, or sensor might tap only portions. (When this diagram was drawn engineers planned to put telephone service on the coaxial cable, along with the TV signal; now they plan two dedicated pairs of lines for phones.) Area controllers (AC) send and receive signals to power blocks, which communicate with outlets, lights, and sensors. Regional controller (RC) coordinates the area controllers. Gas control (GC) mediates the flow of gas, which can be shut off at the main valve or at control manifolds (CM).

**First laboratory Smart House,** in Bowie, MD, is used for breadboarding Smart House components and testing gas appliances.

work of roads, all running willy-nilly behind the walls: Copper wires carry AC power; double strands of copper called twisted-pairs carry the telephone signal; coaxial cable links your television set to an antenna, a VCR, and maybe to a cable-TV service or satellite dish. There may be low-voltage lines for thermostats and doorbells.

It is difficult today for a signal traveling on one of these roads to move to another. It's like driving for miles looking for an intersection, and when you finally find one, it's an overpass or underpass. Conceptually, Smart House would make the roads all run parallel, and provide elegant cloverleaf interchanges so that you could go from one to another whenever and wherever you pleased.

Physically, Smart House starts as a single wiring cable. Electrical engineers call any conductor or group of conductors used to transmit signals between devices a bus. The Smart House cable would supply AC power, low-voltage DC, telephone, audio, video, and high-speed data communication. The cable, a bundle of conductors, would be installed throughout a house by a single subcontractor.

Every service would be available at every outlet. Plug in your television set, and you're connected to the antenna, the cable system, and the VCR, as well as to the electric power. You could plug your toaster—or your telephone—into the same outlet. You could hook up the computer in Johnny's bedroom to the printer in your home office.

With Smart House wiring, switches would no longer physically open and close a circuit to control power flow to an outlet or room light. Instead, they would send signals to a microprocessor in a controller, and it would regulate power flow according to its program. It could be told to turn on the light only if the room is dark and occupied and the wall switch on, for example.

Using switches would be only one way to send a signal to a controlling microprocessor. You could also use a video touch screen, a telephone key pad, an infrared remote control, and sensors (for heat, motion, smoke, gas leaks, water, maybe even for radon or the odor of garlic). With voice-recognition circuits you could simply give orders. Furthermore, one appliance could easily send signals to another.

Connecting a Smart House system to the telephone lines would allow it to communicate with the outside world. You could call your house and ask it to prepare your bath. Or the electric utility could alert your dishwasher when cheap power was available.

The other fundamental aspect of Smart House technology is what the engineers call closed-loop power. "Basically, each appliance, anything that can be plugged in, will contain a communications chip," explained Lane Nichols, manager of power-distribution system development for Smart House Limited Partnership, and a member of the Tiger Team. "The power block associated with each outlet [see diagram] has a chip also." The two would communicate over a dedicated line, a control communication network. "When you plug in the appliance, its chip relays three pieces of information to the power block," Nichols continued. "It gives its identity: 'I am a Sunbeam iron.' It gives its estimated current draw: 'I nominally operate at twelve amps.' And it tells its status on or off."

If everything checks out, the power block would send current to the appliance. Then the signal loop would constantly monitor the appliance. If there is a malfunction— a short, an overload, or a ground fault, for example— power to that outlet would be shut off.

Thus closed-loop power would make Smart Houses safer places to live. If a toddler poked a paper clip into an outlet, no power would be there. Only authorized devices with the right chip can receive electricity. Home wiring is involved in some 300 electrocutions annually, MacFadyen reports. In a Smart House that hazard should be eliminated.

POWER WIRES (3)

TWISTED PAIR FOR CONTROL COMMUNICATION

TWISTED PAIR FOR TELEPHONE

TWISTED PAIR FOR LOW VOLTAGE

Electrical fires should be greatly reduced. If the iron has a frayed cord and shorts, thus drawing too much current, Smart House would cut off the electricity—or wouldn't send any in the first place. One spectator who came to see the Smart House vans told Ken Geremia, Smart House director of public affairs, what such protection could have meant to her. She was scrubbing the walls with a steel-wool soap pad one day, and she wiped it over an outlet. Sparks flew and her clothes caught fire. She suffered second- and third-degree burns over her chest

**One concept for Smart House wiring** calls for a cable to be wrapped around two coaxial cables and covered by a sheathing. Wires are stripped here for clarity only; electricians would snap on insulation-displacement connectors.

and arms. Such an accident wouldn't happen in a Smart House.

Smart House technology would add similar safety to natural gas, for gas outlets also would be closed-loop affairs. A gas control would monitor for gas leaks or improper connections. If it detected an irregularity, it would shut off the gas to that appliance. A Smart House could go further: If a smoke detector sensed smoke, it could cut off the gas at the main valve, for example.

Despite its heavy reliance on electronics, a Smart House would not crash when the power failed. A black box called an uninterruptable power supply (UPS) would switch the house to backup batteries. The UPS would maintain the Smart House logic plus selected functions: Alarms and the pilot for a gas furnace, perhaps.

Homeowners wanting more freedom from blackout worries could add photovoltaic panels or a windmill and keep many more appliances operational. The gas industry is pushing the concept of home cogenerators—natural-gas-powered machines that would generate electricity and also produce heat and hot water.

## Fellow travelers

Few experts doubt that houses will one day have smart-house-type intelligence. Some wonder if it will be Smart House (capital S, capital H) technology, though. There are other shows—or buses—on this road. Today's houses contain what Richard Giddings, manager of homes and buildings research at Honeywell, calls "islands of automation": microprocessor-controlled appliances with limited brains. Manufacturers are now pushing on to achieve product integration—each within its own line. Home automation is also advancing in the form of home-control systems of greater and lesser capabilities.

But what is lacking today are common standards—design specifications that would make controllers and appliances physically and logically compatible. Standards also would mean that the same microprocessor chip could be mass-produced cheaply.

Setting standards is one goal of Smart House. It is also a goal of the Electronic Industries Association (EIA), a powerful trade group with a membership that ranges from consumer-electronics companies to electric utilities. Smart House is designing a Smart House Bus; EIA is writing a Consumer Electronics Bus standard.

The Consumer Electronics bus standard would cover the signals used in three main areas of home electronics: wireless communications (infrared remote control), long-range communications (coaxial cable, twisted-pair wire, or fiber optics), and communications via existing house wiring. Presently none of these standards is written and accepted. "We hope to announce all of them by the end of the year," says Thomas K. Lauterback, vice president of communications at EIA/Consumer Electronics Group.

Theoretically, Smart House could accept the EIA standards. "Whenever they do something that is applicable to our system design, we will use it," says Chuck Gutenson, vice president for engineering at Smart House Limited Partnership. "But we won't wait around to hear what the standard is going to be."

Timing is one problem. Another may be the issue of exclusivity: The EIA wants to publish a standard for everyone to use. Smart House wants to license its proprietary technology, initially to three manufacturers in each product area. Both might be able to have their way: "We've identified about forty areas we want to try to patent that are not related to anything EIA is doing," Mark Gutenson says.

Thickening the plot, the Japanese and the Europeans are also working on their own standards for home automation. So the world may end up with three—or more—standards. One solution: Adapters—interface plugs that would allow non-compatible appliances to communicate with each other.

Like Smart House, the EIA began its Consumer Electronics Bus effort in 1984. Both groups have issued several overly optimistic schedules for completion.

At the 1984 seminar where MacFadyen introduced the Smart House concept, he predicted that the first Smart Houses—5,000 of them—would be ready for sale by 1987. When that year arrived nothing much beyond the bread-boarded vans had materialized. Pundits have a name for hardware and software that never progresses beyond promise or prototype: They call it "vaporware."

"Perhaps we went public too early," admits Keith Phillips, a recent recruit to the Smart House organization. Last year, though, things started rolling.

● The National Electrical Code was amended to allow Smart-House-type wiring.

● Smart House Limited Partnership completed a $10 million capitalization plan by selling limited partnerships, mostly to large home builders.

● The first laboratory Smart House, co-sponsored by the Gas Research Institute (GRI), the NAHB National Research Center, and Smart House Limited Partnership, was built in a new 51-acre National Research Home Park in Bowie, Maryland, next-door to company headquarters. Partly a test house for Smart House systems, it will also host industry testing of new gas technologies. Chief among them: Semi-rigid gas piping, a pet project that GRI is piggybacking onto Smart House because both need the approval of code bodies. With easier-to-install piping, GRI foresees quick-connect gas outlets throughout the house.

## Tiger team

Also in 1987, the Tiger Team—10 to 20 engineers from Smart House, Amp, AT&T, Brintic, Honeywell, and Square D—met at Honeywell in Minnesota to set the initial design parameters for the technology. Gutenson was responsible for making sure the team ran smoothly. "Our job, simply put, is to think about all the hard questions and get the right answers so that when we introduce a product it will be the inevitable product," he summarized when I visited the Honeywell lab.

Smart House technology must do all the wizardry it's supposed to do while satisfying the needs of competing manufacturers and of both the electric and gas industries. And it must be buildable, affordable, and reliable. The latter is a big concern, market research has shown. "If you ask folks, 'How could this thing crash and burn,' you hear about reliability," Phillips reported. " 'Now my furnace can go kablooey, or my TV can go kablooey. You're telling me my house can go kablooey? No thanks,' " he mimed.

To enhance reliability the design team chose to avoid centralized control. "We don't have a single computer sitting there running the house. There are a number of area controllers, each handling a different branch. So if one has a problem, you don't lose the whole house," Gutenson explained.

## Fiber phobia

Another decision the team had to make was whether the wiring cable should include fiber optics. "Just about all of us would have liked to use fiber," Gutenson said. Phil

Zumsteg, a Honeywell engineer lent to the Tiger Team (and the strongest advocate of fiber), ticked off the pros: "Fiber has tremendous bandwidth—information-carrying capacity. That would mean a significant reduction in the wiring. Fiber is not subject to electromagnetic interference for the most part; a signal you put in on one end is not likely to be changed much when it comes out the other. And by adding a different frequency of light, I can double the capacity, literally for free."

Nevertheless, Zumsteg lost that round. "One problem is the cost of termination," Gutenson explained. Everywhere you want to connect a device to the optical fiber you need an optical transducer. They are expensive; connecting them is expensive; and you'd need a lot of them (the team estimates 256) in an average house.

Another consideration was installation. "No one knows what kind of problems you'd run into installing fiber in a house," Gutenson said. "You'd get these two-hundred-pound contractors yanking on the end, running the fiber around sharp corners—what would it do to the quality of the transmission path?" They couldn't predict.

So the Tiger team settled on coaxial cable for distributing audio, video, and high-speed data. "The coax has abundant bandwidth for all the things we can imagine doing," Gutenson said.

Once they gave up fiber optics (at least for now), they had to determine whether the coax could be part of the wiring cable. "We're determined to integrate it," Gutenson said. "But there may be problems: That would bring the radio-frequency signals close to the data-communications network, and we're concerned that there will be cross talk between the two." Preliminary tests give them cause for optimism, but a much more thorough evaluation is about to be launched. If those tests indicate potential problems, the designers will try to find better ways to shield the coax.

When you have all kinds of devices ("nodes," as the engineers call them) sharing a common conductor you have to determine the protocol, or electronic rules, by which each gets its signal on and off the bus. The Tiger Team considered several approaches for the control communications network, which is to run on twisted-pair wires.

One is a contention protocol. "It's like a human conversation," Gutenson said. "Any node just decides for itself when to start talking. They're all contending for the same bus and they can conflict, just as you and I might start to say something at the same time. With humans you kind of look at each other and decide who will talk. With a contention protocol you have to emulate that electronically."

The advantage: The bus is only used when a signal is sent. "So you get an efficient use of the bandwidth," Gutenson explained. A disadvantage: Chips that can electronically referee debts are fairly complex—and expensive. And everything attached to the bus would need one. So the contention protocol was overruled.

## Wait your turn

"The protocol we selected for the communications bus is one of the oldest protocols available: Fixed, time-slotted, time-division multiplexing," said Gutenson. "You allocate all of the nodes on a bus an equal amount of time. The controller sends out a synchronizing signal so that they all start at once. Each node has a number, and each must wait his turn. If number six on the bus has a message, he has to wait (though microseconds only) for slot six to come along. The controller knows the message came from number six because it's in that slot."

The advantage: It's an inexpensive technology. "And it does exactly what we want to do," Gutenson emphasized. A possible problem: Time-slotted multiplexing is an inefficient way to use the bus. "Even if a node has nothing to say, he still gets a slot. That means the communications network is always running like crazy. And to service all the nodes on a branch you need a high data rate." The higher the data rate, the more likely you are to have noise problems—electromagnetic interference. "So we are afraid the communications network might cause interference on your AM radio," Gutenson explained.

With the testing they have done so far, they're pretty sure time-slotted time-division multiplexing will be a workable protocol for the control communications network. "We've identified some problems," Gutenson noted. "But for every one we've found so far, we think we've found a solution."

In early March the Tiger Team published the first set of specifications. Now the engineers and the 10 manufacturers who have signed Smart House research and licensing agreements must flesh out the details and resolve problems that arise, Gutenson noted. "We're beginning to see the light at the end of the tunnel, and we're reasonably sure it isn't the train."

## When and how much?

In 1989, 20 prototype houses, all built with the cooperation of utilities and local home-builders associations, are to be launched. These will be distributed throughout the United States, with a couple in Canada, Ken Geremia reports. Then 50 to 150 demonstration Smart Houses are scheduled for 1990. These will be put up by builders who will show them as model homes and eventually sell them. By the following year a few thousand will have been built for sale.

"By 1995 to 1997, when half the new homes built are using it, Smart House technology will be the de facto standard," Geremia predicts.

How much will a Smart House cost? "Guesstimates say $7,000 to $10,000 more than a comparable 'dumb' house [but a dumb house with only basic AC wiring]," Geremia answers. "That would include the wiring, receptacles, and controlling hardware."

But higher initial cost would be offset by operational savings, Geremia points out. "Maybe ten to forty percent energy savings, depending on location, lifestyle, and how the homeowners take advantage of Smart House capabilities." There should be a reduction in insurance premiums also, and utilities may give incentives to homeowners who let them control certain appliances to reduce peak loads. Balancing higher mortgage payments against lower operating costs, Geremia predicts a Smart Home-owner's outlay should be anywhere from break-even to an additional $60 a month.

In 1991 the plan is to introduce Smart House technology into multi-family housing, and by around 1994 to have a retrofit technology available. Would that require tearing out the walls of your house? Probably not. Designers envision a flat wiring cable that perhaps could run behind a recess in a baseboard. The Smart House staff sees the retrofit market as lucrative: "Only two percent of the housing gets rebuilt each year," Keith Phillips points out. "The other ninety-eight percent is clamoring for upgrading"—by V. Elaine Gilmore. Main illustration by Mario Ferro.

# shock
# stopper

Each year, according to the National Safety Council, more than 300 people are electrocuted at home. Amazingly, the small amount of power it takes to light a seven-watt Christmas-tree bulb can kill an adult. Think your home is safe? Not if it has older non-grounding electrical outlets. These have only two slots, instead of three, and with such outlets the risk of being severely shocked by a ground fault while using plug-in electrical tools and appliances is only an insulation's thickness away (see sidebar).

To protect yourself and your family against all-too-common ground-fault shock hazards of two-slot receptacles, your home electrical system may need updating. If you are familiar with electrical wiring, you can tackle this update yourself. Otherwise, hire a licensed electrician.

The National Electrical Code (NEC) lists three options for replacing a two-slot outlet: Replace with another two-slot outlet (no help with ground faults); replace with a three-slot outlet that is truly grounded; or use a receptacle-type ground-fault circuit interrupter (GFCI). The method you may use depends on your house wiring.

If your house wiring provides some means of grounding a replacement outlet within the outlet box, a two-slot outlet *must* be replaced only with a three-slot grounding outlet (NEC Section 210–7[d]). Some of these sell for as little as forty cents apiece. (Grounded receptacle GFCIs may be used, too.)

The required means of grounding consists of a bare or green-insulated wire in a nonmetallic-cable wiring system or the continuous metal covering of an armored-cable or conduit system.

To find out whether grounding is available at your house's outlets, cut the power to an outlet's circuit at the main service panel. The outlet should be electrically dead. Test it by plugging in a known-to-be-working light or appliance. Or plug in a neon tester (available at any electrical supplier). Be sure to test *both* outlets of a duplex receptacle. Once you're sure that the circuit is dead, remove the cover screw and wall plate. Next, to make sure that no electricity is present inside, apply the neon tester across the exposed lighter-colored terminals on one side of the outlet and the darker-colored terminals on the other side. If the lamp doesn't light, remove the two long No. 10–32 retaining screws that hold the receptacle to its outlet box. Without touching any bare wires (it pays to be cautious around electricity), stretch the receptacle out of the box on its wiring. Pull it far enough to enable you to peer inside the outlet box with a flashlight. You are looking for (1) a bare or green-insulated wire or wires or (2) a metal outlet box served by armored cable or metal conduit. If you find either, a means of grounding is available within the box.

As a double-check, bring a grounded jumper wire near the dead outlet—a car battery jumper cable attached to a continuous metal piping system will do fine. Using a multitester set on "R×1 Ohms," clamp one end of the jumper to one tester lead while touching the other lead to the metal box. If the tester reads zero-ohms resistance, the box is grounded. If any resistance is indicated, however, the box is not grounded.

In all receptacle hookups use standard Code-approved outlet-box makeup procedures. (If your house has aluminum wiring, not copper, special wiring procedures apply.) In any case, every three-slot outlet's hex-head green grounding terminal *must* be connected to a ground. These receptacles may not be installed at any location without grounding.

The very common nonmetallic-sheathed-cable house wiring with white-, black-, and red-insulated wires—but no bare or green-insulated wires—provides no means of grounding. If you find such cable entering the box, you may replace a two-slot outlet *only* with another two-slot outlet or with a receptacle GFCI.

Replacement with a receptacle GFCI solves the ground-fault shock-hazard problem. NEC Section 210–7(d) Exception recognizes that an ungrounded GFCI receptacle does offer a degree of shock protection, even though a tool or appliance plugged into it is not actually grounded. The GFCI receptacle thus protects where the old two-slot receptacle does not.

Receptacle GFCIs in a number of brands are widely sold for $11 to $20. Naturally, the receptacle GFCI you purchase should be listed by Underwriters Laboratories and bear the familiar "UL" designation ("CSA" in Canada).

A GFCI works by monitoring current flow in and out. As long as both are equal, though opposite, nothing happens. But when some current leaks to ground—even as little as six milliamperes—the in-out current becomes unbalanced. This triggers it to cut off the power within a few milliseconds. GFCIs protect only against line-to-ground shocks, not line-to-line or line-to-neutral shocks. Fortunately, the latter are not nearly as common as ground faults.

## Feed-through protection

Most receptacle GFCIs are designed to feed through their protection to other outlets. Two of the five leads or terminal blocks are labeled "line" and two are labeled "load," with the fifth one for grounding. Use of a GFCI in first-receptacle position will protect an entire branch circuit, except the wiring between the service panel and the first receptacle. Instructions with the GFCI tell how to locate the first outlet in a circuit and how to find the house line and load wires. With a GFCI wired for a feed through, you change this first outlet only. All outlets beyond it in the circuit must be left as two slot. Furthermore, a grounding conductor must not be connected between the receptacle GFCI and any outlet supplied from it.

A GFCI may be used in a non-feed-through installation by leaving its load terminals empty or placing wire nuts on the ends of its load leads, as in the second pictorial.

In connecting a receptacle GFCI, be sure to follow the instructions that come with it, though these do not generally cover its specialized use as a replacement for two-slot outlets. For home safety you not only want correct polarity at each GFCI, you want any two-slot outlets served by a feed-through GFCI wired with correct polarity. Check them to be sure. The narrow receptacle slots should be hot and the wide slots should be at ground potential (dead) when the circuit is turned on. Reversed polarity does not affect the operation of a GFCI, however.

Since the outlet box is not grounded, the Code does not require bonding of the receptacle GFCI's grounding lead to the box. This

**Receptacle GFCIs** come with terminals (above) or with leads (the feed-through unit shown in photo on page 180).

means that the grounding lead or terminal is left vacant. Being ungrounded has no effect on the GFCI's function, however. Care must be taken to be sure that it does not contact any uninsulated live parts inside the outlet box. If it's a lead, thread a wire nut on it; if a terminal, run the empty hex-head binding screw down tightly. And when mounting the receptacle to the box, be certain that any live wires are kept away.

To work properly, receptacle GFCIs need a "ground reference." In a properly wired house, this is provided by the service panel's neutral busbar, which is bonded—electrically connected—to the main panel enclosure and through this to the house grounding-electrode system. Most often, the grounding electrode is a buried water pipe.

If spare capacity is available, a circuit with grounding may be extended by adding additional wiring and outlets. An ungrounded circuit, whether it has GFCI or not, may not be extended. New outlets must be served by equipment-grounding conductors.

Remember to test all your GFCIs periodically as is directed in the instructions.

While your GFCI update does not provide grounding, it does give extremely sensitive, fast-acting ground-fault protection that can save someone's life. Still, having ground-fault protection is no reason for careless handling of electrical tools and appliances when you are wet or grounded. Using good electrical sense is still your best protection—
*by Richard Day.*

# upgrading telephone systems

With recent advances in telephone technology, home telephone systems can do much more than reach out to family and friends. Some of the new capabilities include links between computers inside and outside the home, ways to receive and transmit printed material through phone lines, phone-based intercoms and home-security systems.

But even if you're not looking to add these capabilities, you can still take advantage of the new simplicity of the modular phone equipment that is now generally available in hardware and electronics stores. With this gear you don't have to be a wiring expert to add more phone lines or otherwise upgrade your telephone system.

## Surveying your phone system

Most home telephone systems installed or modified after 1974 consist of *modular* components that are linked with plug-in connections. If you can't unplug your phone from the wall fixture or "jack," or it's attached by a large four-prong plug, the installation is hard-wired and predates modular design.

You can convert hard-wired jacks for use with the modular plugs on modern equipment with snap-on converter kits, as shown in the illustration. Kits are available for less than $5 at telephone supply and home center stores.

Continue the survey by determining the wiring layout in your house. First, find where the outside telephone line enters your home. In newer houses and ones that have had the phone system recently modified, you'll find a small plastic box called the *network interface*. This is the boundary between the telephone company's wires and your system. Your phone system connects to the interface with a modular plug. If you can't find the interface, the phone company will provide one or advise you on how to upgrade your system.

It's a good idea to have a network interface installed even if you're not upgrading the system because it helps pinpoint problems in phone service. If there's a problem in your system, unplug your phone line from the interface, and plug a phone into the box. If you don't hear a dial tone or if the sound is distorted, the problem is in phone company's lines, and they'll have to fix it at no charge. Clear transmission means there's a problem in your wiring system, and you're responsible for getting it fixed.

From the interface, follow the phone line through the house. In most homes, a single wire runs from the

*Reprinted by permission of Homeowner magazine.*

network interface directly to a phone jack. If each extension jack is wired in sequence, that is, if a single wire comes out of each jack and runs to the next, yours is a *loop-wiring* system. While this is the easiest way to wire phones, any problem in the line will affect all the phones in the house.

The other common residential wiring system is *home-run wiring*. In it, the interface is connected to a junction box from which as many as four separate lines run to phone jacks throughout the house. With this layout, a problem in one line won't affect the entire system. This is especially important when you depend on phone links for computer modems or security systems.

## Adding phone jacks

When working with phone wires, disconnect your line at the network interface to prevent injury from electrical shock. Even if you're simply plugging in adapters, you can get shocked if the phone rings while you're working. To be safe, take a phone off the hook.

There are several ways to add extension phones, but there is a limit to

**It takes only** a few minutes to convert a hard-wired jack to a modular one. To install adapter kits with color-coded, snap-on connections, snip the phone cord as shown in the illustration, and attach the connectors. Some kits have color-coded wires with spade lugs at their ends, which are screwed underneath the terminals.

ART BY CARL DE GROOTE

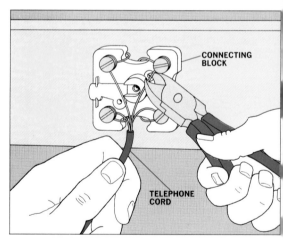

**The adapter kit** serves as the new jack cover. Some very old telephones with lighted dials get AC voltage from a transformer that is plugged in to an outlet nearby. You should unplug the transformer before converting the jack.

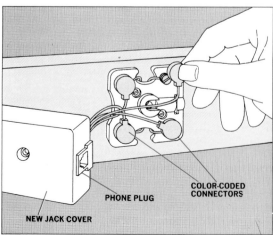

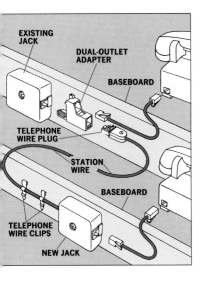

EXISTING JACK

DUAL-OUTLET ADAPTER

BASEBOARD

TELEPHONE WIRE PLUG

STATION WIRE

BASEBOARD

TELEPHONE WIRE CLIPS

NEW JACK

**A dual-outlet adapter** lets one jack serve two phones. Or it lets you loop-wire a new jack to an existing one.

**A junction box** acts as a distribution point for jacks in a home-run wiring system. Plug-in junction boxes, such as the one shown in this illustration, let you create a home-run subsystem from an existing jack.

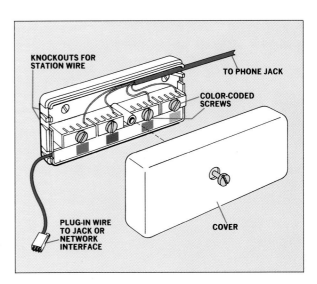

KNOCKOUTS FOR STATION WIRE

TO PHONE JACK

COLOR-CODED SCREWS

PLUG-IN WIRE TO JACK OR NETWORK INTERFACE

COVER

he number of telephones or other devices a single line can accommodate. When a line is overloaded, transmission quality breaks down.

As a rule of thumb, five pieces of equipment is the limit for each incoming line. But telephone service varies, and it's best to contact your local telephone company and discuss your plans. The service representative will probably ask you to add up the *ring equivalency numbers* (REN) stamped on each piece of equipment you want to use on the line. If the total adds up to less than the local limit, you can make the connections you want.

The simplest way to add an extension phone is to install a *dual-line* adapter in an existing jack (shown in the illustration on page 183). Plug the original phone into one portion of the adapter and a 25-foot telephone extension cord into the other. When you add a phone, most local phone companies ask that you register it with them and supply the REN and FCC number.

One way to add a new jack is to loop-wire it to an existing jack using telephone *station wire.* Station wire comes in 50-foot rolls, which is the maximum distance recommended between jacks. Either run the wire along baseboards or other moldings, or route it through walls, ceilings and floors. For a surface application, run the wire from the existing jack to the desired location, securing it along the way with plastic phone-wire clips.

To the end of the wire nearest the original jack, attach a *telephone wire plug* (see the illustration on page 183) by cutting the cable and inserting the end into the plug. By design, the plug automatically makes the connection,

so there's no need to strip the wire. Insert the plug into the original jack using a dual-line adapter if the jack already services a phone. At the other end of the wire, attach a modular jack. You'll find that the wires and terminals are color-coded for easy installation. Attach the jack to the wall and plug in the phone.

Another method for wiring an extension phone employs a *plug-in*

*junction box* (see the illustration on page 183), which allows you to convert a loop-wire to a home-run wiring system or create a home-run sub-system using an existing jack. Connect a telephone wire plug to the network interface or to an existing jack. Then attach station wire as shown in the illustration on page 183 to service each of the extension jacks—
*by John Warde.*

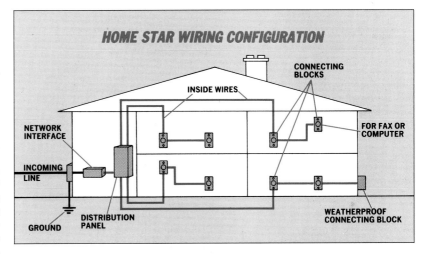

**HOME STAR WIRING CONFIGURATION**

CONNECTING BLOCKS

INSIDE WIRES

FOR FAX OR COMPUTER

NETWORK INTERFACE

INCOMING LINE

GROUND

DISTRIBUTION PANEL

WEATHERPROOF CONNECTING BLOCK

**AT&T has developed** a wiring system called Home Star to accommodate the sophisticated telecommunications equipment now available for home use. The system employs enhanced capacity cable, which can carry more than one line and connect more than one device with a single cable. In addition, the wiring is controlled from a central distribution panel. From the panel, separate wires are routed to each room in the house, as shown in the illustration above, making it easy to add one, two or even three extra lines and sophisticated equipment, such as FAX machines, electronic key system telephones and security equipment, without changing the original wiring layout.

Home star is designed for new construction. The new distribution panel can also be installed in an existing house, but you'll have to rewire the house with advanced capacity cable to enjoy the full benefits of Home Star.

# Index

184